EU AND US COMPETITION LAW: DIVIDED IN UNITY?

Markets and the Law

Series Editor:
Geraint Howells, University of Manchester, UK

Markets and the Law is concerned with the way the law interacts with the market through regulation, self-regulation and the impact of private law regimes. It looks at the impact of regional and international organizations (e.g. EC and WTO) and many of the works adopt a comparative approach and/or appeal to an international audience. Examples of subjects covered include trade laws, intellectual property, sales law, insurance, consumer law, banking, financial markets, labour law, environmental law and social regulation affecting the market as well as competition law. The series includes texts covering a broad area, monographs on focused issues, and collections of essays dealing with particular themes.

Other titles in the series

Financial Regulation in Africa
An Assessment of Financial Integration Arrangements in African Emerging and Frontier Markets
Iwa Salami
ISBN 978 0 7546 7985 1

The Tobacco Challenge
Legal Policy and Consumer Protection
Geraint Howells
ISBN 978 0 7546 4570 2

Introduction to Business Law in Russia
Vladimir Orlov
ISBN 978 0 7546 7755 0

EU and US Competition Law: Divided in Unity?

The Rule on Restrictive Agreements and Vertical Intra-brand Restraints

CSONGOR ISTVÁN NAGY
University of Szeged and Budapest University of Technology and Economics, Hungary

Routledge
Taylor & Francis Group
LONDON AND NEW YORK

First published 2013 by Ashgate Publishing

2 Park Square, Milton Park, Abingdon, Oxfordshire OX14 4RN
52 Vanderbilt Avenue, New York, NY 10017

Routledge is an imprint of the Taylor & Francis Group, an informa business

First issued in paperback 2020

British Library Cataloguing in Publication Data
Nagy, Csongor István, 1979–
EU and US competition law : divided in unity? : The rule on restrictive agreements and vertical intra-brand restraints. – (Markets and the law)
1. Antitrust law – European Union countries. 2. Antitrust law – United States.
3. Restraint of trade – European Union countries. 4. Restraint of trade – United States.
5. Antitrust law (International law) 6. Conflict of laws – Antitrust law.
I. Title II. Series
343.2'40721–dc23

Library of Congress Cataloging-in-Publication Data
Nagy, Csongor István, 1979–
EU and US competition law, divided in unity? : the rule on restrictive agreements and vertical intra-brand restraints / by Csongor Istvan Nagy.
p. cm.—(Markets and the Law)
Includes bibliographical references and index.
ISBN 978-1-4094-4230-1 (hardback)
1. Antitrust law—United States. 2. Antitrust law—Europan Union countries. 3. Restraint of trade—United States. 4. Restraint of trade—Europan Union countries. 5. Antitrust law (International law) 6. Conflict of laws—Antitrust law. I. Title. II. Title: European Union and United States competition law, divided in unity?

K3850.N34 2013
343.2407'21–dc23

2012024266

ISBN 978-1-4094-4230-1 (hbk)
ISBN 978-0-367-60181-2 (pbk)

Contents

Acknowledgements

I am profoundly grateful to my wife Zsófia and my son Nimród for their patience, understanding, tolerance and support.

I am grateful to the Central European University's Legal Studies Department for supporting my S.J.D. studies and the writing of this book.

Table of legislation

EU regulations

Commission Regulation (EC) No 2790/1999 of 22 December 1999 on the application of Article 81(3) of the Treaty to categories of vertical agreements and concerted practices. OJ [1999] L 336/21.

Commission Regulation (EC) No 1400/2002 of 31 July 2002 on the application of Article 81(3) of the Treaty to categories of vertical agreements and concerted practices in the motor vehicle sector. OJ [2002] L 203/30.

Council Regulation (EC) No 1/2003 of 16 December 2002 on the implementation of the rules on competition laid down in Articles 81 and 82 of the Treaty. OJ [2003] L 1/1.

Commission Regulation (EC) No 772/2004 of 27 April 2004 on the application of Article 81(3) of the Treaty to categories of technology transfer agreements. OJ [2004] L 123/11.

Commission Regulation (EU) No 330/2010 of 20 April 2010 on the application of Article 101(3) of the Treaty on the Functioning of the European Union to categories of vertical agreements and concerted practices. OJ [2010] L 102/1.

Commission Regulation (EU) No 461/2010 of 27 May 2010 on the application of Article 101(3) of the Treaty on the Functioning of the European Union to categories of vertical agreements and concerted practices in the motor vehicle sector. OJ [2010] L 129/52.

EU guidelines and notices

Guidelines on vertical restraints. OJ [2000] C 291/1.

Guidelines on the applicability of Article 81 of the EC Treaty to horizontal cooperation agreements. OJ [2001] C 3/2.

Commission Notice on agreements of minor importance which do not appreciably restrict competition under Article 81(1) of the Treaty establishing the European Community (de minimis). OJ [2001] C 368/13.

Guidelines on the application of Article 81 of the EC Treaty to technology transfer agreements. OJ [2004] C 101/2.

Guidelines on the application of Article 81(3) of the Treaty. OJ [2004] C 101/97.

Guidelines on vertical restraints. OJ [2010] C 130/1.

Guidelines on the applicability of Article 101 of the Treaty on the Functioning of the European Union to horizontal co-operation agreements. OJ [2011] C11/1.

Supplementary guidelines on vertical restraints in agreements for the sale and repair of motor vehicles and for the distribution of spare parts for motor vehicles. OJ [2010] C 138/16.

US guidelines

Federal Trade Commission (FTC) and Antitrust Division of the U.S. Department of Justice (DOJ) Guidelines for Collaborations Among Competitors, April 2000.

List of abbreviations

1/2003/EC Regulation	Council Regulation (EC) No 1/2003 of 16 December 2002 on the implementation of the rules on competition laid down in Articles 81 and 82 of the Treaty. OJ [2003] L 1/1.
AG	Advocate General
Article 81	Article 81 of the Treaty Establishing the European Community (equivalent of Article 101 between 1 May 1999 and 1 December 2009)
Article 85	Article 85 of the Treaty establishing the European Community (equivalent of Article 101 before 1 May 1999)
Article 101	Article 101 of the Treaty on the Functioning of the European Union*
BER	Commission Regulation (EU) No 330/2010 of 20 April 2010 on the application of Article 101(3) of the Treaty on the Functioning of the European Union to categories of vertical agreements and concerted practices. OJ [2010] L 102/1.
CFI	Court of First Instance (as from 1 December 2009: General Court)
Commission	European Commission
DoJ	United States Department of Justice
ECJ	Court of Justice (before 1 December 2009: Court of Justice of the European Communities)
FTC	Federal Trade Commission
GC	General Court (before 1 December 2009: Court of First Instance)
Guidelines on Article 101(3)	Guidelines on the application of Article 81(3) of the Treaty. OJ [2004] C 101/97.

* In the book the new numbers introduced by the Treaty of Lisbon will be used, which are applicable as from 1 December 2009. Nevertheless, the original texts of the quotations remain unchanged.

Guidelines on Horizontal Cooperation Agreements	Guidelines on the applicability of Article 101 of the Treaty on the Functioning of the European Union to horizontal co-operation agreements. OJ [2011] C 11/1.
Guidelines on the Assessment of Technology Transfer Agreements	Guidelines on the application of Article 81 of the EC Treaty to technology transfer agreements. OJ [2004] C 101/2.
Guidelines on Vertical Restraints	Guidelines on vertical restraints. Official Journal C 130, 19.05.2010, p. 1
MVBER	Commission Regulation (EC) No 1400/2002 of 31 July 2002 on the application of Article 81(3) of the Treaty to categories of vertical agreements and concerted practices in the motor vehicle sector. OJ [2002] L 203/30.
New MVBER	Commission Regulation (EU) No 461/2010 of 27 May 2010 on the application of Article 101(3) of the Treaty on the Functioning of the European Union to categories of vertical agreements and concerted practices in the motor vehicle sector. OJ [2010] L 129/52.
Notice on Agreements of Minor Importance	Commission Notice on agreements of minor importance which do not appreciably restrict competition under Article 81(1) of the Treaty establishing the European Community (*de minimis*). OJ [2001] C 368/13.
Old BER	Commission Regulation (EC) No 2790/1999 of 22 December 1999 on the application of Article 81(3) of the Treaty to categories of vertical agreements and concerted practices. OJ [1999] L 336/21.
Old Guidelines on Horizontal Cooperation Agreements	Guidelines on the applicability of Article 81 of the EC Treaty to horizontal cooperation agreements. OJ [2001] C 3/2.
Old Guidelines on Vertical Restraints	Guidelines on vertical restraints. OJ [2000] C 291/1.
RPF	Resale Price Fixing
RPM	Resale Price Maintenance

Section 1	Section 1 of the Sherman Act
Section 2	Section 2 of the Sherman Act
TEU	Treaty on the European Union
TFEU	Treaty on the Functioning of the European Union
TTBER	Commission Regulation (EC) No 772/2004 of 27 April 2004 on the application of Article 81(3) of the Treaty to categories of technology transfer agreements. OJ [2004] L 123/11.

Chapter I
Introduction

Competition law is probably the most globalized field of law, certainly because it uses the same world-language: economics. Nevertheless, under the surface of superficial unity, competition laws diverge very significantly in terms of legal thinking, analytical structure and allocation of burden of proof. This book demonstrates, through the example of vertical intra-brand restraints, how the treatment of restrictive agreements in the world's two leading competition law jurisdictions differs, and evaluates comprehensively the two regulatory patterns from this comparative perspective.

'Antitrust policy toward vertical restraints is the biggest substantive issue facing antitrust',[1] the most controversial question being the treatment of intra-brand restrictions. While economic common sense suggests that the most important competition problems are triggered by inter-brand restrictions, where the reseller's freedom is restricted in how to deal with competing brands, and intra-brand restraints, where the reseller's freedom is restricted in how to deal with the brand concerned, are less harmful, it is intra-brand restraints that are subject to the harshest treatment: from vertical agreements solely, intra-brand restraints have figured on the list of hardcore restrictions.

Recently, this field experienced sweeping changes. In 2007, a highly divided US Supreme Court, in a four-to-five judgment, overruled a century-old precedent: since then RPF has been subjected to an effects-analysis (rule of reason) on this side of the Atlantic; nonetheless, the treatment of RPF seems to have remained rather intact in the EU, notwithstanding some changes in the Commission's style. Accordingly, the foregoing developments have entailed a remarkable divergence between the two empires of antitrust and RPF has remained 'one of the most controversial areas of competition law and policy'.[2]

Likewise, US antitrust law treats territorial exclusivities laxly, while in the EU absolute territorial protection is chased with fire and sword, albeit restrictions on active promotion (relative territorial protection) are, similarly, subject to effects-analysis. Nonetheless, the purpose of market integration (single market imperative) is said to justify this deviation from sound economics in the EU.

---

1 Richard A. Posner, *Vertical Restraints and Antitrust Policy*, 72 University of Chicago Law Review 229, 229 (2005).

2 *OECD Policy Roundtable* 2008 on *Resale Price Maintenance*, DAF/COMP (2008) 37, (2009) 9.

Besides the divergence between the two sides of the Atlantic, there is a tension also between mainstream economics and EU competition law; a tension that had been present also in US antitrust law before 2007.

The backbone of the book comprises of the detailed comparison of EU competition and US antitrust law. 'Antitrust law is an American tradition, as should always be remembered when comparisons are made and guidance is sought for the European law. Comparative law in this area is more than a fascinating intellectual game; it is a valuable tool; and indeed to the European lawyer an essential one.'[3] Economics serves an important role when evaluating the results of the comparative analysis.

The book's structure rests on two pillars: the analysis of the rule on restrictive agreements (Chapters II-IV) and the specific examination of the economics and the law of vertical intra-brand restraints (Chapters V-VII). The book ends with the final conclusions (Chapter VIII).

In the first part of the book, the structure of the rule on restrictive agreements will be considered in the context of vertical intra-brand restrictions. It would be an over-simplification of the problem if the query were reduced to the question whether intra-brand restraints are subject to an outright prohibition or to an effects-analysis. The constituent elements of this rule embrace the concept of agreement and the substance of the prohibition.

Chapter III deals with the notion of agreement, which has a pivotal role as the threshold question of the prohibition on restrictive agreements. A narrow grasp of agreement may enable the unilateral maintenance of prices and of exclusive territories, thus turning the rule on RPF and territorial protection upside down. On the other hand, a too wide notion of agreement may subject genuine unilateral conduct to the application of rules addressed to coordinated behaviour.

As a matter of practice, in US antitrust law the abolition of RPF's *per se* illegality had already been an accomplished fact in 2007, when in *Leegin* the Supreme Court overruled the *per se* illegality rule of *Dr. Miles*: the Supreme Court's holding in *Monsanto* (1984) effectively enabled producers to maintain prices by establishing that the concept of RPF agreement does not cover situations where a producer terminates price-cutters because of discounting, even if this happens after non-discounting dealers' complaining to the producer.

It will be demonstrated that the *Colgate* doctrine of US antitrust law is at variance with the sound economic considerations of vertical intra-brand restraints. In *Colgate*, the Supreme Court established that all traders have the natural right to select their business partners and, hence, to announce in advance the conduct they expect on the part of their dealers and to unilaterally terminate the non-complying ones. The exclusion of the foregoing plights from the ambit of agreement enables producers with some bargaining power to maintain resale prices unilaterally, while

3 René Joliet, The Rule of Reason in Antitrust Law; American, German and Common Market Laws in Comparative Perspective 191 (1967).

the most fundamental proposition of vertical restraints is that they raise problems only if the producer has market power.

The other constituent element of this architecture is the substance of the rule on restrictive agreements, which is analysed in Chapter IV. In EU competition law the bifurcation of Article 101 envisages a two-step analysis with different focuses: Article 101(1) contains a general prohibition on restrictive agreements, while Article 101(3) contains an exception (individual exemption). On the other hand, though the statutory language of Section 1 of the Sherman Act suggests a monistic approach, the rule of reason analysis is also structured. In both regimes, the burden of proof is allocated in the analytical phases differently.

It is submitted that Article 101(1) centres around the competitive process (rivalry), while Article 101(3), centres around productive efficiency. On the other hand, Section 1 uses a monistic analysis focusing on the agreement's effects on consumer welfare.

The structure of Article 101, if properly construed, minimizes the risks of false positives and false negatives, because it allocates the burden of proof according to the agreement's probable effects on consumer welfare. Nevertheless, the construction of Article 101, as applied in practice, is inconsistent, as it blurs the borderline between the focuses of Article 101(1) and Article 101(3). In practice, these two focuses are not clearly distinguished and the analysis under the bifurcated Article 101 is often blurred.

It is submitted that the position that the treatment of RPF in US antitrust law after *Leegin* is, more or less, in line with the treatment in EU competition law – because here the parties have always been able to argue that the agreement meets the requirements of Article 101(3) – is inconsistent with the realities of Article 101: in the rule of reason the plaintiff has to present a *prima facie* case before the burden of proof shifts to the defendant at all, while RPF is condemned under Article 101(1) automatically; object type agreements have never had a realistic chance under Article 101(3); defendants bear a heavier burden of proof under Article 101(3) as compared to the American rule of reason, where the perception is that if substantiated justifications come up, courts tend to decide for the defendant.

The second part of the book examines specifically the economics of vertical intra-brand restraints (Chapter V) and contrasts it with their treatment in US antitrust and EU competition law (Chapters VI and VII). It goes beyond mere contrasting and grasps the conundrum of vertical intra-brand restraints in the context of the architecture of the rule on restrictive agreements: should justifications be considered under Article 101(1) or 101(3)? The Supreme Court's judgment in *Leegin*, where RPF's *per se* condemnation was overruled, also raises a novel point of analysis, especially because it reveals the 'economic views' of the judiciary: while economic scholarship is replete with efficiency theories of intra-brand restraints, one of the most important questions is which will be the 'economics of the courts', i.e. which theories will become part of the effects-analysis before US courts.

It will be argued here that the current treatment of vertical intra-brand restraints in EU competition law, which regards RPF and absolute territorial protection as almost *de facto* falling foul of Article 101, is not in accord with sound economics; economic analysis suggests that such restraints may have both pro- and anti-competitive effects, while EU competition law treats RPF and absolute territorial protection as restraints that are always or almost always harmful. In US antitrust law all intra-brand restraints are subjected to the effects-analysis of the rule of reason.

The treatment of absolute territorial protection in EU competition law is heavily influenced by the purpose of market integration (single market imperative), especially by the notion that private enterprises should not be allowed to rebuild national borders, which were lifted by the common market rules; nevertheless, this approach of EU law is misguided. The argument that European citizens have the natural right to purchase wherever they want in the common market does not justify the outright ban on absolute territorial protection on the wholesale level. Furthermore, since territorial protection seems to be the most efficient method of penetrating new markets, the foregoing ban may even impede market integration. Namely, the outright prohibition of absolute territorial exclusivity is a missing brick in the wall of territorial protection that in some markets can make the entire building crumble. In certain cases, the possibility of restricting active sales does not provide adequate protection against free-riding by parallel traders, which, in fact, execute the active sales themselves.

The final conclusions are summarized in the third part of the book (Chapter VIII). There is an emerging criticism against the almost *de facto* outright prohibition of RPF and absolute territorial protection in the EU, which was reinforced by the *Leegin* judgment. Nevertheless, the rising substantive analysis of vertical intra-brand restraints in EU competition law seems to be misplaced; there is a danger that all analysis related to RPF and absolute territorial protection will be done under Article 101(3). While the advantages of vertical intra-brand restraints relate normally to the enhancement of the competitive process, Article 101(3) centres on (productive) efficiency. Furthermore, the most pressing argument for RPF and absolute territorial protection is that if the producer has low market share and the practice is not widespread, the vertical intra-brand restraint is simply not capable of having any anti-competitive impact; this argument certainly fits the *de minimis* concept of Article 101(1) but has no place under Article 101(3).

Chapter II

Contextual concepts: the devil is in the context? The structure of the rule on restrictive agreements

In this chapter the architecture of the rule on restrictive agreements of EU competition and US antitrust law will be analysed and compared primarily in the context of vertical arrangements.

The structure of Article 101

In EU competition law the basic substantive rules of restrictive agreements are embedded in Article 101, which reads as follows.

> Article 101
>
> 1. The following shall be prohibited as incompatible with the common market: all agreements between undertakings, decisions by associations of undertakings and concerted practices which may affect trade between Member States and which have as their object or effect the prevention, restriction or distortion of competition within the common market, and in particular those which:
>   (a) directly or indirectly fix purchase or selling prices or any other trading conditions;
>   (b) limit or control production, markets, technical development, or investment;
>   (c) share markets or sources of supply;
>   (d) apply dissimilar conditions to equivalent transactions with other trading parties, thereby placing them at a competitive disadvantage;
>   (e) make the conclusion of contracts subject to acceptance by the other parties of supplementary obligations which, by their nature or according to commercial usage, have no connection with the subject of such contracts.
> 2. Any agreements or decisions prohibited pursuant to this article shall be automatically void.
> 3. The provisions of paragraph 1 may, however, be declared inapplicable in the case of:
>   – any agreement or category of agreements between undertakings,
>   – any decision or category of decisions by associations of undertakings,
>   – any concerted practice or category of concerted practices,

> which contributes to improving the production or distribution of goods or to promoting technical or economic progress, while allowing consumers a fair share of the resulting benefit, and which does not:
> (a) impose on the undertakings concerned restrictions which are not indispensable to the attainment of these objectives;
> (b) afford such undertakings the possibility of eliminating competition in respect of a substantial part of the products in question.

In the following, the general rule on restrictive agreements will be analysed in accordance with its conceptual elements. The notion of inter-state trade ('may affect trade between Member States'), despite being a very important rule of jurisdiction, is not examined here. Disregarding the requirement of inter-state trade, Article 101 contains the following conceptual elements:

1. Concept of agreement (agreements, decisions by associations of undertakings and concerted practices).
2. Substance of the rule on restrictive agreements (all agreements that are anti-competitive are, in principle, prohibited).
   - The distinction between agreements anti-competitive by object and anti-competitive by effect.
   - General prohibition on restrictive agreements:[1] anti-competitiveness (prevention, restriction or distortion of competition) – what is the content that must not be agreed to according to the general prohibition on restrictive agreements?
   - The system of exemption (cooperation is sometimes more efficient than competition): individual exemption, block exemptions.[2]

---

1 *Cf.* the German concepts of '*Kartellverbot*' and '*Freistellung*', where, in principle, all agreements restricting competition are prohibited (*Kartellverbot*) but may be exempted under certain circumstances (*Freistellung*). In this book the term 'rule on restrictive agreements' embraces both the general prohibition on restrictive agreements and the notion of exemption, while the term 'general prohibition on restrictive agreements' parallels the meaning of the German term '*Kartellverbot*'.

2 The Commission had legal monopoly to grant individual exemptions under Article 101(3) for several decades. Accordingly, Article 101(3) had no direct effect and its application was not automatic. Nevertheless, Regulation 1/2003/EC abolished the notification system and the Commission's legal monopoly and conferred direct effect on Article 101(3), see Regulation 1/2003/EC, Article 1(1)-(2). Accordingly, as from 1 May 2004, there is an *ex lege* individual exemption system in force, i.e. agreements meeting the requirements of Article 101(3) are *ipso iure* exempted, 'no prior decision to that effect being required'. Regulation 1/2003/EC, Article 1(1)-(2).

The structure of Section 1

In US antitrust law, the basis of the rule on restrictive agreements is Section 1 of the Sherman Act.

> Section 1
> Every contract, combination in the form of trust or otherwise, or conspiracy, in restraint of trade or commerce among the several States, or with foreign nations, is declared to be illegal. Every person who shall make any contract or engage in any combination or conspiracy hereby declared to be illegal shall be deemed guilty of a felony, and, on conviction thereof, shall be punished by fine not exceeding $100,000,000 if a corporation, or, if any other person, $1,000,000, or by imprisonment not exceeding 10 years, or by both said punishments, in the discretion of the court.[3]

The conceptual structure of US antitrust law's rule on restrictive agreements is more sparely built than that of EU competition law. First, in US antitrust law there is no system of exemption but all exceptions to the general prohibition on restrictive agreements are to be found within the body of Section 1. Second, US antitrust law, as applied in the judicial practice, does not distinguish between 'object' and 'effect' restraints but the dividing line is between the categories of *per se* illegality and rule of reason. The sharpness of the dividing line has recently been eroded by the Supreme Court's introduction of the so-called 'quick look' (abbreviated or truncated rule of reason), according to which the defendants get a very limited chance to submit justifying arguments even if the agreement mirrors the features of one of the categories of agreements that are treated as *per se* illegal, and courts are ready to have a quick look at the proffered justifications. If the latter seem to give the impression of being plausible, a full-blown rule of reason may follow, where, however, the defendant bears the burden to prove pro-competitive effects, the anti-competitive ones being assumed.

Section 1 of the Sherman Act contains an 'inter-state commerce' clause too; nevertheless, similarly to EU competition law, this clause will not be covered by the forthcoming analysis.

The structure of Section 1 is to be conceptualized as follows:

1. Concept of agreement (contract, combination, conspiracy).
2. General rule on restrictive agreements.
    - *Per se* rules and rule of reason.
    - The structure and balancer of rule of reason analysis.
    - The concept of 'quick look'.

3 15 USC 1.

Comparative summary

The threshold question of both EU competition and US antitrust law is the notion of agreement. The significance of the concept of agreement is clearly demonstrated by the differences between EU competition and US antitrust law. As shown in the forthcoming chapter, in EU law there is a danger that the very wide notion of vertical agreement extends the prohibition also to genuine unilateral conduct, while in US antitrust law the producer may smooth the restraint over by referring to unilateralism.

The second constituent element of both systems is the substance of the rule on restrictive agreements and the categorization of agreements according to their competitive/anti-competitive nature. In this regard, there is a salient difference between EU competition and US antitrust law. While EU law operates with two different, though undefined, notions of substantive analysis, the first being in Article 101(1) and the second being in Article 101(3), US antitrust law has a single blender that is expected to embrace all considerations. Accordingly, contrary to US antitrust law's monistic grasp, there are two different and complementary substantive tests in EU competition law. Intuition suggests that the combination of these two tests embraces the analysis that is included in the monistic test of US antitrust law. Intuition also suggests that the two tests of EU competition law have different focuses.

Chapter III

The threshold of the prohibition on restrictive agreements: the concept of agreement, contract, combination and conspiracy

While competition lawyers usually prefer discussing the issue of what can be agreed to in a vertical relationship, the question when the parties are regarded as having agreed to a particular measure seems to have similar practical significance, *viz* it is the concept of agreement that triggers off, or precludes, the antitrust law analysis. In real life, the interpretation of the notion of agreement determines whether a measure running counter to the principles that define the content of the law on restrictive agreements can be implemented.

Vertical agreements between producers and distributors in EU competition law: a thought crime?

The concept of agreement in EU law is an extremely wide notion obviously transgressing the colloquial meaning of the term, especially in case of vertical relations. In the following, the definition of agreement will be analysed in detail due to its paramount importance regarding the evaluation of the treatment of vertical restraints.

Article 101(1) embraces not only agreements but also concerted practices (and decisions of associations of undertakings). The ECJ confirmed in *Pioneer* that concerted practice can exist even between undertakings in a vertical relationship.[1]

1 Joined Cases 100 to 103/80 *SA Musique Diffusion française and others v Commission* [1983] ECR 1825, paras 79-80. ('Thus it is not disputed that Mr. Setton did indeed bring to the meeting the results of three test purchases which undertakings managed by him had made from British customers of Shriro and that he insisted on the neet to put a stop to parallel imports to France. Moreover, it is not disputed that Mr. Todd's letter to his customers were a direct consequence of that meeting and not of later contacts with Mr. Setton. In those circumstances, Pioneer, which had called the meeting and presided over it, must accept responsibility for that consequence, regard being had to the position which it occupies in relation to its national distributors, as described above. It must therefore be concluded that the Commission was justified in finding that Pioneer had participated in two concerted practices.')

In the following, all forms of vertical cooperation will be analysed jointly, as the distinction between agreement and concerted practice has no practical significance, i.e. it is irrelevant whether a particular collusion is treated as an agreement or a concerted practice;[2] and the vast majority of vertical cases centres around the notion of agreement.

In EU competition law, the concept of agreement is an extremely wide category, which also covers apparently unilateral behaviour.[3] Both the Commission and EU courts use a very flexible definition, especially if it comes up in a vertical context. Lead by the purpose of market integration, the ECJ often applied Article 101 to cases where, at least in colloquial sense, there were no mutual subjective elements (consensus) between the parties and, hence, the existence of an agreement was dubious.[4] These cases concerned undertakings with no dominant position, who were, accordingly, not addressed by Article 102 but who tried to partition the common market along national borders, eliminate parallel trade or sought to maintain different prices in different Member States. The extension of the concept of agreement has been frequently motivated by the desire to catch arguably unilateral practices that fall foul of the purpose of market integration.[5] Nevertheless, these considerations, inspired by the final purpose of EU competition law, should not, at least in theory, influence the interpretation and application of the concept of agreement. The existence of an agreement is independent from its alleged aim or effect on competition.[6] The question is whether there was some consensus between the parties and not whether one of the parties had motives that are antipathic for EU law.

The concept of agreement has experienced a smooth move since its early days: at the outset, EU courts had an artificially wide grasp of agreement, which was later on corrected and confined. The purview of 'agreement' is, however, still extremely wide.

Before riding the waves of the history of this jurisprudence it is useful to get equipped with a conceptual compass. It is submitted that there are two theories that enable the conversion of the producer's unilateral behaviour into the synallagmatic relationship between the former and its distributors: the concept of 'continuous

2 Joanna Goyder, EU Distribution Law 21 (4th ed., 2005).

3 *See* Joanna Goyder, EU Distribution Law 20 (4th ed., 2005).

4 Morten Broberg and Peter Stig Jakobsen, *The Concept of Agreement in Article 81 E.C.: on the Manufacturers' Right to Prevent Parallel Trade within the European Community*, 23(3) European Competition Law Review 127, 128 (2002).

5 Ioannis Lianos, *Collusion in Vertical Relations under Article 81 EC*, 45 Common Market Law Review 1027, 1037 (2008).

6 *Contra* Ioannis Lianos, *Collusion in Vertical Relations under Article 81 EC*, 45 Common Market Law Review 1027, 1036 (2008) (arguing that 'it would be erroneous to assess the definition of the concept of agreement in competition law in disconnection from the aims pursued by Article 81; which implies that because the aims of competition law are not similar to those of contract law, the requirement of concurrence of wills or mutual consent fulfils a different objective and should therefore be interpreted differently from contract law').

business relationship'[7] (or 'ongoing business relations') and the concept of 'tacit acquiescence (assent)'. According to the first theory, the permanent business relationship between the producer and the distributor, especially in case of selective distribution, may qualify as a distribution framework agreement that authorizes the producer to make certain decisions relating to the whole distribution system, which – despite their unilateral nature – thus become part of the consensual space between the parties, i.e. the unilateral calls and declarations of the producer are automatically treated as part of the agreement between the parties. The second theory is based on the argument that distributors tacitly acquiesce in the call of the producer, who might have requested them not to sell under a certain price or not to sell to customers from a particular territory. Nevertheless, it is questionable whether the distributor's mere silence suffices: may an agreement be established on the basis of the bare fact that the distributor failed to oppose the circular of the producer or it is also necessary that the producer's unilateral call materializes in the distributor's conduct?

The first leading case[8] in respect of the concept of agreement in a vertical context is *AEG-Telefunken*,[9] where the ECJ held that in a selective distribution system[10] the notion of agreement encompasses the unilateral conduct of the producer where the

---

7 *See* Case COMP/37.975 *PO/Yamaha* Commission decision of 16.07.2003 (unpublished but available at http://ec.europa.eu/competition/antitrust/cases/decisions/37975/en.pdf), para 87. ('Instructions given by Yamaha's subsidiaries to their contractual distributors within the official network also constitute agreements and/or concerted practices and are not unilateral acts which would escape the prohibition contained in Article 81(1) of the Treaty and 53(1) of the EEA Agreement. According to the established case law, admission to a distribution network implies that the contracting parties explicitly or implicitly accept the distribution policy of a manufacturer. The circulars and instructions are therefore part of the agreements between Yamaha's subsidiaries and their authorised dealers, since they are to be regarded as part of a set of continuous business relations based on an existing general agreement. Admission to Yamaha's network, governed by an agreement drawn up in advance, implies acceptance by distributors of the policy communicated by Yamaha which they have followed by adjusting their behaviour in the market according to these instructions.') *See* Valentine Korah and Denis O'Sullivan, Distribution Agreements under the EC Competition Rules 286 (2002). *See also* Ioannis Lianos, *Collusion in Vertical Relations under Article 81 EC*, 45 Common Market Law Review 1027, 1037 (2008) (stressing that distribution networks 'can be conceived as hybrid institutions separate from the model of the "market", but falling short of establishing a "hierarchy" or firm').

8 This was, nevertheless, not the very first case in this question. The ECJ had already dealt with the issue of whether the producer's unilateral declarations could qualify as an agreement in *BMW Belgium SA*, where it regarded the circular of the manufacturer as being caught in the net of Article 101(1). Joined Cases 32/78, 36/78 to 82/78 *BMW Belgium SA and others v Commission* [1979] ECR 2435, paras 28-30.

9 Case 107/82 *Allgemeine Elektrizitäts-Gesellschaft AEG-Telefunken AG v Commission* [1983] ECR 3151.

10 Selective distribution is normally used for marketing branded goods. The gist of this scheme is that the producer sells only to selected distributors chosen on the basis of certain criteria usually related to the nature of the brand itself. Members of the distribution

latter refuses to admit new distributors to the scheme. The Court based its decision on the 'continuous business relationship' theory. The refusal of the producer to admit an additional distributor to the system was regarded as part of the business relationship between the former and the dealers that were already part of the selective distribution system, and, thus, it was caught in the net of Article 101(1). The Court considered that when a new distributor is admitted the acceptance by the producer is based on the tacit or actual agreement between the members of the scheme that they acquiesce in the producer's business policy in this regard. This notion encompasses, *inter alia*, that the producer can exclude from the system all distributors who – while complying with the qualitative requirements of the selective distribution scheme – do not obey the producer's general business policy. It follows from the foregoing that decisions relating to adherence to the selective distribution scheme are to be evaluated in the context of the business relationship between the authorized distributors and the producer:

> even refusals of approval are acts performed in the context of the contractual relations with authorized distributors inasmuch as their purpose is to guarantee observance of the agreements in restraint of competition which form the basis of contracts between manufacturers and approved distributors.[11]

Reacting to the applicant's defence that the refusals did not represent systematic business policy and they amounted to sporadic instances, the Court, in fact, held that once the Commission proves that some distributors occasionally happened to have been excluded despite complying with the qualitative criteria of the selective distribution system, the burden of proof shifts to the undertaking: it is the latter who has to prove that the occasional exclusions do not represent a systematic business strategy.[12] The Court considered that the restricted number of the infringements did not imply that the practice was not part of the undertaking's business policy: such a conclusion could be reached only if it was established that notwithstanding the sporadic occasions this was not the strategy of the applicant.[13]

After *AEG-Telefunken* it was equivocal what bearing the common interest of the parties has on the way the existence of agreement is established. The Court's

---

scheme can sell only to final consumers or to distributors that are also admitted to the system. *See Guidelines on Vertical Restraints*, para 174.

11 Paras 38-39.

12 *See* Morten Broberg and Peter Stig Jakobsen, *The Concept of Agreement in Article 81 E.C.: on the Manufacturers' Right to Prevent Parallel Trade within the European Community*, 23(3) European Competition Law Review 127, 129 (2002).

13 Para 46. ('It follows that the non-systematic nature of the infringements is not necessarily proved by their relatively restricted number and the possibility that there has been a systematic use of the conditions for admission in a manner incompatible with Community law can be rules out only after it has been established that there was no general policy on the part of AEG or its subsidiaries designed to exclude re-sellers who were too aggressive or to influence prices.')

reasoning did not mention this but in this case the producer and the authorized dealers had the same interest: maintaining prices. Nevertheless, the ECJ's judgment in *Ford-Werke AG and Ford of Europe Inc.*[14] suggests that it is irrelevant whether the producer and the distributors have common or conflicting interests regarding the agreement.[15] According to the fact pattern, the subsidiary of a motor vehicle producer refused to supply German distributors with right-hand drive cars. The reason was that prices in the United Kingdom were significantly higher than in Germany and there was an increasing demand for such cars in Albion, which stimulated parallel trade. The producer, in order to protect its British distributor, informed the German dealers that it was not going to accept orders for right-hand drive cars, and, henceforth, such motor vehicles were to be purchased from the British distributor.[16] The ECJ held that the foregoing conduct comes within the purview of Article 101. According to the Court's explanation,

> agreements which constitute a selective distribution system and which (...) seek to maintain a specialized trade capable of providing specific services for high-technology products are normally concluded in order to govern the distribution of those products for a certain number of years. Because technological developments are not always foreseeable over such a period of time, those agreements necessarily have to leave certain matters to be decided later by the manufacturer.[17]

The fact pattern before the bench was said to be such a situation: the selective distribution agreement authorized the producer to decide future questions, and it acted accordingly. Thereafter, the ECJ practically repeated its statements made in *AEG-Telefunken*: the unilateral nature of the producer's conduct was only ostensible since the behaviour formed part of the business relationship between the producer and the distributors, and by entering the distribution system the latter implicitly accepted the producer's business policy regarding the question of what kind of models would be supplied to the German market.[18]

Ford also argued that even if it could be established that there was an agreement between the parties, such an agreement could not be regarded as part of the

14 Joined Cases 25/84 and 26/84 *Ford-Werke AG and Ford of Europe Inc. v Commission*, [1985] ECR 2725.

15 In this case there was a conflict of interest between the producer and the distributors concerning the business policy concerned. *See* Morten Broberg and Peter Stig Jakobsen, *The Concept of Agreement in Article 81 E.C.: on the Manufacturers' Right to Prevent Parallel Trade within the European Community*, 23(3) European Competition Law Review 127, 130 (2002); Richard Whish, Competition law 108 (2009).

16 Para 6. It is noteworthy that this case dealt with the individual exemption of the distribution framework agreement. The Commission investigated the stopping of deliveries in this context and refused to grant individual exemption to the framework agreement on this ground.

17 Para 20.

18 Paras 21-22.

distribution framework agreement but was independent from that. Namely, the framework agreement did not touch upon the trade in right-hand drive cars but these vehicles were supplied in the frame of a separate arrangement applicable solely to such cars. The Court, nevertheless, held that the blocking of the deliveries occurred in the context of the distribution framework agreement itself. The ECJ underpinned its position with the following arguments: the distributors of the two contractual arrangements were the same and the incriminated circular sent by the producer was addressed exclusively to dealers who were part of the framework agreement.[19]

The *Ford-Werke AG and Ford of Europe Inc.* judgment reveals the artificial amplification of the concept of agreement. Namely, the foregoing jurisprudence suggests that in case of a selective distribution system all the producer's unilateral acts are to be treated as part of the agreement, even if the scope of the framework agreement does not embrace the product in question. What is more, the termination of the supply of right-hand drive cars did not require express or tacit assent on the part of the distributors, nay, from the point of view of the implementation of the producer's strategy the distributors' market conduct was perfectly irrelevant.

In *Sandoz*[20] the ECJ expanded further the concept of agreement. According to the Commission's position, since the producer systematically dispatched invoices bearing the phrase 'export prohibited', and the distributors failed to object to this indication, the export-ban became part of the framework agreement between the parties.

> Consequently, the invoice cannot be seen as the expression of a merely unilateral act but forms part of such an agreement of which it constitutes the documentary evidence. The fact that the invoices have been constantly and systematically used leads to the conclusion that [the producer's,] Sandoz PF's clients implicitly agreed with it and accepted it. Hence the words 'export prohibited', which appear on the invoices used by Sandoz PF, represent, with regard to Article 85 a contractual clause forming an integral part of the agreement on which Sandoz PF and its customers base their transactions. This is confirmed by the presence, on the front of the invoices, of certain other commercial clauses relevant to clients. The fact that Sandoz PF claims that these clauses are void or simply respecting the Italian Civil Code does not affect their nature as sales conditions.[21]

It is very important to stress that in this case, as opposed to both *AEG-Telefunken* and *Ford-Werke AG and Ford of Europe Inc.*, there was no written agreement between the parties. Although the Commission was perfectly right, and confirmed

19 Paras 23-25.

20 Case C-277/87 *Sandoz prodotti farmaceutici SpA v Commission* [1990] ECR I-45. The case concerned pharmaceutical products in relation to which there are considerable price differences between Member States, due to national price regulations. This situation issues in flourishing parallel trade.

21 87/409/EEC *Sandoz* [1987] OJ L 222/28, paras 26-27.

by the ECJ, when saying that such a circumstance certainly does not prevent the ascertainment of an agreement according to Article 101, as the existence of an agreement is attested by the parties' continuous business relationship,[22] it cannot be disregarded that in the case at stake, as opposed to both *AEG-Telefunken* and *Ford- Werke AG and Ford of Europe Inc.*, there was no framework agreement one could have screwed out of the producer to shape the content of the parties' business relationship by unilateral acts. Furthermore, in *Sandoz* there was no selective distribution scheme in relation to which the producer could have been deemed to have governance rights in order to preserve the consistency, image and reputation of the brand. It follows from the Commission decision and its judicial affirmation that if the producer expresses its will towards the distributors systematically and the latter do not object, the producer's communication becomes part of the agreement between the parties. In this regard it is irrelevant whether the dealers act in accordance with the producer's wish, or whether the behaviour wished by the producer is in the dealers' interest. Namely, the Commission did not examine whether the dealers acted according to the call on the invoices ('export prohibited'), while their interest in re-exporting the goods was obvious.[23]

The EU institutions opened Pandora's box with the artificial dilatation of the concept of agreement, which did actually cast the shadow of stifling suspicion on the producer's unilateral acts. The justification of such an approach is questionable both from a conceptual and an economic point of view. Namely, competition law prohibitions related to unilateral conduct are embedded in Article 102, which, nevertheless, applies only to dominant undertakings. With the incomprehensible dilatation of the concept of agreement, EU competition law in fact imposed obligations on non-dominant undertakings that were shaped to govern undertakings with significant market power. The ECJ's recent judicial practice, certainly due to the foregoing considerations, tried to move back the genie into the bottle and virtually overruled some elements of the above jurisprudence, the principles of which were to be refined, remarkably. However, for the time being no breakthrough has been experienced and the concept of agreement has remained a bodiless and vague notion.

The ECJ's judgment in *Bayer*[24] was the first considerable step in this regard. In the context of the producer's endeavour to hinder parallel trade, the Court held that there is no agreement if the producer reduces the quantity delivered to the distributors or answers the orders of the latter only to the extent that is necessary for satisfying the demand in the local market. Thus, in the absence of dominant position, the producer's business policy does not fall foul of EU competition law.

---

22 Para 25.

23 *Cf.* Morten Broberg and Peter Stig Jakobsen, *The Concept of Agreement in Article 81 E.C.: on the Manufacturers' Right to Prevent Parallel Trade within the European Community*, 23(3) European Competition Law Review 127, 131 (2002).

24 Joined Cases C-2/01 and C-3/01 *Bundesverband der Arzneimittel-Importeure eV and Commission v Bayer AG* [2004] ECR I-23. *See* Christopher Brown, Note, *Bayer v Commission: the ECJ agrees*, 25(7) European Competition Law Review 386 (2005).

The fact pattern was the following. There were significant differences between Member States as regards the prices of pharmaceuticals, primarily due to price regulation. The difference between the UK, on the one hand, and the French and Spanish markets, on the other, was 40 per cent, creating a spawn for parallel trade and resulting in an almost 50 per cent decrease in the UK distributor's turnover.[25] In order to eliminate parallel trade, the producer of the medicine (Adalat) refused to supply the ever-increasing orders of the French and Spanish distributors and supplied them with only the quantity it considered necessary for satisfying their own local markets. The producer thus prevented the dealers from over-importing and then re-exporting any excess to the UK.[26]

The Commission condemned Bayer for inserting an export ban into the commercial relationship with the wholesalers.[27] The Commission's decision also said that Bayer endeavoured to identify the exporting wholesalers, and if one of them happened to re-export, Bayer reduced the quantity delivered. From these circumstances the Commission inferred that Bayer was only willing to supply wholesalers with the proviso that these wholesalers accepted the export ban, i.e. it forced the wholesalers to acquiesce in the export ban and they did so, tacitly.[28] The producer delivered the goods with reference to the export ban and reduced the quantity automatically once it was proved that the wholesaler exported.

The GC quashed the Commission's decision referring to the latter's failure to prove the existence of an agreement. The distributors' behaviour, namely, did not mirror any acceptance of an export ban. Using different practices, the wholesalers still endeavoured to obtain significant volumes of Adalat and to export them. Therewith, the Commission also failed to prove that Bayer actually required any guarantee from the distributors agreeing that they refrain from re-exporting.[29] The GC disapproved the Commission's argument that the agreement between the parties could be deduced from the very circumstance that the wholesalers did not terminate their business relations with Bayer after having become aware of the latter's anti-export business policy. The GC also gave a definition of agreement, based on the requirement of the existence of mutual subjective elements.

> The proof of an agreement between undertakings within the meaning of Article 85(1) of the Treaty must be founded upon the direct or indirect finding of the existence of the subjective element that characterises the very concept of an agreement, that is to say a concurrence of wills between economic operators on the implementation of a policy, the pursuit of an objective, or the adoption of a given line of conduct on the market, irrespective of the manner in which the parties' intention to behave on the market in accordance with the terms of that

25 Para 3.

26 Para 4.

27 96/478/EC *ADALAT* [1996] OJ L 201/1, para 184.

28 *Id.* at paras 155-188.

29 Case T-41/96 *Bayer AG v Commission* [2000] ECR II-3383, paras 111-157.

> agreement is expressed (…). The Commission misjudges that concept of the concurrence of wills in holding that the continuation of commercial relations with the manufacturer when it adopts a new policy, which it implements unilaterally, amounts to acquiescence by the wholesalers in that policy, although their de facto conduct is clearly contrary to that policy.[30]

The GC also emphasized that the evil envisaged by the producer should not affect the way the agreement is defined.

> [P]rovided he does so without abusing a dominant position, and there is no concurrence of wills between him and his wholesalers, a manufacturer may adopt the supply policy which he considers necessary, even if, by the very nature of its aim, for example, to hinder parallel imports, the implementation of that policy may entail restrictions on competition and affect trade between Member States.[31]

The ECJ upheld the GC's judgment, confirming the latter's reasoning. The Court held that an agreement exists only when the call of one of the parties receives express or tacit acquiescence from the other party. This is all the more the case if the parties have conflicting interests.

> For an agreement within the meaning of Article 85(1) of the Treaty to be capable of being regarded as having been concluded by tacit acceptance, it is necessary that the manifestation of the wish of one of the contracting parties to achieve an anti-competitive goal constitute an invitation to the other party, whether express or implied, to fulfil that goal jointly, and that applies all the more where, as in this case, such an agreement is not at first sight in the interests of the other party, namely the wholesalers.
>
> Therefore, the Court of First Instance was right to examine whether Bayer's conduct supported the conclusion that the latter had required of the wholesalers, as a condition of their future contractual relations, that they should comply with its new commercial policy.[32]

The ECJ also distinguished the fact pattern of *Bayer* from *AEG-Telefunken* and *Ford-Werke AG and Ford of Europe Inc.*: it emphasized that in these cases there was a pre-existing agreement and the main question was whether the measures of the producer could be added into the agreement.[33] In one word, the Court said that *AEG-Telefunken* and *Ford-Werke AG and Ford of Europe Inc.* were based on

30 Para 173.

31 Para 176.

32 Joined Cases C-2/01 and C-3/01 P *Bundesverband der Arzneimittel-Importeure eV and Commission v Bayer AG* [2004] ECR I-23, paras 102-103.

33 Para 144.

the 'continuous business relationship' theory, while *Bayer* was, and should be, examined on the basis of the 'tacit acquiescence (assent)' theory. The ECJ also tried to distinguish the fact pattern of *Bayer* from *Sandoz* but in fact it unequivocally overruled the latter, though in a very euphemistic manner. The Court held that *Sandoz* did not support the proposition that there was an agreement if the distributor continued to send orders to the producer after the latter had expressed the wish to restrict export. An agreement presupposes assent on the side of the distributor, which must be at least tacit.[34] This language in fact eliminates the authority of *Sandoz* since their tacit acquiescence was derived from the distributors' failure to object to the permanent use of the 'export prohibited' phrase on the invoices and because they continued to send orders to the producer.

It is worth citing AG Tizzano's opinion, which stresses that an agreement in this context presupposes an offer or call on the side of the producer. If no offer is made, there is nothing to be accepted, and, hence, no agreement can come into existence. This was the element that, according to Tizzano, distinguished *Sandoz* from *Bayer*: in *Sandoz* there was indeed an offer properly made by the producer, which could be considered to have been implicitly accepted.[35]

In *Bayer*, the ECJ made a very important contribution to the concept of agreement, however, the scope of the judgment is rather limited since here the producer acted unilaterally, and the implementation of its business strategy did not require the distributors' cooperation. The producer could and did implement the business policy in a strictly unilateral manner by simply reducing the quantity supplied. Thus, after satisfying the local market the wholesalers had no excess capacity that could have been exported. The Commission failed to prove that Bayer required its distributors not to take part in parallel trade.

In *Volkswagen*, the EU judiciary had another chance to elucidate the concept of agreement. The fact pattern – contrary to *Bayer* – concerned unilateral behaviour where the producer wanted the distributors to act in a certain way. Volkswagen instructed its German dealers not to give, or to give restricted, discounts for the Volkswagen Passat model. The Commission characterized this unilateral call which had materialized in circulars as an agreement aiming at fixing the resale price and, accordingly, violating EU competition law.[36] The piquancy of the case is that the Commission based its decision on the theory of 'continuous business relationship', while not even mentioning the theorem of 'tacit acquiescence'. Later on, this turned out to be fatal. According to the Commission, the agreement between the parties establishing a selective distribution system authorized the producer to make unilateral decisions, which subsequently, became part of the agreement between the parties. The Commission considered that as the distributors implicitly accepted the producer's marketing policy by signing the distribution agreement, there was

---

34 Para 142.

35 Opinion of AG Tizzano in Joined Cases C-2/01 and C-3/01 *Bundesverband der Arzneimittel-Importeure eV and Commission v Bayer AG* [2004] ECR I-23, paras 60-61.

36 2001/711/EC *Volkswagen* [2001] OJ L 262/14.

nothing to prevent the application of Article 101. Nonetheless, the Commission did not investigate whether the dealers' behaviour effectively mirrored the call of the producer. Indeed, the proof of the latter would not have been necessary if the argument of 'continuous business relationship' had worked and if the producer's business policy had become part of the parties' agreement. Nevertheless, as both the GC and the ECJ took issue with the Commission's point that the unilateral call of the producer became part of the parties' 'continuous business relationship', the Commission's failure to examine whether the dealers' behaviour actually corresponded to the producer's wish sealed the decision's fate.

The GC held that 'the concept of agreement (…) centres around the existence of a concurrence of wills between at least two parties, the form in which it is manifested being unimportant so long as it constitutes the faithful expression of the parties' intention'.[37] While unilateral behaviour is not caught by Article 101,

> a distinction should be drawn between cases in which an undertaking has adopted a genuinely unilateral measure, and thus without the express or implied participation of another undertaking, and those in which the unilateral character of the measure is merely apparent. Whilst the former do not fall within Article 81(1) EC, the latter must be regarded as revealing an agreement between undertakings and may therefore fall within the scope of that article. That is the case, in particular, with practices and measures in restraint of competition which, though apparently adopted unilaterally by the manufacturer in the context of its contractual relations with its dealers, nevertheless receive at least the tacit acquiescence of those dealers …[38]

The GC analysed both above theories of agreement formation. It held that the theory of 'continuous business relationship' is applicable only if the framework agreement, being the container of the business relationship, effectively authorizes the producer to shape the business relations between the parties through unilateral acts.

> [A] contractual variation could be regarded as having been accepted in advance, upon and by the signature of a lawful dealership agreement, where it is a lawful contractual variation which is foreseen by the contract, or is a variation which, having regard to commercial usage or legislation, the dealer could not refuse. By contrast, it cannot be accepted that an unlawful contractual variation could be regarded as having been accepted in advance, upon and by the signature of a lawful distribution agreement. In that case, acquiescence in the unlawful contractual variation can occur only after the dealer has become aware of the variation desired by the manufacturer.[39]

---

37 Case T-208/01 *Volkswagen v Commission* [2003] ECR II-5141, para 32.

38 Para 35.

39 Para 45. *See* paras 45-46 and 61-63.

According to the GC the distribution agreement did not authorize the producer to supplement the consensual relationship between the parties. Nonetheless, the GC followed a novel approach in this regard: it examined the issue of authorization not in general but in the context of the distribution agreement in question, i.e. the GC suggested that it is required that the distribution agreement virtually empowers the producer to make additions to the agreement. The framework agreement creating a continuous business relationship is in itself not sufficient to make the unilaterally expressed business policy part of the permanent business relationship. After having concluded that the framework agreement contained no specific authorization, the GC proceeded on the basis of the 'tacit acceptance' theory or, in order to be precise, would have proceeded since – as no investigation was carried out in this regard – the Commission failed to prove that the rebuked call was in fact followed.[40]

The ECJ affirmed the approach of the GC with some corrections reiterating the GC's most important statements.

> The will of the parties may result from both the clauses of the dealership agreement in question and from the conduct of the parties, and in particular from the possibility of there being tacit acquiescence by the dealers in a call from the manufacturer (…). In the present case, with respect to the first possibility, the Commission inferred that there was a concurrence of wills between the parties solely on the basis of the clauses of the dealership agreement in question. The Court of First Instance then had to proceed, as it did, to consider whether those calls were explicitly contained in the dealership agreement or, at the very least, whether the clauses of that agreement authorised motor vehicle manufacturers to make such calls.[41]

The ECJ agreed with the GC that the application of the 'continuous business relationship' theory requires the determination of 'whether the calls at issue were part of the overall commercial relationship between Volkswagen and its dealers, [and] the Court of First Instance should have considered whether they were provided for or authorised by the clauses of the dealership agreement, taking account of the aims pursued by that agreement *per se*, in the light of the economic and legal context in which the agreement was signed'.[42] The Court also endorsed the GC's approach of making a 'specific assessment of the dealership agreement'[43] and relying 'on the wording of the clauses'.[44, 45]

40 Para 38.

41 Paras 39-40.

42 Para 48.

43 Para 52.

44 Para 53.

45 Para 4 of the ECJ's judgment summarized the relevant clauses of the distribution agreement: 'Under Clause 4(1) of the dealership agreement in its September 1995 and January 1998 versions, Volkswagen grants the dealer a contract territory for the range of vehicles and for customer service. In return, the dealer undertakes to promote sales and the

The ECJ rectified the GC's judgment in one regard. The Court noted

> that its case-law does not indicate that the compliance or non-compliance of the contractual clauses in question with the competition rules is necessarily decisive in that examination. It follows that the Court of First Instance erred in law in finding (...) that clauses which comply with the competition rules may not be regarded as authorising calls which are contrary to those rules. The possibility that a call which is contrary to the competition rules may be regarded as being authorised by seemingly neutral clauses of a dealership agreement cannot be automatically excluded. Consequently, the Court of First Instance could not, without making an error of law, refrain from examining the clauses of the dealership agreement individually, taking account, where applicable, of all other relevant factors, such as the aims pursued by that agreement in the light of the economic and legal context in which it was signed.[46]

Similarly to the GC, the ECJ did not examine the issue of tacit acquiescence, repeating the reasons employed by the former.

> With respect to the second possibility, that is, in the absence of relevant contractual provisions, the existence of an agreement within the meaning of Article 81(1) EC presupposes the dealers' explicit or tacit acquiescence to the measure adopted by the motor vehicle manufacturer (...). In the present case, since the Commission did not rely on there being explicit or tacit acquiescence by the dealers, this second possibility is not relevant for the present dispute.[47]

The question is still open: what is the law of the land after *Bayer* and *Volkswagen*? Thus much is certain that these judgments eliminated some parts of the earlier jurisprudence. *Bayer* made it unequivocal that the producer's genuine unilateral action is not caught by Article 101. Thereby, those elements of the producer's

---

customer service intensively in his specific area and to exploit its market potential to the best of his ability. Under Clause 2(6) (January 1989 version) or Clause 2(1) (September 1995 and January 1998 versions) of the dealership agreement, the dealer undertakes "to defend and promote in every way the interests of Volkswagen AG, of the Volkswagen distribution organisation and of the Volkswagen brand". It is also stipulated that "the dealer will comply with all instructions issued for the purposes of the agreement regarding the distribution of new Volkswagen cars, the stocking of replacement parts, customer service, sales promotion, advertising, training, and the ensuring of quality in each area of Volkswagen's business". Finally, under Clause 8(1) of the dealership agreement, "Volkswagen AG will issue non-binding price recommendations concerning retail prices and discounts".'

46 Paras 43-45. However, the ECJ also established in para 54 that this error did 'not affect the soundness of the conclusion reached by the Court of First Instance, to the effect that the calls at issue in the present case cannot be regarded as constituting an "agreement" within the meaning of Article 81(1) EC'.

47 Paras 46-47.

business policy that do not require the distributors' subsequent behaviour can avoid competition law scrutiny under Article 101. The ECJ also made it clear in *Bayer* that the mere silence of the distributors cannot be considered as acceptance. The latter proposition was confirmed by the Court in *Volkswagen*. Therewith, in *Volkswagen* the Court went further and exceeded the propositions of *Bayer* by holding that even if the producer does not want to, or does not have a chance to, implement the chosen business policy through unilateral conduct and tries to enjoin a particular behaviour on its dealers, an agreement comes into existence only if there is a pre-existing agreement between the parties that virtually authorizes the producer to determine mandatory patterns of conduct, unilaterally, *or* the distributors accept the call of the producer, though tacitly. In this regard the dealers' actual conduct may be taken into account in order to establish whether there was acquiescence.[48]

The applicability of the 'continuous business relationship' theory requires the analysis of the concrete provisions of the distribution framework agreement taking into account its legal and economic context. The fact that a general framework agreement exists is far from sufficient. Contrary to earlier practice, the conclusion of the distribution framework agreement, even in case of selective distribution, in itself, does not imply that the distributors authorize the producer to determine mandatory patterns of conduct.[49] Quite the contrary, the authorization must be virtual, though not necessarily express; and hypothetical or visionary authorization is not sufficient. The GC and ECJ judgments in *Volkswagen* are so much the more

48 Ali Nikpay, Jonathan Faull and Lars Kjølbye, *Chapter 3: Article 81*, *in* The EC Law of Competition § 3.76 (Jonathan Faull and Ali Nikpay ed., 2007). *See* Case T-168/01 *GlaxoSmithKline Services Unlimited v Commission* [2006] ECR II-2969, para. 83. ('That evidence may consist of direct evidence, taking the form, for example, of a written document (…), or, failing that, indirect evidence, for example in the form of conduct (…).') *See also* Ali Nikpay, Jonathan Faull and Lars Kjølbye, *Chapter 3: Article 81*, *in* The EC Law of Competition § 3.82 (Jonathan Faull and Ali Nikpay ed., 2007). ('[T]he way in which the ECJ distinguished *Bayer* from its judgment in *Sandoz* suggests that the European Courts may not require much more than passive acquiescence in cases where the supplier has sought the cooperation of dealers.')

49 *See* Case T-208/01 *Volkswagen v Commission* [2003] ECR II-5141, para 47. ('The Court considers that the Commission is proceeding from a mistaken interpretation of the case-law which it cites in support of its case, when it argues that, according to the *AEG*, *Ford*, *BMW* and *Volkswagen* judgments, it is not necessary, at least in the case of selective distribution systems such as the one in this case, to look for acquiescence to a manufacturer's call in the conduct adopted by the dealer in the context of that call (for example after its receipt), and that such acquiescence ought to be regarded as having been established as a matter of principle by the mere fact that the dealer has entered the distribution network'); Mario Filipponi, Luc Peeperkorn and Donncadh Woods, *Chapter 9: Vertical Agreements*, *in* The EC Law of Competition § 9.30 (Jonathan Faull and Ali Nikpay ed., 2007); Vivien Rose and Peter Roth, *Article 81(1)*, *in* Bellamy & Child's European Community Law of Competition § 2.025 (Peter Roth and Vivien Rose ed., 2008).

interesting for the cognoscente competition lawyer as the fact pattern concerned an exclusive and selective distribution system and EU courts declared in this context that the authorization has to be virtual. Namely, *AEG-Telefunken* and *Ford-Werke AG and Ford of Europe Inc.* dealt with selective distribution schemes when amplifying the theory of 'visionary authorization' with a fabulous conceptual and logical feat. In the light of the factual situation in *Volkswagen* it is, however, clear that this judgment is applicable not only to selective distribution schemes but also to distribution systems at large.

In this regard, the GC's judgment in *General Motors*[50] should be mentioned, which seems to go counter to the foregoing ECJ practice, hence representing questionable authority. Although the GC's judgment reached the ECJ on appeal, the appellant surprisingly failed to raise the issue of lack of agreement; thus, the ECJ had no chance to amplify its position. In General Motors, the producer, *inter alia*, excluded export sales from its bonus system. The Commission's decision, confirmed by the GC, characterized this conduct as an agreement on the basis of the theory of 'continuous business relationship'.[51]

The ambit of Section 1: contract, combination and conspiracy

US antitrust law went through a similarly arduous path as EU competition law did for the sake of working out a workable definition for 'agreement'; unfortunately with similar ill-success. Nonetheless, the American judiciary's starting-point was completely the opposite. In *Colgate*[52] the US Supreme Court declared that the unilateral behaviour, which is certainly, *per definitionem*, not caught by Section 1, encompasses a situation where the producer makes to the public a general statement about the hoped for behaviour of the distributors, in this case about resale prices, and breaks off business relations with dealers falling short of these expectations. Apparently, this very loose freedom of action holes the ship of *per se* illegality in vertical relationships since it makes all prohibitions on vertical restraints easily evadable.[53] Hence, the Supreme Court, later on, tried to qualify the initially very broad scope of the *Colgate* exception, but this endeavour entailed complete obscurity. Be that as it may, the judicial practice moved in the direction of an ever broader concept of agreement. Nevertheless, it would be obviously an over-simplification to say that US antitrust and EU competition law met in the middle.

50 Case T-368/00 *General Motors Nederland BV and Opel Nederland BV v Commission* [2003] ECR II-4491; Case C-551/03 *General Motors BV, formerly General Motors Nederland BV and Opel Nederland BV v Commission* [2006] ECR I-3173.

51 Para 98.

52 *United State v Colgate & Co.*, 250 U.S. 300 (1919).

53 By the way, this ship sank in the meantime. In *Leegin*, the Supreme Court eliminated the last citadel of *per se* illegality in vertical relations. 127 S.Ct. 2705 (2007).

Immunity for Colgate *unilateralism*

Though cited in papers and chapters on Section 2 monopolization, *Colgate* was a genuine Section 1 case: albeit the indictment ran only against Colgate & Co., it made no reference to monopoly but proceeded solely upon the theory of an unlawful combination.[54] The defendant, Colgate & Co. was engaged in manufacturing soap and toilet articles and selling them throughout the US. Colgate wanted the prices of its products to be uniform on the level of distribution and circulated letters, telegrams and lists, which suggested charging uniform prices. It urged its dealers to adhere to these prices and it indicated to them that no sales would be made to those who did not follow the pricing policy, and in fact, Colgate refused to supply those dealers who deviated from its pricing lists. The Supreme Court proceeded from the freedom of action of the businessmen and held that unilateral conduct is basically not caught by Section 1 of the Sherman Act and the manufacturer is entitled to announce in advance that it will not supply those resellers that do not follow the price lists recommended by the manufacturer and to break off business relations with those dealers that do not comply with the recommended prices.[55] According to the Supreme Court, as long as it is not attempting to monopolize, an undertaking's freedom of contract is not subject to restrictions but it can freely choose its contracting partners.[56] The Sherman Act's purpose is to prevent monopolies and combinations from coming into existence, and it does not envisage restricting the conduct of market operators in other respects. The fact that Colgate exploited the market and restricted competition on the downstream level, thus causing a considerable price increase, did not make its conduct illegal.

> In the absence of any purpose to create or maintain a monopoly, the [Sherman] act does not restrict the long recognized right of trader or manufacturer engaged in an entirely private business, freely to exercise his own independent discretion as to parties with whom he will deal; and, of course, he may announce in advance the circumstances under which he will refuse to sell. The trader or manufacturer, on the other hand, carries on an entirely private business, and can sell to whom he pleases.

The holding of *Colgate* was subsequently confined in several respects. It was obvious that the *Colgate* privilege could serve as a tool to circumvent the *per se* illegality of RPF. The veil of unilateralism may in several cases, if shaped smartly, conceal a resale price-fixing scheme. This danger was to be tackled and since the Supreme Court has refused to overrule *Colgate*, the traditional right of the trader to

54 *United State v Colgate & Co.*, 250 U.S. 300, 302 (1919).

55 250 U.S. 300.

56 *See* Csongor István Nagy, *Refusal to Deal and the Doctrine of Essential Facilities in US and EC competition law: a Comparative Perspective and a Proposal for a Workable Analytical Framework*, 32(5) European Law Review 664, 667 (2007).

choose its trading partners was to be reconciled with the prohibition of Section 1. It lies at the heart of *Colgate* that there is no antitrust law violation if the manufacturer makes a public announcement about the prices it considers preferable and simply refuses to supply distributors that do not observe this price list. Nonetheless, if the producer goes further he may come within the purview of Section 1. Accordingly, the question emerges: how should 'announcement/refusal plus'[57] situations be defined and distinguished from bare 'announcement/refusal' plights?

Before analysing the subsequent case-law spelling out the limits of *Colgate*, one of the basic features of this jurisprudence is to be premised. First, Chicago school theories identifying legitimate rationales for RPF seem to have raised the sympathy of the Supreme Court towards these arrangements. Despite not overruling *Dr Miles* for almost a century, the Supreme Court's approach concerning agreements in RPF cases was admittedly impregnated by Chicago school theories, and this triggered a rather relaxed approach.[58] As a corollary, even though an agreement may be concluded either explicitly or implicitly, an RPF agreement comes into existence only if there is consensus relating specifically to prices. Terminating the distributorship because of the dealer's discounting does not qualify as an RPF agreement. No RPF agreement can be inferred automatically, even if termination occurs after the complaints of other dealers. When distributor 'A' urges the producer to terminate distributor 'B' and the producer acts accordingly, the agreement between 'A' and the producer aims at terminating the discounter's distributorship and not at maintaining the resale price; nevertheless, such a situation is one of the *indicia* of RPF. Since resale price fixing and minimum resale price fixing were *per se* illegal according to the later-overruled *Dr. Miles*, the extraction of 'agreements to terminate' from the realm of RPF and defining them as a possibly independent agreement transferred them to the 'rule of reason' box.

In *Monsanto* the Supreme Court gave the following general definition of agreement.

> The correct standard is that there must be evidence that tends to exclude the possibility of independent action by the manufacturer and distributor. That is, there must be direct or circumstantial evidence that reasonably tends to prove that the manufacturer and others had a conscious commitment to a common scheme designed to achieve an unlawful objective.[59]

Agreement implied in fact: subsequent implementation does not suffice

Two years after *Colgate* the Supreme Court in *Cudahy*[60] faced a case that concerned the nucleus of the whole 'agreement' problem. After *Colgate* it remained obvious

57 *Russell Stover Candies, Inc. v FTC*, 718 F.2d 256 (1983).

58 *See Monsanto Co. v Spray-Rite Service Corp.*, 465 U.S. 752, 762-763 (1984).

59 *Id.* at 768.

60 *Frey & Son v Cudahy Packing Co.*, 256 U.S. 208, 41 S.Ct. 451 (1921).

that all express agreements involving either written or oral communication come within the scope of Section 1;[61] what is more, even implied agreements are caught in the net. However, it was still dubious what the latter involves. An agreement may be implied in the acts of the parties mainly in two ways. First, the call of one of the parties, typically the producer, is accepted neither in writing nor orally but through indicative behaviour addressed to the party making the call: by way of example, the distributor nods assent to the producer's orally presented plan. This case certainly comes under Section 1. Second, the distributor may also adhere without saying a single word or making any direct indication of intent to the producer by simply doing what he was asked to do. It may also amount to an agreement if the producer states that it wishes a 10 per cent price increase on retail level and next day the prices increase, though 'by accident'. In *Cudahy* the Supreme Court seems to have taken a restrictive approach towards the concept of agreement, what is not a surprise, given the fact that otherwise it would have brought *Colgate*'s relevance into question. The Court held that – even though 'the essential agreement, combination or conspiracy might be implied from a course of dealing or other circumstances'[62] – once the producer's conduct is characterized by *Colgate* type unilateralism, it is, in itself, not sufficient for establishing a Section 1 violation to prove that the distributors in fact acted according to the wish of the producer. If the producer confines itself to making a declaration on the (expected) business policy and is refusing to sell to the recalcitrant dealers, there is no agreement under Section 1, even if shown that all distributors are following the producer's call. In this regard, it is irrelevant that the distributors expressed no dissent from the producer's business plan or their attention was called to the business plan on many different occasions.[63]

---

61 *See U.S. v A. Schrader's Son*, 252 U.S. 85, 40 S.Ct. 251 (1920).

62 *Frey & Son v Cudahy Packing Co.*, 256 U.S. 208, 41 S.Ct. 451, 451-452 (1921).

63 The Supreme Court condemned the following jury instruction: 'I can only say to you that if you shall find that the defendant indicated a sales plan to the wholesalers and jobbers, which plan fixed the price below which the wholesalers and jobbers were not to sell to retailers, and you find defendant called this particular feature of this plan to their attention on very many different occasions, and you find the great majority of them not only expressing no dissent from such plan, but actually co-operating in carrying it out by themselves selling at the prices named, you may reasonably find from such fact that there was an agreement or combination forbidden by the Sherman Anti-Trust Act.' 256 U.S. 208, 210-211 (1921). 'The crucial question is whether respondents' conduct toward petitioner stemmed from independent decision or from an agreement, tacit or express. To be sure, business behavior is admissible circumstantial evidence from which the fact finder may infer agreement. (...) But this Court has never held that proof of parallel business behavior conclusively establishes agreement or, phrased differently, that such behavior itself constitutes a Sherman Act offense. Circumstantial evidence of consciously parallel behavior may have made beavy inroads into the traditional judicial attitude toward conspiracy; but "conscious parallelism" has not yet read conspiracy out of the Sherman Act entirely.' *Theatre Enterprises, Inc. v Paramount Film Distributing Corp.*, 346 U.S. 537,

The foregoing approach was confirmed in *Monsanto*,[64] where the Supreme Court observed that 'the manufacturer can announce its resale prices in advance and refuse to deal with those who fail to comply. And a distributor is free to acquiesce in the manufacturer's demand in order to avoid termination.'[65] It is worthy of note that in *Russell Stover* the court of appeals discharged the producer where 97.4 per cent of the distributors complied with the announced minimum prices, whereas the producer did not go beyond unilaterally announcing the minimum prices and consistently refused to sell to price-cutters.[66]

With the foregoing narrow grasp of agreement, the realm of unilateralism enjoying immunity from Section 1 was heavily widened. Nevertheless, in the light of the courts' subsequent jurisprudence the concept of agreement seems to have recaptured some counties from the realm of unilateralism.

Wholesalers may be called not to discount but should not be called to terminate discounters

In *Beech-Nut Packing*[67] the Supreme Court held that it is an 'announcement/refusal plus' situation and thus beyond the reach of *Colgate* if the producer refuses to sell to wholesalers who do not refuse to supply retailers not adhering to the pricing schedule. Here, the 'plus' element relied in the circumstance that the wholesalers were also involved, even though the relationship between the producer and the wholesalers seems to have been characterized by *Colgate* type unilateralism. The Court condemned the producer's conduct towards the retailers due to the fact that the former made unilateral declaration to the wholesalers asking them not to sell to renitent retailers and broke up business relations with wholesalers not acting as wished, while the wholesalers acted accordingly. The decision rested mainly on effect-based reasons. Put at its simplest, the Court said that even though what the producer did does not amount to an agreement it has the very same effects, thus such conduct is to be condemned.

> From this course of conduct a court may infer – indeed, cannot escape the conclusion – that competition among retail distributors is practically suppressed for all who would deal in the company's products are constrained to sell at the suggested prices. (…) Nor is the inference overcome by the conclusion (…) that the merchandising conduct of the company does not constitute a contract or contracts whereby resale prices are fixed, maintained, or enforced. The specific facts found show suppression of the freedom of competition by methods in which

540-541 (1954). *See Klein v American Luggage Works, Inc.*, 323 F.2d 787, 791 (1963). *Cf. Black Gold, Ltd. v Rockwool Industries, Inc.*, 729 F.2d 676, 685-687 (1984).

64 *Monsanto Co. v Spray-Rite Service Corp.*, 465 U.S. 752 (1984).

65 *Id.* at 761.

66 *Russell Stover Candies, Inc. v FTC*, 718 F.2d 256, 257 (1983).

67 *FTC v Beech-Nut Packing Co.*, 257 U.S. 441 (1922).

> the company secures the co-operation of its distributors and customers, which are quite as effectual as agreements express or implied intended to accomplish the same purpose. By these methods the company, although selling its products at prices satisfactory to it, is enabled to prevent competition in their subsequent disposition by preventing all who do not sell at resale prices fixed by it from obtaining its goods.[68]

A similar fact pattern reached the bench in *Bausch & Lomb*[69] where the Supreme Court endorsed *Beech-Nut Packing*.

> As in the Beech-Nut case, there is more here than more acquiescence of wholesalers in Soft-Lite's published resale price list. The wholesalers accepted Soft-Lite's proffer of a plan of distribution by cooperating in prices, limitation of sales to and approval of retail licensees. That is sufficient. (…) So far as the wholesalers are concerned, Soft-Lite and its officers conspired and combined among themselves and with at least some of the wholesalers to restrain commerce by designating selected wholesalers as sub-distributors of Soft-Lite products, by fixing resale prices and by limiting the customers of the wholesalers to those recommended by the wholesalers and approved by Soft-Life – all in violation of the Sherman Act. (…) Whether this conspiracy and combination was achieved by agreement or by acquiescence of the wholesalers coupled with assistance in effectuating its purpose is immaterial.[70]

The approach of *Beech-Nut Packing* was also confirmed and amplified in *Parke Davis*[71] where the Supreme Court stated again that the producer loses the protection granted by *Colgate* if it calls its wholesalers to cut off relations with discounting retailers and the former actually do adhere,[72] even if the producer's behaviour towards the wholesalers is characterized by *Colgate* unilateralism.

> Parke Davis did not content itself with announcing its policy regarding retail prices and following this with a simple refusal to have business relations with any retailers who disregarded that policy. (…) Although Parke Davis' originally announced wholesalers' policy would not under *Colgate* have violated the Sherman Act if its action thereunder was the simple refusal without more to deal with wholesalers who did not observe the wholesalers' Net Price Selling Schedule, that entire policy was tainted with the 'vice of illegality,' (…) when

68 *Id.* at 455.

69 *U.S.* v *Bausch & Lomb Optical Co.*, 321 U.S. 707 (1944).

70 *Id.* at 723.

71 *U.S.* v *Parke, Davis & Co.*, 362 U.S. 29 (1960).

72 It is to be stressed that the Court made no indication that the wholesalers' actual adherence would be a requirement; however, in the above cases (*Beech-Nut Packing*, *Bausch & Lomb* and *Parke Davis*) the wholesaler, in fact, did so.

> Parke Davis used it as the vehicle to gain the wholesalers' participation in the program to effectuate the retailers' adherence to the suggested retail prices.[73]

Interestingly, the Court's reasoning revealed the tension between the legalistic and transcendent *Colgate* doctrine protecting a fundamental freedom recognized of old, on the one hand, and the economic assessment of the effects, on the other hand. The Court, while refusing to overrule *Colgate*, tried to go as far as possible without destroying the core of the above freedom.

> True, there results the same economic effect as is accomplished by a prohibited combination to suppress price competition if each customer, although induced to do so solely by a manufacturer's announced policy, independently decides to observe specified resale prices. So long as Colgate is not overruled, this result is tolerated but only when it is the consequence of a mere refusal to sell in the exercise of the manufacturer's right 'freely to exercise his own independent discretion as to parties with whom he will deal.' (…) When the manufacturer's actions, as here, go beyond mere announcement of his policy and the simple refusal to deal, and he employs other means which effect adherence to his resale prices, this countervailing consideration is not present and therefore he has put together a combination in violation of the Sherman Act. Thus, whether an unlawful combination or conspiracy is proved is to be judged by what the parties actually did rather than by the words they used.[74]

The foregoing discloses that the Court attempted to reconcile effect-based sound economic considerations with a right that became part of antitrust law due to legal tradition instead of economic justification. Nonetheless, the problem with the above reconciliation is that making a unilateral declaration to the wholesalers calling them not to supply recalcitrant retailers is not any more effective than the producer's unilateral refusal to supply the retailers. Accordingly, from the perspective of the effects there is no difference between the conduct discharged of antitrust condemnation in *Colgate* and the scenario convicted in *Beech-Nut Packing*. The only dissimilarity is a circumstance that should not make a difference: in the first

73 *U.S. v Parke, Davis & Co.*, 362 U.S. 29, 45-46 (1960). The District Court's judgment in *Dart Drug* found no violation of antitrust law where the producer's announcement/refusal was addressed directly to the retailers without using the wholesalers as 'messengers'. The Court held that 'the Colgate doctrine still applied, despite all its limitations and restrictions, to a simple refusal to sell to a customer who will not resell at prices suggested by the seller and that this is permissible under the Sherman Act. It is a natural inference from that statement that a simple refusal to sell to an individual customer for any purpose or for any reason is permissible, provided there is no attempt to induce others to follow that course.' *Dart Drug Corp. v Parke, Davis & Co.*, 221 F.Supp. 948, 949-950 (1963), aff'd 344 F.2d 173 (1965).

74 *U.S. v Parke, Davis & Co.*, 362 U.S. 29, 43-44 (1960).

case the producer sells directly to the retailers, while in the latter wholesalers are employed for supplying them. Nonetheless, from an antitrust perspective it should not matter how many levels the distribution scheme has. The producer's business decision on whether to sell directly to the retailers or to employ wholesalers should be based on sound economic considerations and not on the desire to avoid antitrust law. The above formalistic distinction constitutes a misguided incentive: the fear of antitrust scrutiny may drive producers to inefficient decisions by building up a two-tiered distribution system (producer-retailers) also in cases where a three-tiered scheme (producer-wholesalers-retailers) would be more efficient.

In *Leegin*, however, the Supreme Court held that the fixing of the minimum resale price is to be analysed under the rule of reason and, hence, the above problem lost its practical significance.[75]

The involvement of a third party also triggers combination

In *Albrecht*,[76] which is more well-known for its overruling the *per se* illegality of maximum resale price fixing, the Supreme Court generalized the holding of *Beech-Nut Packing* and *Parke Davis* by condemning a producer's conduct where instead of wholesalers, other (competing) undertakings were involved. Owing to the petitioner's charging more than the suggested maximum retail price the publisher of a newspaper hired a company to solicit subscriptions from the customers of the former and hired another company to deliver the newspaper to those who switched. The carrier that took over the route knew 'that respondent would not tolerate overcharging and (…) [understood] that he might have to return the route if petitioner discontinued his pricing practice'.[77] The Supreme Court, basing its reasoning on *Parke Davis*, came to the conclusion that the publisher, the company soliciting subscriptions from the renitent dealer's customers and the carrier constituted a combination:

> If a combination arose when Parke, Davis threatened its wholesalers with termination unless they put pressure on their retail customers, then there can be no doubt that a combination arose between respondent, Milne, and Kroner to force petitioner to conform to the advertised retail price.[78]

75 *Leegin Creative Leather Products, Inc. v PSKS, Inc.*, 127 S.Ct. 2705 (2007).

76 *Albrecht v Herald Co.*, 390 U.S. 145 (1968).

77 *Id.* at 147-148.

78 *Id.* at 148-150. ('When respondent learned that petitioner was overcharging, it hired Milne to solicit customers away from petitioner in order to get petitioner to reduce his price. It was through the efforts of Milne, as well as because of respondent's letter to petitioner's customers, that about 300 customers were obtained for Kroner. Milne's purpose was undoubtedly to earn its fee, but it was aware that the aim of the solicitation campaign was to force petitioner to lower his price. Kroner knew that respondent was giving him the customer list as part of a program to get petitioner to conform to the advertised price, and

The problem of the telltale distributor

A typical case of refusal to deal as a disciplinary measure in the vertical line is when the complaining of a competing distributor antedates the termination of the distributorship. After some decades of ambiguity, the Supreme Court finally addressed this issue in *Monsanto*,[79] where it held that termination following complaints is, in itself, not sufficient for establishing an agreement. '[S]omething more than evidence of complaints is needed. There must be evidence that tends to exclude the possibility that the manufacturer and non-terminated distributors were acting independently.'[80]

The Court based the above conclusion on several arguments. After emphasizing the difference between concerted and independent action, the Supreme Court made a distinction between vertical price and non-price restraints. While admitting that it is not easy to make a clear distinction because they often have the same economic effects, the Court stressed that characterization is to be done cautiously, taking into account its consequences.[81] Namely, at the time when *Monsanto* was decided the *per se* illegality rule of *Dr. Miles* for vertical price restraints was still valid and, hence, it made a difference whether an agreement was characterized as a price or a non-price restraint. Therewith, the Court's grasp of agreement seems to have been heavily impregnated by the free-rider rationale and a considerable sympathy towards RPF; nevertheless, this sympathy was not sufficient to overturn a long standing precedent.

> [T]he fact that a manufacturer and its distributors are in constant communication about prices and marketing strategy does not alone show that the distributors are not making independent pricing decisions. A manufacturer and its distributors have legitimate reasons to exchange information about the prices and the reception of their products in the market. Moreover, it is precisely in cases in

---

he knew that the might have to return the customers if petitioner ultimately complied with respondent's demands. He undertook to deliver papers at the suggested price and materially aided in the accomplishment of respondent's plan.')

79 *Monsanto Co. v Spray-Rite Service Corp.*, 465 U.S. 752 (1984).

80 *Id.* at 764. *See Pink Supply Corp. v Hiebert, Inc.*, 612 F.Supp. 1334, 1341-1342 (1985). With the foregoing position the Supreme Court, in fact, invalidated some earlier lower court precedents. *E.g. Girardi v Gates Rubber Co. Sales Division, Inc.*, 325 F.2d 196, 199-200 (1963) ('From this it seems plain that if Oranges, a competitor of Girardi, objecting to the latter's cutting of the prices suggested by Gates in its catalog, persuaded Gates to cancel Girardi, or cooperated with it in eliminating Girardi from the field because of his price cutting, then Girardi would have made a sufficient case to require the questions of fact to be submitted to the jury, and it would be error to dismiss the action as was done here.')

81 'Nevertheless, it is of considerable importance that independent action by the manufacturer, and concerted action on nonprice restrictions, be distinguished from price-fixing agreements, since under present law the latter are subject to *per se* treatment and treble damages.' *Monsanto Co. v Spray-Rite Service Corp.*, 465 U.S. 752, 763 (1984).

> which the manufacturer attempts to further a particular marketing strategy by means of agreements on often costly nonprice restrictions that it will have the most interest in the distributors' resale prices. The manufacturer often will want to ensure that its distributors earn sufficient profit to pay for programs such as hiring and training additional salesmen or demonstrating the technical features of the product, and will want to see that 'free-riders' do not interfere. (…) Thus, the manufacturer's strongly felt concern about resale prices does not necessarily mean that it has done more than the *Colgate* doctrine allows.[82]

The Court's reasoning reveals that the same arguments were used for creating a relaxed definition of agreement that served as a basis for lifting the *per se* illegality of vertical non-price restraints in *Sylvania*. The Court appears to have had in mind a situation where the producer inserts non-price restraints into the vertical agreement in the form of pre-sale or point-of-sale services but the non-observation of these obligations by a dealer becomes apparent due to the latter's discounting and at the same time it is also the discounting that raises other dealers' suspicion of the discounter's free-riding. The language of the judgment gives the reader the idea that the concept of vertical price agreement embraces only those cases where there is a virtual consensus specifically relating to the price. A combination to exchange price data between the producer and the distributors or an agreement to terminate a discounting distributor after complaints from other dealers is not a vertical price restraint.

> On a claim of concerted price-fixing, the antitrust plaintiff must present evidence sufficient to carry its burden of proving that there was such an agreement. If an inference of such an agreement may be drawn from highly ambiguous evidence, there is a considerable danger that the doctrines enunciated in *Sylvania* and *Colgate* will be seriously eroded. Permitting an agreement to be inferred merely from the existence of complaints, or even from the fact that termination came about 'in response to' complaints, could deter or penalize perfectly legitimate conduct.[83]

82 *Monsanto Co. v Spray-Rite Service Corp.*, 465 U.S. 752, 762-763 (1984).

83 *Monsanto Co. v Spray-Rite Service Corp.*, 465 U.S. 752, 763-764 (1984). ('As Monsanto points out, complaints about price-cutters "are natural – and from the manufacturer's perspective, unavoidable – reactions by distributors to the activities of their rivals." Such complaints, particularly where the manufacturer has imposed a costly set of nonprice restrictions, "arise in the normal course of business and do not indicate illegal concerted action." (…) Moreover, distributors are an important source of information for manufacturers. In order to assure an efficient distribution system, manufacturers and distributors constantly must coordinate their activities to assure that their product will reach the consumer persuasively and efficiently. To bar a manufacturer from acting solely because the information upon which it acts originated as a price complaint would create an irrational dislocation in the market. (…) In sum, "[t]o permit the inference of concerted action on the basis of receiving complaints alone and thus to expose the defendant to treble damage

Afterwards, the Court unfolded the correct legal test in this regard.

> The correct standard is that there must be evidence that tends to exclude the possibility of independent action by the manufacturer and distributor. That is, there must be direct or circumstantial evidence that reasonably tends to prove that the manufacturer and others had a conscious commitment to a common scheme designed to achieve an unlawful objective. Under this standard, the evidence in this case created a jury issue as to whether Spray-Rite was terminated pursuant to a price-fixing conspiracy between Monsanto and its distributors ...[84]

The above lines of *Monsanto* were further amplified in *Business Electronics*,[85] which elucidated the foregoing points. According to the fact pattern, one of the distributors complained to the producer about another distributor's low prices and the producer subsequently terminated the discounter. Even though the distribution agreements contained no price maintenance clause, the producer published a list of suggested minimum resale prices. The Supreme Court proceeded from the point that terminating a price-cutter even after complaints is not tantamount to fixing a concrete or minimum resale price. These are two different kinds of agreements. The delimitation was rather important as RPF was *per se* illegal, while agreements to terminate were to be judged according to their effects (rule of reason). The Supreme Court dismissed the argument that termination for price-cutting and agreements on resale price go hand in hand and hence, the *per se* illegality of the former would be justified by the reason of preventing the latter.[86]

The Court's strongest argument was that inferring resale price fixing merely from the termination of a price-cutter would heavily frustrate the purpose pursued in *Sylvania*, i.e. prevention of free-riding. Such a wide approach would, namely,

> threaten to dismantle the doctrine of GTE Sylvania. Any agreement between a manufacturer and a dealer to terminate another dealer who happens to have

---

liability would both inhibit management's exercise of independent business judgment and emasculate the terms of the statute."')

84 *Monsanto Co. v Spray-Rite Service Corp.*, 465 U.S. 752, 763-764 and 768 (1984).

85 *Business Electronics Corp. v Sharp Electronics Corp.*, 485 U.S. 717 (1988).

86 *Business Electronics Corp. v Sharp Electronics Corp.*, 485 U.S. 717, 731 (1988). ('Finally, we do not agree with petitioner's contention that an agreement on the remaining dealer's price or price levels will so often follow from terminating another dealer 'because of [its] price cutting' that prophylaxis against resale price maintenance warrants the District Court's *per se* rule. Petitioner has provided no support for the proposition that vertical price agreements generally underlie agreements to terminate a price cutter. That proposition is simply incompatible with the conclusion of GTE Sylvania and Monsanto that manufacturers are often motivated by a legitimate desire to have dealers provide services, combined with the reality that price cutting is frequently made possible by "free riding" on the services provided by other dealers. The District Court's *per se* rule would therefore discourage conduct recognized by GTE Sylvania and Monsanto as beneficial to consumers.')

> charged lower prices can be alleged to have been directed against the terminated dealer's 'price cutting.' In the vast majority of cases, it will be extremely difficult for the manufacturer to convince a jury that its motivation was to ensure adequate services, since price cutting and some measure of service cutting usually go hand in hand.[87]

In *Business Electronics*, the Supreme Court seems to have conceptualized *Sylvania* differently from conventional wisdom. The conventional reading of *Sylvania* is that it brought vertical non-price restraints under the rule of reason heading, while leaving the *per se* prohibition for vertical price restraints intact. Nevertheless, the Court in *Business Electronics*, building upon *Monsanto*, made clear that *Sylvania*'s message also includes that the free-rider rationale is not only one of the arguments that led to the releasing of vertical non-price restraints from *per se* illegality but it is a principle generally recognized in antitrust law, or at least concerning vertical agreements. Accordingly, *Sylvania* is also relevant from the point of view of characterizing a restraint as either price or non-price. The Court's line of reasoning may be summarized as follows. All vertical restraints are to be judged according to their effects. Even price restraints may have positive effects, i.e. prevention of free-riding, though their imminent tendency of facilitating cartelization, and thus reducing inter-brand competition pulls them out of the rule of reason. However, this holds true only for agreements that specifically fix the price. An agreement to terminate a price-cutter is to be evaluated under the rule of reason standard since such an arrangement may prevent free-riding while being insufficient to promote cartelization.[88]

87 *Business Electronics Corp. v Sharp Electronics Corp.*, 485 U.S. 717, 727-728 (1988).

88 *Business Electronics Corp. v Sharp Electronics Corp.*, 485 U.S. 717, 726-727 (1988). ('Our approach to the question presented in the present case is guided by the premises of GTE Sylvania and Monsanto: that there is a presumption in favor of a rule-of-reason standard; that departure from that standard must be justified by demonstrable economic effect, such as the facilitation of cartelizing, rather than formalistic distinctions; that interbrand competition is the primary concern of the antitrust laws; and that rules in this area should be formulated with a view towards protecting the doctrine of GTE Sylvania. (…) There has been no showing here that an agreement between a manufacturer and a dealer to terminate a "price cutter," without a further agreement on the price or price levels to be charged by the remaining dealer, almost always tends to restrict competition and reduce output. Any assistance to cartelizing that such an agreement might provide cannot be distinguished from the sort of minimal assistance that might be provided by vertical nonprice agreements like the exclusive territory agreement in GTE Sylvania, and is insufficient to justify a *per se* rule. Cartels are neither easy to form nor easy to maintain. Uncertainty over the terms of the cartel, particularly the prices to be charged in the future, obstructs both formation and adherence by making cheating easier.')

Threats, warnings and coerced adherence

Besides establishing that termination following dealer complaints is not sufficient to support the inference of an agreement,[89] the Supreme Court in *Monsanto* – as mentioned above – also defined the proper standard for establishing an agreement.[90] Accordingly, the evidence must exclude the possibility of independent action (on the part of the manufacturer and the distributor), i.e. 'there must be direct or circumstantial evidence that reasonably tends to prove that the manufacturer and others had a conscious commitment to a common scheme designed to achieve an unlawful objective'.[91]

Since under the foregoing standard 'the evidence in (…) [the] case created a jury issue as to whether Spray-Rite was terminated pursuant to a price-fixing conspiracy between Monsanto and its distributors',[92] the fact pattern is very informative. According to the Court, the following circumstances created substantial evidence of combination and enabled the jury to reasonably conclude that Monsanto and some of its dealers were parties to an agreement.

> There was testimony from a Monsanto district manager, for example, that Monsanto on at least two occasions in early 1969, about five months after Spray-Rite was terminated, approached price-cutting distributors and advised that if they did not maintain the suggested resale price, they would not receive adequate supplies of Monsanto's new corn herbicide. (…) When one of the distributors did not assent, this information was referred to the Monsanto regional office, and it complained to the distributor's parent company. There was evidence that the parent instructed its subsidiary to comply, and the distributor informed Monsanto that it would charge the suggested price. (…) Evidence of this kind plainly is relevant and persuasive as to a meeting of minds.[93]

After *Monsanto*, the question of how to draw a bright line between *Colgate* type situations and coerced agreements still remained unanswered. It is obvious that a prior complaint from a dealer does not convert the termination of a discounter into an agreement. Nonetheless, what if the distributor defers and follows the producer's

89 *Business Electronics Corp. v Sharp Electronics Corp.*, 485 U.S. 717, 758 (1988).

90 For an antecedent 'coerced agreement' case *see Yentsch v Texaco, Inc.*, 630 F.2d 46, 53-54 (1980). ('While evidence of exposition, persuasion, argument, or pressure is alone insufficient to establish coercion, (...), threats of termination, as long as they secure adherence to the fixed price, have been deemed to trespass beyond the boundaries of *Colgate*, thereby triggering a finding of an illegal combination. (...) Thus, such threats were also adequate proof of firm enforcement. (...) The coercive atmosphere may have been enhanced by a policy of price surveillance.') *Jack Walters & Sons Corp. v Morton Bldg., Inc.*, 737 F.2d 698, 707 (1984).

91 *Monsanto Co. v Spray-Rite Service Corp.*, 465 U.S. 752, 768 (1984).

92 *Id.* at 768.

93 *Id.* at 765.

business policy: is there a coerced agreement based on threat and warning? Note that a general threat informing dealers that in case of non-compliance with the producer's business policy they will be terminated comes under *Colgate* immunity. Consequently, only private or direct communications should matter. Nevertheless, it would be senseless to claim that announcements to the public are exempted, while declarations aimed at particular addressees are not. A logical reading of *Monsanto* could be that the dividing line lies in the cause of the announcement/statement: the question is whether the producer makes a general statement about his own business policy including the potential consequences of non-compliance or it simply reacts to a particular price-cutting where he raises the attention of the discounter to the business policy and solicits compliance under penalty of termination. The latter is the area where the producer's unilateral declarations and the dealer's subsequent compliance may establish an agreement. It is worthy of note that a general announcement combined with actual compliance on the side of the distributors is, in itself, not sufficient to establish a Section 1 case.[94]

In order to establish an agreement, the frequency and the assertive nature of the warnings are to be taken into consideration together with the dealer's subsequent behaviour.[95] A causal link between the threat and the behaviour is to be inferred from the circumstances in order to establish a coerced agreement case.

Comparative summary

The above parallel analysis of the concepts of agreement in a vertical relationship reveals the utmost significance of this threshold question. Divergent grasps of agreement may entail a very considerable difference between two regulatory regimes even if regarding the substance of the prohibition, i.e. what content is prohibited, both systems are on a common ground. The role of the concept of agreement is so pivotal that it may convert a system that is facially based on the *per se* illegality of RPF into a *de facto* rule of reason scheme. It is not an exaggeration to assert that the practical dethronement of the *per se* prohibition of RPF had already been an accomplished fact when in *Leegin* the Supreme Court transferred vertical minimum price fixing into the rule of reason box. Obviously, the abolition of the *per se* prohibition in US antitrust law did make a difference; nevertheless, the change was far from being a turnaround. The hostile attitude towards RPF received a mortal wound already in 1984 (*Monsanto*), while the old rule yielded up its soul in 2007 (*Leegin*).

Naturally, both EU competition and US antitrust law cover express agreements. Similarly, none of them brings into the purview of the law on restrictive agreements business strategies implemented unilaterally, e.g. reduction of the quantity supplied in order to prevent re-export. Though initially this had not been the case in EU

94 *Frey & Son v Cudahy Packing Co.*, 256 U.S. 208, 41 S.Ct. 451 (1921).

95 *World of Sleep, Inc. v La-Z-Boy Chair Co.*, 756 F.2d 1467, 1475-1476 (1985).

competition law, in *Bayer* the ECJ announced that genuine unilateral conduct is certainly not covered by Article 101, i.e. unilateral refusal to supply or reduction of the quantity supplied is not an agreement.

Nonetheless, the two legal systems follow a completely different approach concerning tacit agreements (agreements implied in fact). The permissive approach followed by US antitrust law may be explained with the tradition-based *Colgate* doctrine and the favourable position taken regarding intra-brand vertical restraints; the latter had remarkable influence on the way 'agreement' was defined in vertical cases.

EU competition law contains two theories for condemning vertical tacit agreements: 'continuous business relationship' and 'tacit acquiescence (assent)'. Pursuant to the old reading of the first theory, if there is a permanent business relationship between the parties, even genuine unilateral producer declaration may become part of the parties' vertical relationship, thus coming within the purview of Article 101. In *Volkswagen*, the ECJ refused the old reading and took a definite stance establishing that the 'continuous business relationship' theory works only if the framework distribution agreement virtually authorizes the producer to render certain decisions and make them part of the parties' business relationship. Though no express authorization is required, the power conferred on the producer should not be visionary. In US antitrust law, no such theory is perceivable. Nevertheless, it is submitted that on this side of the Atlantic such an approach would be in conformity with the case-law only if the producer had clear and unambiguous authorization, resembling a contractual incorporation theory.

The second theory of EU competition law, i.e. 'tacit acquiescence (assent)', has its counterpart in US antitrust. Nevertheless, in the latter the concept of tacit acquiescence has a rather limited scope and significance. In EU law, partially due to the long-lasting reign of the approach that grasped the 'continuous business relationship' theory as one requiring only visionary authorization, there has been no coercive need to elaborate the theory of tacit acquiescence; indeed, cases interpreting this theory are quite rare. Thus, several questions of interpretation are still open. One thing remains certain: silence infers no consent. Nonetheless, it is questionable whether actual distributor compliance attached to the producer's call reveals an agreement according to Article 101. The ECJ's *Volkswagen* judgment suggests an affirmative answer. In US antitrust, the actual compliance of the dealers does not implicate an agreement. According to the *Colgate* doctrine, a producer is free to announce in advance the behaviour he expects from the dealers and to terminate non-complying traders. The fact that almost all dealers act in conformity with the producer's contemplated strategy does not prove the existence of an agreement. Post-*Colgate* case-law has made it clear that not only public but also private communication having concrete addressees may come under the immunity of unilateralism; what is more, recurrent warnings may also avoid Section 1 scrutiny if their frequency, intensity and the subsequent conduct of the dealer do not result in a coerced agreement.

Evaluation

Admitting that there is no perfect answer for the above problem, it is to be stressed that both systems have considerable shortcomings. The most obvious drawback of the American approach is that it is favourable to producers with market power since these are the ones that are capable of coercing compliance through the threat of refusing to supply. Producers with minor bargaining power simply cannot exploit the chances provided by *Colgate*. Nonetheless, it is the scenarios where the producer possesses some market power that are, or at least should be, the virtual targets of the prohibitions concerning vertical restraints. One of the basic arguments for the more flexible treatment of vertical intra-brand restraints is that these agreements have normally no anti-competitive consequences where the producer lacks market power. Now, granting more give to producers with some market power seems to be perverse. Exclusionary behaviour accomplished by dominant market operators may be caught by Section 2. Nevertheless, *Colgate* immunity gives *carte blanche* to undertakings with market power not reaching the level of dominance targeted by Section 2. On the other hand, small producers, if wanting to influence their dealers, would definitely need the arsenal of contract law, which they had been deprived of before *Leegin* as Section 1 agreements were legally not enforceable.

Another problem with the *Colgate* doctrine before *Leegin* eliminated the *per se* condemnation of RPF, was that it induced producers to engage in a very costly strategy in order to maintain prices. Obviously, legal prohibitions make it costly for the addressees to pursue the forbidden activity, and it is natural and welcome that those who endeavour to circumvent legal prohibitions encounter considerable costs. The problem with the *Colgate* doctrine was that from two strategies having the very same economic effects it interdicted one, while granting legality to the other. What is more, the method permitted was more expensive than the one prohibited. Producers were virtually allowed to maintain prices but they were prevented from doing this in the most efficient way. Intuition suggests that the most efficient way of maintaining prices is to enter into legally enforceable covenants, and regular monitoring, guarded warnings and careful communication are more expensive and less efficient from an economic point of view.

In this context, submitting that the proper standard is the ‘call plus compliance’ test, the logical flaw of EU competition law seems to be that it does not interdict attempts to coerce but it condemns successfully implemented coercion: a producer can urge its dealers not to discount or not to sell outside the contract territory but this act is illegal only if it is effective and the call is complied with.

It could be argued that another loophole in the system is the *Bayer* phenomenon: the producer has no power to enjoin the distributors from re-exporting, and thus from ensuring the territorial partitioning of the common market, but he may reduce the quantity supplied to the extent that it covers only the needs of the distributor’s local market. Accordingly, in the absence of dominant position,[96] the producer may accomplish with unilateral behaviour what cannot be reduced to an agreement.[97] Nevertheless, this argument seems to be odd, as Article 101, clearly, addresses agreements and not producer motivation. The question is, or should be, whether there is an agreement, and not what the motives of the producer are.

The root of the problem relies in the peculiarities of the vertical relations. Vertical intra-brand restraints in many cases, contrary to the producer's stake and irrespective of the interests of the entire distribution system, do not serve the distributors' individual interests, or at least they involve a chance for opportunistic behaviour. Hence, in cases where distributors comply with the producer's call some kind of an agreement may be inferred as there is hardly any other reasonable explanation for the dealers' acting contrary to their best interests but the possibly coerced assent to the producer's business policy. Although this meeting of minds may not amount to an agreement in US antitrust law, the consensual character of the arrangement cannot be denied.

The starting point of both US antitrust and EU competition law is that market operators, in principle, should determine their market behaviour, independently.[98] The distributor is certainly not acting independently if it behaves in the way envisaged by the producer simply because of the consequences of non-compliance. Theoretically, it is plausible to argue that the call of the producer combined with the actual compliance of the distributors does amount to an agreement, provided the independence of the distributor's action can be excluded. Put it another way, if the producer calls distributors to act in a certain way, including both public announcement and direct communication, and distributors do act in this way because of the call, the existence of an agreement cannot be denied since the parties do not act independently. Accordingly, the only way to escape competition law condemnation is to prove that the distributor would have acted in the incriminated manner anyway. In this regard the self-interests of the distributors should have a central role.

In US antitrust law, the *Colgate* doctrine baffles the above logic. Nonetheless, the *Colgate* doctrine is based on a categorical imperative (*quasi* fundamental freedom), which is external to the concept of agreement. Put it simple, the *Colgate* defence works not because *Colgate* situations could not be brought under the 'agreement' heading but because the trader has a natural right to select his trading partners and this natural right would be frustrated if the trader was condemned

96 At the same time, it may be an Article 102 case if a dominant undertaking refuses to meet ordinary orders with the view of putting a stop to parallel exports. *See* Case C-468/06 to C-478/06 *Sot. Lelos kai et altera v GlaxoSmithKline*, [2008] ECR I-07139.

97 Naturally, there might be a difference between the two tools of territorial partitioning: reducing the quantity supplied is a less precise tool and requires more detailed market information on the side of the producer than an agreed export-ban is and does.

98 *See* Case C-209/07 *Competition Authority v Beef Industry Development Society Ltd and Barry Brothers (Carrigmore) Meats Ltd.* [2008] ECR I-08637, para 34.

when making a preliminary call and, afterwards, receiving compliance from the distributors. Another feature of US antitrust law merits attention: the Supreme Court's reasoning in *Monsanto* revealed that the hostility towards the rule of *per se* illegality of RPF heavily influenced the way the concept of agreement was shaped. Due to the concept of *stare decisis*, it was more *comme il faut* to channel all unrest regarding the *per se* rule into the concept of agreement than to overrule it. For the time being, this phenomenon lost its significance as in *Leegin* the *per se* illegality of RPF was overruled. Nevertheless, it seems to be inconsistent to define the concept of agreement depending on the content the parties agreed to.

Since in EU competition law neither the *categoricus imperativus* of *Colgate*, nor the binding authority of *stare decisis* have a decisive influence, and it is submitted that the concept of agreement should embrace all situations where independence of action is missing. Accordingly, the application of the 'tacit acquiescence' theory presupposes an 'announcement/call plus actual compliance' situation. The 'continuous business relationship' theory has already been rephrased by the ECJ so as to cover only situations where the producer is virtually authorized to amend or supplement the business relationship between the parties. Nevertheless, in the absence of such a mandate, the Commission or the plaintiff is required to prove actual compliance. Moreover, it is submitted that all debate about and hostility towards the *per se* condemnation of RPF should be channelled into the concept of anti-competitiveness and should leave the concept of agreement intact.

Chapter IV
The substance of the rule on restrictive agreements

EU competition law

In EU competition law the substance of the rule on restrictive agreements has three layers. The first encompasses the object/effect dichotomy. Resembling the *per se*/rule of reason dualism of US antitrust, agreements that are anti-competitive by object are automatically condemned under Article 101(1), while other agreements can be condemned only if they have anti-competitive effects and merit a full-blown analysis of the market context. The second layer comprises the anti-competitiveness to be investigated under the 'effect' analysis of Article 101(1). Here, the question is whether there is a reasonableness (or 'rule of reason') standard embedded in Article 101(1). The 'object' pigeonhole contains, namely, pre-defined categories of agreements the anti-competitiveness of which is conclusively presumed, albeit these are less firm than the US antitrust categories of *per se* illegal agreements. The third layer is the balancers of Article 101(1) and Article 101(3), i.e. what are the different focuses of analysis under these provisions. Since in the EU the substance of the law on restrictive agreements is twofold, Article 101 – having two prongs: Article 101(1) and Article 101(3) – would enable a more differentiated analysis than Section 1. Although it is unsettled what the focus of analysis is under Article 101(1) and under Article 101(3), it is submitted that Article 101(1) centres around competition in the colloquial sense (i.e. competitive process or rivalry), while Article 101(3) is the proper place for efficiency justifications.

Object or effect

EU competition law prohibits those agreements that have an anti-competitive object *or* effect. This delicate distinction is of utmost importance. Namely, if an agreement is anti-competitive by object, there is no need to examine its effects but it can be condemned simply on its face;[1] there is no need to examine the market

1 *See* Mario Filipponi, Luc Peeperkorn and Donncadh Woods, *Chapter 9: Vertical Agreements*, *in* THE EC LAW OF COMPETITION § 9.40 (Jonathan Faull and Ali Nikpay ed., 2007). Interestingly, the above proposition concerning agreements anti-competitive by object was first pronounced in a vertical case. Joined Cases 56/64 and 58/64 *Consten and Grundig v Commission* [1964] ECR 299. p. 342. ('[T]here is no need to take account of the concrete effects of an agreement once it appears that it has as its object the prevention, restriction or distortion

position of the parties, the structure of the market, entry barriers etc.[2] 'Restrictions of competition by object are those that by their very nature have the potential to restrict competition within the meaning of Article 101(1). It is not necessary to examine the actual or potential effects of an agreement on the market once its anti-competitive object has been established.'[3] On the contrary, if an agreement is not anti-competitive by object, its effects are to be scrutinized, i.e. the market consequences of the arrangement are to be analysed. Effects may be actual or potential, direct or indirect; however, they always require the analysis of the agreement's market context.[4]

---

of competition.') Case C-209/07 *Competition Authority v Beef Industry Development Society Ltd and Barry Brothers (Carrigmore) Meats Ltd.*, [2008] ECR I-08637. para 16. *Cf.* VALENTINE KORAH AND DENIS O'SULLIVAN, DISTRIBUTION AGREEMENTS UNDER THE EC COMPETITION RULES 59 (2002). ('The law and practice relating to exclusive distribution was developed in the 1960s before any other aspect of competition law. The Commission's earliest decisions in 1964 related to exclusive distribution systems, most of which included export restraints to prevent poaching in other dealers' territories.') Case C-209/07 *Competition Authority v Beef Industry Development Society Ltd and Barry Brothers (Carrigmore) Meats Ltd* [2008] ECR I-8637, para 16. ('In deciding whether an agreement is prohibited by Article 81(1) EC, there is (…) no need to take account of its actual effects once it appears that its object is to prevent, restrict or distort competition within the common market (…). That examination must be made in the light of the agreement's content and economic context ….')

2 *Cf.* Ali Nikpay, Jonathan Faull and Lars Kjølbye, *Chapter 3: Article 81*, *in* THE EC LAW OF COMPETITION 222 and 223 (Jonathan Faull and Ali Nikpay ed., 2007). ('However, no agreement is automatically restrictive by object: agreements must be assessed in their legal and economic context.') (Nevertheless, it cannot be concluded that 'an extensive analysis of actual or likely effects of an agreement is necessary for it to be restrictive by object.'); *Guidelines on Article 101(3)*, para 22.

3 *Guidelines on Horizontal Cooperation Agreements*, para 24. *See* Case C-209/07 *Competition Authority v Beef Industry Development Society Ltd and Barry Brothers (Carrigmore) Meats Ltd.* [2008] ECR I-08637, para 16. ('In deciding whether an agreement is prohibited by Article 81(1) EC, there is (…) no need to take account of its actual effects once it appears that its object is to prevent, restrict or distort competition within the common market'.)

4 Joined Cases 56/64 and 58/64 *Consten and Grundig v Commission* [1964] ECR 299, p. 342; Case C-277/87 *Sandoz Prodotti Farmaceutici v Commission* [1990] ECR I-45; Case C-219/95 P *Ferriere Nord v Commission* [1997] ECR I-4411, paras 14-15; Case C-49/92 *Commission v Anic Partecipazioni SpA* [1999] ECR I-4125, para 99; Case C-199/92 *Hüls AG v Commission* [1999] ECR I-4287, para 178; Joined Cases T-374/94, T-375/94, T-384/94 and T-388/94 *European Night Services Ltd (ENS) et altera v Commission* [1998] ECR II-3141, para 136. ('[I]n assessing an agreement under Article 85(1) of the Treaty, account should be taken of the actual conditions in which it functions, in particular the economic context in which the undertakings operate, the products or services covered by the agreement and the actual structure of the market concerned (…), unless it is an agreement containing obvious restrictions of competition such as price-fixing, market-sharing or the control of outlets….')

The above classification is done on the basis of pre-determined categories[5] and certainly not on the basis of the parties' subjective intentions.[6] There is a very intimate connection between the classification as 'object' type or 'effect' type agreement, on the one hand, and the substance of anti-competitiveness pursued or allegedly pursued by the cooperation, on the other. It is very important to stress that although the foregoing differentiation between object and effect resembles US antitrust law's dichotomy of *per se* illegality and rule of reason and, roughly speaking, such parallelism exists in practice, it would be misleading to put an equality sign between the two regimes.[7] In EU competition law, *per se* condemnation is legally restricted to

---

5 The categories of object and effect type agreements may change from time to time. The case-law of the ECJ 'indicate[s] that the broad headings used in the object box (...) may require refinement from time to time to exclude from the "object" category some types of agreements that are not so obviously restrictive of competition as others. The size and content of the object box is capable of change over a period of time, as the Community Courts are called on to consider, or perhaps to reconsider, the restrictive nature of particular types of agreements. This process of categorisation and recategorisation is natural and to be expected, and has a parallel in the US where the courts are from time to time called upon to determine whether a particular type of agreement should be tested according to a *per se* or a rule of reason standard. However the fact that such a process takes place does not call into question the underlying "object or effect" distinction contained in Article 81(1).' Richard Whish, Competition law 122 (2009).

6 *See* Richard Whish, Competition Law 116 (2009). ('There are some types of agreement the anti-competitiveness of which can be determined simply from their object; the word "object" in this context means not the subjective intention of the parties when entering into the agreement, but the objective meaning and purpose of the agreement considered in the economic context in which it is to be applied.'); Vivien Rose and Peter Roth, *Article 81(1)*, *in* Bellamy and Child's European Community Law of Competition § 2.096 (Peter Roth and Vivien Rose ed., 2008). ('The 'object' of the agreement is to be found by an objective assessment of the aims of the agreement in question, and it is unnecessary to investigate the parties' subjective intentions.'); Jakob Schröter, Kommentar zum Europäischen Wettbewerbsrecht 259 (2003). ('Der Begriff des Bezweckens hat einen objektiven Character. Die subjektiven Vorstellungen der Parteien treten demgegenüber zurück.')

7 Richard Whish, Competition law 131 (2009). On the issue of the European rule of reason *see* Valentine Korah, *Rule of reason: apparent inconsistency in the case law under Article 81*, 1 Competition Law Insight 24 (2002); René Joliet, The Rule of Reason in Antitrust Law; American, German and Common Market Laws in Comparative Perspective 77-106 (1967); Mark Clifford Schechter, *The Rule of Reason in European Competition Law*, 1982(2) Legal Issues in European Integration 1 (1982); Ian Forrester and Christopher Norall, *The Laicization of Community Law: Self-help and the Rule of Reason: How Competition Law is and could be Applied*, 21 Common Market Law Review 11 (1984); Valentine Korah, *EEC Competition Policy – Legal Form or Economic Efficiency*, 39 Current Legal Problems 85 (1986); James S. Venit, *Brave New World: the Modernization and Decentralization of Enforcement under Articles 81 and 82 of the EC Treaty*, 40 Common Market Law Review 545 (2003); Donald L. Holley, *EEC Competition Practice; a Thirty-Year Retrospective*, 16 Fordham International Law Journal 342 (1992/1993); Valentine Korah, *The Rise and Fall of Provisional Validity: The Need for a Rule of Reason in EEC Antitrust*, 3 Northwestern

Article 101(1),[8] as no agreement can be excluded from the perspective of benefiting from Article 101(3). Agreements having an anti-competitive object might benefit from an individual or block exemption,[9] albeit this seems to be rather a theoretical perspective with a negligible practical chance.[10] In practice there is a considerable convergence between the above EU competition and US antitrust law concepts because object type restrictions are normally not covered by block exemption regulations due to their being treated as hardcore, and it is also highly unlikely that they could fulfil the requirements of Article 101(3) on an individual basis.

It should be stressed that the concept of object type agreements is, as a matter of fact, not tantamount to US antitrust law's *per se* illegality. The *per se* character of object type agreements is limited to Article 101(1): no elaborate inquiry is needed in order to establish that the agreement runs counter Article 101(1). Nevertheless, in principle, all agreements (or as Article 101(3) literally says: 'any agreement') may be a candidate for an Article 101(3) exemption; at least theoretically. In *Matra Hachette SA v Commission* the GC held that

> in principle, no anti-competitive practice can exist which, whatever the extent of its effects on a given market, cannot be exempted, provided that all the

---

Journal of International Law and Business 320 (1981); Ernst Steindorff, *Article 85 and the Rule of Reason*, 21 Common Market Law Review 639 (1984).; Luc Gyselen, *Vertical Restraints in the Distribution Process: Strength and Weakness of the Free Rider Rationale under EEC Competition Law*, 21 Common Market Law Review 647 (1984); Richard Whish and Brenda Sufrin, *Article 85 and the Rule of Reason*, 7 1987 Yearbook of European Law 1 (1988); Jan Peeters, *The Rule of Reason Revisited: Prohibition on Restraints of Competition in the Sherman Act and in the EEC Treaty*, 37 American Journal of Comparative Law 521 (1989); G. Wils, *'Rule of Reason': Une Regle Raisonnable en Droit Communautaire?*, 26 Cahiers de Droit Européen 19 (1990); Pietro Manzini, *The European Rule of Reason: Crossing the sea of doubt*, 23 European Competition Law Review 392 (2002); Phedon Nicolaides, *The Balancing Myth: The Economics of Article 81(1) and (3)*, 32(2) Legal Issues of Economic Integration 123 (2005).

8 Case T-14/89 *Montedipe SpA v Commission* [1992] ECR II-01155, para 265. (Agreements clearly violating Article 101(1) 'must be regarded as an infringement per se of the competition rules'.); Case T-148/89 *Tréfilunion SA v Commission* [1995] ECR II-01063, para 109. ('Agreements clearly violating Article 81(1) 'must be regarded as an infringement per se of the competition rules (…).')

9 Case T-17/93 *Matra Hachette SA v Commission* [1994] ECR II-595, para 85.

10 Block exemption regulations consistently treat agreements anti-competitive by object as hard-core and exclude them from the 'safe harbour' of the block exemption. On the other hand, such agreements do not have a real chance to survive under Article 101(3). *See* Valentine Korah and Denis O'Sullivan, Distribution Agreements under the EC Competition Rules 233 (2002). (Noting in the context of vertical agreements that '[i]n brief, although *Matra Hachette* suggests that no restriction of competition is beyond exemption, there appears to be no real possibility of redeeming the so-called "hardcore" restraints'.)

> conditions laid down in Article 85(3) of the Treaty are satisfied and the practice in question has been properly notified to the Commission.[11]

In *Competition Authority v Beef Industry Development Society Ltd and Barry Brothers (Carrigmore) Meats Ltd*,[12] the ECJ encountered a horizontal hardcore agreement (market-sharing and output limitation) in a preliminary reference. The question posed by the national court was whether such an agreement is anti-competitive by object and thus automatically contrary to Article 101(1). Albeit the ECJ was not express in saying that even a horizontal hardcore agreement (market-sharing and output limitation) may be, at least theoretically, eligible for an exemption under Article 101(3), the language of the judgment suggests this clearly; but it also suggests that this is rather a theoretical possibility. The ECJ refused to consider certain arguments of the Beef Industry Development Society under Article 101(1), stating that '[i]t is only in connection with Article 81(3) EC that matters such as those relied upon by BIDS *may, if appropriate*, be taken into consideration for the purposes of obtaining an exemption from the prohibition laid down in Article 81(1) EC'.[13] At another point of the judgment, the Court seems to be rather sceptical about the chance to justify a horizontal hardcore agreement under Article 101(3): 'such matters *may, at the most,* be relevant for the purposes of the examination of the four requirements which have to be met under Article 81(3) EC in order to escape the prohibition laid down in Article 81(1) EC'.[14] It is to be emphasized that the national court's preliminary question addressed solely Article 101(1), hence, for procedural reasons the Court, in principle, had no competence to decide on the applicability of Article 101(3) to a horizontal hardcore agreement. This is a circumstance that is certainly relevant from the perspective of the judgment's interpretation.

Nevertheless, object type, i.e. hardcore, agreements are very unwelcome guests under Article 101(3): one may hardly find any example where they benefited from an exemption. In practical terms, the door is open but they should not try to enter. Nonetheless, it is to be emphasized that there may be exceptions; it could be argued that some agreements did meet the conditions of Article 101(3), notwithstanding the fact that they were considered as anti-competitive by object. It seems that the position that even 'object' restrictions have a realistic, though very exceptional, chance to fulfil the requirements of Article 101(3) is getting stronger.[15] At the

---

11 Case T-17/93 *Matra Hachette SA v Commission* [1994] ECR II-595, para 85.

12 Case C-209/07 *Competition Authority v Beef Industry Development Society Ltd and Barry Brothers (Carrigmore) Meats Ltd* [2008] ECR I-8637.

13 Para 21. Emphasis added.

14 Para 39. Emphasis added.

15 *See* Richard Whish, Competition law 150-151 (2009); *Guidelines on Vertical Restrains*, para 47. (Emphasizing that although hardcore agreements are presumptively caught by Article 101(1) and unlikely to fulfil the conditions of Article 101(3), this is a rebuttable presumption.)

same time, it is dubious whether the cases that could be raised as examples for the exemption of object-type agreements involved genuine naked restrains and, hence, a real anti-competitive object.

In these cases[16] the Commission was normally not explicit about the anti-competitive object of the arrangement but condemned it under Article 101(1) after some withheld effect analysis without specifying whether these agreements were anti-competitive by object or by effect; at the same moment, notwithstanding the obscure language, the analysis under Article 101(1) was rather summary. In *Société Air France/Alitalia Linee Aeree Italiane SpA*,[17] the cooperation was spiced with some ancillarity. In *Reims II*,[18] the Commission did not establish that the agreement had an anti-competitive object but it paid scant attention to this question, and after a brief explanation it reached Article 101(3). In this case European public postal operators agreed to the amount of terminal dues, which one party has to pay to another for the onward delivery of letters, the addressee of which is in the latter's territory. '[T] erminal dues are the price the PPO [public postal operator] in the country of origin pays to the PPO in the country of destination for the service of delivering cross-border mail.'[19] Nevertheless, the Commission came to the conclusion that 'this Agreement fails to be considered as an agreement fixing selling prices within the meaning of Article 81(1) of the EC Treaty and Article 53(1) of the EEA Agreement.'[20] The reason was that the agreement was not concluded by 'sellers' but by 'sellers' and 'buyers'. Accordingly, the Commission came to the conclusion that 'the REIMS II Agreement is a price-fixing agreement with unusual characteristics'.[21] The *Visa International – Multilateral Interchange Fee* decision declares that 'the Commission does not consider the MIF agreement to be a restriction of competition by object'.[22] The multilateral interchange fee (MIF) is the amount the acquiring banks pay to the issuing banks. In *MasterCard* the Commission was less straight about the characterization of MIF but stated that it is needless to take a clear position, as the agreement, due to the parties' market power, was certainly anti-competitive by effect.[23]

Another familiar concept of EU competition law is hardcore agreements, which is, nevertheless, a term unknown for the language of Article 101. The

---

16 *E.g.* RICHARD WHISH, COMPETITION LAW 150-151 (2009), refers to *Société Air France/Alitalia Linee Aeree Italiane SpA*, *Reims II* and *Visa International – Multilateral Interchange Fee*.

17 2004/841/EC *Société Air France/Alitalia Linee Aeree Italiane SpA*, Commission decision of 7 April 2004, not published in the OJ.

18 1999/695/EC OJ [1999] L 275/17.

19 *Id.* at para 63.

20 *Id.* at para 63.

21 *Id.* at para 65.

22 2002/914/EC OJ [2002] L 318/17, para 69.

23 Case No COMP/34.579 – *MasterCard*, COMP/36.518 – *EuroCommerce*, COMP/38.580 – *Commercial Cards* (19.12.2009), not published in the OJ, para 407. Interestingly, in the US the 11th Circuit refused to condemn MIF as *per se* illegal. *National Bancard Corporation (NaBANCO) v VISA U.S.A., Inc.*, 596 F.Supp. 1231 (1984).

term 'hardcore restraints' is the telegraphese name of agreements that are anti-competitive by object under Article 101(1) and are highly unlikely to be saved under Article 101(3). While in principle all agreements have the chance to meet the requirements of Article 101(3) and it cannot be said that a particular type of agreement is automatically excluded from the perspective of an exemption,[24] it is very unlikely that a hardcore agreement could fulfil these conditions.[25] In this sense the notion of hardcore restraints is wider than the concept of 'object' type agreements, as the latter relates only to Article 101(1); nevertheless, the two terms cannot be sensibly distinguished because hardcore agreements are anti-competitive by object and *vice versa*. Thus, the analysis under Article 101(1) and that under Article 101(3) converge as far as quick condemnation is concerned. Restrictions by object and restriction that are by their very nature anti-competitive are two designations for the same group of agreements and are part of the terminology of Article 101(1).[26] On the other hand, the concept of hardcore restrictions, although it designates the very same species of agreements, has a much broader application as it is a notion used both under Article 101(1) and Article 101(3).[27]

The *Guidelines on Article 101(3)* give a concise summary of restraints that, in a horizontal context, are treated as anti-competitive by object: price-fixing, output limitation and sharing of markets or customers.

> In the case of horizontal agreements restrictions of competition by object include price fixing, output limitation and sharing of markets and customers.'[28]

---

24 Case T-17/93 *Matra Hachette SA v Commission* [1994] ECR II-595, para 85; Case T-168/01 *GlaxoSmithKline Services Unlimited v Commission* [2006] ECR II-02969, para 233.

25 Frank Wijckmans, Filip Tuytschaever and Alain Vanderelst, Vertical Agreements in EC Competition Law § 2.134 (2006). ('[H]ardcore restrictions (…) are almost by way of definition banned by EC competition law.'); Ali Nikpay, Jonathan Faull and Lars Kjølbye, *Chapter 3: Article 81*, *in* The EC Law of Competition § 3.405 (Jonathan Faull and Ali Nikpay ed., 2007). ('Article 81 does not contain a *per se* rule. However, this fact is not as significant as it might seem: restrictions of competition that can be qualified as "hardcore" are very unlikely to fulfil the conditions of Article 81(3).') ('However, the absence of *per se* rule introduces a useful check on hard-core lists: if in a significant number of cases hardcore restrictions do satisfy the conditions of Article 81(3), the restriction in question should be re-classified. A restriction should only be classified as hardcore if upon individual assessment such agreements would almost always be prohibited. Naked cartels, for instance, clearly satisfy this test.') *See also* Case 28/77 *Tepea BV v Commission* [1978] ECR 01391, para 57; Case 35/83 *BAT Cigaretten-Fabriken GmbH v Commission* [1985] ECR 363, para 41.

26 *See* Case C-306/96 *Javico International and Javico AG v Yves Saint Laurent Parfums SA (YSLP)* [1998] ECR I-1983, paras 14 and 20-21.

27 *See Guidelines on Article 101(3)*, para 23; Mario Filipponi, Luc Peeperkorn and Donncadh Woods, *Chapter 9: Vertical Agreements*, *in* The EC Law of Competition § 9.41 (Jonathan Faull and Ali Nikpay ed., 2007).

28 *Guidelines on Article 101(3)*, para 23.

> Restrictions of competition by object are those that by their very nature have the potential of restricting competition. These are restrictions which in light of the objectives pursued by the Community competition rules have such a high potential of negative effects on competition that it is unnecessary for the purposes of applying Article 81(1) to demonstrate any actual effects on the market. This presumption is based on the serious nature of the restriction and on experience showing that restrictions of competition by object are likely to produce negative effects on the market and to jeopardise the objectives pursued by the Community competition rules. Restrictions by object such as price fixing and market sharing reduce output and raise prices, leading to a misallocation of resources, because goods and services demanded by customers are not produced. They also lead to a reduction in consumer welfare, because consumers have to pay higher prices for the goods and services in question.[29]

The 2011 *Guidelines on Horizontal Cooperation Agreements* contain the same enumeration;[30] an approach also followed by the *Old Guidelines on Horizontal Cooperation Agreements* as well.[31]

A similarly authoritative summary is to be found in the Commission *Guidelines on Vertical Restraints* about the vertical agreements that are treated as anti-competitive by object in EU competition law. In this regard, the *Guidelines* refer to the list in Article 4 of the BER and provide that '[w]here such a hardcore restriction is included in an agreement, that agreement is presumed to fall within Article 101(1). It is also presumed that the agreement is unlikely to fulfil the conditions of Article 101(3).'[32] Article 4 reads as follows:

> Article 4
> Restrictions that remove the benefit of the block exemption – hardcore restrictions.
> The exemption provided for in Article 2 [of the BER] shall not apply to vertical agreements which, directly or indirectly, in isolation or in combination with other factors under the control of the parties, have as their object:
> (a) the restriction of the buyer's ability to determine its sale price, without prejudice to the possibility of the supplier to impose a maximum sale price or recommend a sale price, provided that they do not amount to a fixed or minimum sale price as a result of pressure from, or incentives offered by, any of the parties;
> (b) the restriction of the territory into which, or of the customers to whom, a buyer party to the agreement, without prejudice to a restriction on its place of establishment, may sell the contract goods or services, except:

---

29 *Guidelines on Article 101(3)*, para 21.

30 *Guidelines on Horizontal Cooperation Agreements*, paras 128 and 205.

31 *Old Guidelines on Horizontal Cooperation Agreements*, paras 18 and 25.

32 *Guidelines on Vertical Restraints*, para 47. Regulation 2790/1999 OJ [1999] L 336/21. *See Old Guidelines on Vertical Restraints*, para 7.

> (i) the restriction of active sales into the exclusive territory or to an exclusive customer group reserved to the supplier or allocated by the supplier to another buyer, where such a restriction does not limit sales by the customers of the buyer,
> (ii) the restriction of sales to end users by a buyer operating at the wholesale level of trade,
> (iii) the restriction of sales by the members of a selective distribution system to unauthorised distributors within the territory reserved by the supplier to operate that system, and
> (iv) the restriction of the buyer's ability to sell components, supplied for the purposes of incorporation, to customers who would use them to manufacture the same type of goods as those produced by the supplier;
>
> (c) the restriction of active or passive sales to end users by members of a selective distribution system operating at the retail level of trade, without prejudice to the possibility of prohibiting a member of the system from operating out of an unauthorised place of establishment;
> (d) the restriction of cross-supplies between distributors within a selective distribution system, including between distributors operating at different level of trade;
> (e) the restriction, agreed between a supplier of components and a buyer who incorporates those components, of the supplier's ability to sell the components as spare parts to end-users or to repairers or other service providers not entrusted by the buyer with the repair or servicing of its goods.

Nevertheless, it seems that the reference to the enumeration of Article 4 goes too far. 'In the absence of horizontal elements, vertical restraints have only been held to constitute restrictions by object where they are used to impede parallel trade within the Community or enforce resale price maintenance.'[33]

In accordance with the above, the *Guidelines on Article 101(3)* provide as follows:

> As regards vertical agreements the category of restrictions by object includes, in particular, fixed and minimum resale price maintenance and restrictions providing absolute territorial protection, including restrictions on passive sales.[34]

Accordingly, there seems to be some inconsistency between the above Commission instruments. The *Guidelines on Vertical Restraints* refer to Article 4 of the BER and consider restraints enumerated there as hardcore. This list, nevertheless, embraces not only the fixing of concrete or minimum prices and absolute territorial protection, but also some restraints in selective distribution agreements, as defined in Article

33 Mario Filipponi, Luc Peeperkorn and Donncadh Woods, *Chapter 9: Vertical Agreements*, *in* THE EC LAW OF COMPETITION § 9.46 (Jonathan Faull and Ali Nikpay ed., 2007).

34 Para 23.

4(c) and 4(d), and restraints on the supplier of spare parts, as defined in Article 4(e). On the other hand, other Commission instruments confine automatic condemnation under Article 101(1) to the fixing of concrete or minimum resale price and to absolute territorial protection. All in all, the latter seems to be the valid approach.[35]

In sum, from intra-brand restrictions the fixing of concrete or minimum resale price and absolute territorial protection are anti-competitive by object, while the fixing of the maximum resale price, recommended prices and relative territorial protection come under the 'effect' heading. The *Guidelines on Vertical Restraints* contain one exception in this regard: even an absolute territorial protection clause may be lawful for two years if it is necessary for 'grubbing' a new market.[36]

Does Article 101(1) contain a 'rule of reason'? – The test of (anti-)competitiveness

An agreement is prohibited by Article 101(1) only if its object or effect is anti-competitive. Even though Article 101(1) distinguishes between three types of anti-competitiveness (prevention, restriction and distortion of competition), this enumeration is rather descriptive. Hence, for the sake of simplicity, the terms 'anti-competitiveness' and 'anti-competitive' will be used as an all-in category.

The concept of anti-competitiveness is central to the evaluation of 'effect' type agreements. Obviously, its role is similarly important regarding 'object' type agreements, as well, though not on the level of the individual agreements' assessment but on the abstract level of defining the categories of agreements that are anti-competitive by object. Namely, anti-competitiveness is the key issue when defining the categories of agreements that fall into the 'object' box; nonetheless, no elaborate inquiry into the circumstances is needed once the agreement qualifies as anti-competitive by object.

As regards the concept of anti-competitiveness, the pivotal question is whether there is a 'rule of reason' type logic embedded in Article 101(1). Naturally, Article

---

35 *See* RICHARD WHISH, COMPETITION LAW 120 (2009); Ali Nikpay, Jonathan Faull and Lars Kjølbye, *Chapter 3: Article 81*, *in* THE EC LAW OF COMPETITION § 3.150 (Jonathan Faull and Ali Nikpay ed., 2007). *Green Paper on Vertical Restraints in EC Competition Policy.* COM (96) 721 final. 22 January 1997, para 276. ('The policy of treating resale price maintenance and impediments to parallel trade as serious violations of the competition rules would continue. It is proposed that they be treated as *per se* contrary to Article 85(1), as long as the agreement, concerted practice or decision concerned may affect trade between Member States. They are also unlikely to benefit from an exemption under Article 85(3).'); Mario Filipponi, Luc Peeperkorn and Donncadh Woods, *Chapter 9: Vertical Agreements*, *in* THE EC LAW OF COMPETITION § 9.46 (Jonathan Faull and Ali Nikpay ed., 2007); *Cf.* JOANNA GOYDER, EU DISTRIBUTION LAW 27 (4th ed., 2005). (Adding non-compete clauses to the genre of agreements anti-competitive by object.) *Contra* Matthew Bennett and A. Jorge Padilla, *Article 81 EC Revisited: Deciphering European Commission Antitrust Goals and Rules*, *in* COMPETITION POLICY IN THE EU 46 (Xavier Vives ed., 2009). (Designating all the five restraints enumerated in Article 4 as hardcore.)

36 Para 61.

101(3) must contain a reasonableness standard by definition. Nevertheless, it is a vexed question whether already Article 101(1) contains such a standard; of course, such a standard would be applicable only to agreements that are anti-competitive by effect.

In order to make clear that the question is not whether Article 101(1) imports the American rule of reason or any of its mutants,[37] the European standard will be designated by the name of 'competitiveness' (or 'anti-competitiveness').[38] Below, the term 'reasonableness' (or European 'rule of reason') implies that there is a substantive analysis under Article 101(1), where the pros and cons of the agreement can be contrasted, without giving any indication about the focus of this analysis. The term 'competitiveness' (or 'anti-competitiveness'), as demonstrated below, implies that there is a reasonableness standard under Article 101(1) that centres around rivalry (competitive process).

The question whether a 'rule of reason' standard is contained in Article 101(1) is unsettled. The ECJ has not spoken yet, albeit it endorsed the 'market context' approach and the concept of 'comparison' (counter-factual) in its judicial practice, suggesting that some sort of a rule of reason does exist under Article 101(1). The Commission adopted the 'rule of reason' approach to a limited extent.[39] On

---

37 *See* Richard Whish, Competition Law 131 (2009). (Taking the position that it is spurious to argue that US rule of reason could be incorporated into EU competition law. 'EC competition law is different in many ways from US law, not least in that it has the bifurcation of Article 81(1) and Article 81(3), which does not exist in the Sherman Act, and that it is concerned with the promotion of a single market as well as with "conventional" competition law concerns.'); Pietro Manzini, *The European Rule of Reason – Crossing the Sea of Doubt*, 23 European Competition Law Review 392, 395 (2002). ('If the evaluation of the overall effects of an agreement on competition can be limited to paragraph 1, paragraph 3 risks appearing superfluous. Not to contravene the effet utile, this last provision should pursue different purposes from those related to the protection of a well-balanced system of competition within the market. Unfortunately these purposes are far from being evident.'); Vincent Verouden, *Vertical Agreements and Article 81(1) EC: the Evolving Role of the Economic Analysis*, 71 Antitrust Law Journal 525, 564 (2003) ('[I]t is necessary to clearly distinguish the economic approach of the European Courts under Article 81(1) from the rule of reason as it is applied in the United States, as the European approach does not constitute a full competition-based analysis that assesses an agreement's net impact on competition and prices.'); Doris Hildebrand, The role of economic analysis in the EC competition rules 235 (1998).

38 *See* Richard Whish and Brenda Sufrin, *Article 85 and the Rule of Reason*, 7 Yearbook of European Law 1 (1987); Geert Wils, *'Rule of reason': une règle raisonnable en droit communautaire?*, 26 Cahiers de Droit Européen 19 (1990).

39 *See White Paper on Modernisation of the Rules Implementing Article 85 and 86 of the EC Treaty.* Commission Programme 99/027. COM (99) 101 final. OJ [1999] C 132/1, para 57. ('The Commission has already adopted this approach to a limited extent and has carried out an assessment of the pro- and anti-competitive aspects of some restrictive practices under Article 85(1). This approach has been endorsed by the Court of Justice. However, the structure of Article 85 is such as to prevent greater use being made of this approach: if more systematic use were made under Article 85(1) of an analysis of

the other hand, the GC has clung to the position that EU competition law does not contain a rule of reason and the pro- and anti-competitive effects cannot be contrasted under Article 101(1). Nevertheless, the GC, in fact, does not do what it says: the GC actually does endorse an approach that amounts to the balancing of the pro- and anti-competitive effects when it says that the competitive situations with and without the agreement are to be compared in order to determine whether the agreement is anti-competitive or not. Such an approach follows a rule of reason logic; of course: not the American one. All in all, the ECJ's reluctance to take sides in the question of rule of reason and the GC's outright refusal against any reference to the 'rule of reason' seem to be inconsistent with what EU courts in fact do. The EU judiciary endorsed under Article 101(1) several arrangements that notwithstanding their obviously restrictive nature were reasonable (or pro-competitive). In *Société Technique Minière* an exclusivity clause[40] in *Pronuptia* certain restraints related to franchising,[41] in *Metro* a selective distribution agreement,[42] in *Nungesser* an exclusive licence,[43] and in *Remia* a non-compete obligation attached to a sale of business[44] were considered to be in accord with Article 101(1). In *Gøttrup-Klim*, the ECJ held that an agricultural cooperative's rule providing that the members of the cooperative may not have membership in another cooperative complies with Article 101(1).[45]

Numerous theories emerged that tried to give a reasonable explanation on the substantive analysis under Article 101(1) and to conceptualize the above jurisprudence. Nevertheless, some of these theories were only partially successful.

An interpretation of the above jurisprudence on Article 101(1)'s substantive analysis could be that the Court did not establish a general approach but simply acknowledged the conventional wisdom about certain business arrangements, e.g. franchising and sale of business. Accordingly, 'the European Courts appear to have taken the "common sense" view that certain forms of activity such as franchising (*Pronuptia*) and the sale of a business (*Remia*) were legitimate activities which would have been harmed by an overly expansive application of Article 81(1)'.[46]

---

the pro and anti-competitive aspects of a restrictive agreement, Article 85(3) would be cast aside, whereas any such change could be made only through revision of the Treaty.')

40 Case 56/65 *Société Technique Minière (L.T.M.) v Maschinenbau Ulm GmbH (M.B.U.)* [1966] ECR 235.

41 Case 161/84 *Pronuptia de Paris GmbH v Pronuptia de Paris Irmgard Schillgallis* [1986] ECR 353.

42 Case 26/76 *Metro SB-Großmärkte GmbH and Co. KG v Commission* [1977] ECR 1875.

43 Case 258/78 *L.C. Nungesser KG and Kurt Eisele v Commission* [1982] ECR 2015, para 57.

44 Case 42/84 *Remia BV and others v Commission* [1985] ECR 2545, paras 19-20.

45 Case C-250/92 *Gøttrup-Klim e.a. Grovvareforeninger v Dansk Landbrugs Grovvareselskab AmbA.*, [1994] ECR I-5641.

46 Ali Nikpay, Jonathan Faull and Lars Kjølbye, *Chapter 3: Article 81*, *in* THE EC LAW OF COMPETITION § 3.252 (Jonathan Faull and Ali Nikpay ed., 2007).

Other theories, while trying to give an overall explanation for arrangements not covered by Article 101(1), are at fault for a test that could help in assessing arrangements not having been adjudicated yet by EU courts; they explain past decisions but fail to give a comprehensive guidance for future cases. According to one of these theories, the above cases are the projections of a qualitative appreciability test applied as a precursor of a more general *de minimis* rule. This concept of qualitative appreciability is asserted to embrace, for instance, the grant of an exclusive licence, restrictions that are the inherent part of franchising systems, obligations that are necessary for protecting intellectual property rights and ancillary restrictions in general.[47]

The *Guidelines on Article 101(3)* suggest the existence of the concept of 'objective necessity', considering that 'certain restraints may in certain cases not be caught by Article 81(1) when the restraint is objectively necessary for the existence of an agreement of that type or that nature'.[48] Nevertheless, the *Guidelines* do not shed light on the question: which are the agreements that come under the scope of the 'objective necessity' theory. This approach resembles the theory of ancillary restraints, which provides that all restraints that are ancillary to a legitimate end (main transaction) are lawful. Again, the flaw of this theory is that it does not give us hints about the question how to identify those main transactions that are legitimate and are capable of justifying restraints that are ancillary to them.

Last but not least, the jurisprudence of the EU courts under Article 101(1) may be conceptualized as the projection of the European 'rule of reason': both Article 101(1) and Article 101(3) contain a substantive analysis, though with different focuses, where the pros and cons can and should be contrasted.[49] While there is a

47 Lennart Ritter and W. David Braun, European Competition Law: a Practitioner's Guide 274 (3d ed., 2005).

48 Para 18(2) of the *Guidelines on Article 101(3)* suggests the existence of the concept of 'objective necessity'. ('However, certain restraints may in certain cases not be caught by Article 81(1) when the restraint is objectively necessary for the existence of an agreement of that type or that nature. Such exclusion of the application of Article 81(1) can only be made on the basis of objective factors external to the parties themselves and not the subjective views and characteristics of the parties. The question is not whether the parties in their particular situation would not have accepted to conclude a less restrictive agreement, but whether given the nature of the agreement and the characteristics of the market a less restrictive agreement would not have been concluded by undertakings in a similar setting.') *See* Frank Wijckmans, Filip Tuytschaever and Alain Vanderelst, Vertical Agreements in EC Competition Law § 2.161-2.166 (2006). (Drawing the conclusion from the foregoing provision of the *Guidelines* that 'certain intra-brand restrictions of competition, irrespective of whether they are part of a main agreement which is restrictive or non restrictive of competition in the sense of Article 81(1) EC, may still be outside the scope of Article 81(1) EC because they are objectively justified.')

49 AG Léger in his opinion delivered in *Wouters*, while acknowledging that there are 'learned disputes concerning the definition of (…) [the concept of rule of reason] or the advisability of its introduction into Community law', treated the above cases as examples

considerable controversy both in the jurisprudence of EU courts and in European scholarship, it is submitted that Article 101(1) contains a competitiveness standard, which serves as a basis for comparing the pro- and anti-competitive effects. The requirement to analyse the context and effects of the agreement necessarily implies that these counter-moves (pro- and anti-competitive effects) are to be balanced. The phraseological reluctance of the GC in some cases cannot disguise what the GC actually said. The purpose of the analysis conducted under Article 101(1) is certainly different from the aim of Article 101(3).[50] Nonetheless, both provisions embrace a peculiar 'rule of reason' test, which in the aggregate enable the analysis of all the circumstances that are examined under the American rule of reason: i.e. everything goes into the blender; however, in a more structured way.[51]

Hereunder, the jurisprudence of the EU courts will be analysed.[52] First, the concept of appreciability will be discussed, which is the minimum standard of reasonableness. Second, it will be demonstrated that while the ECJ has not endorsed the rule of reason under Article 101(1) expressly, it introduced two analytical tools, i.e. the 'market context' approach and the concept of 'comparison', which

---

where the ECJ 'made limited application of the rule of reason'. AG Léger's Opinion in *J. C. J. Wouters, J. W. Savelbergh and Price Waterhouse Belastingadviseurs BV v Algemene Raad van de Nederlandse Orde van Advocaten, intervener: Raad van de Balies van de Europese Gemeenschap* [2002] ECR I-01577, para 103. VALENTINE KORAH AND DENIS O'SULLIVAN, DISTRIBUTION AGREEMENTS UNDER THE EC COMPETITION RULES 293 and 297 (2002). (Arguing that a rule of reason type analysis should be made under Article 101(1).) OKEOGHENE ODUDU, THE BOUNDARIES OF EC COMPETITION LAW 98, 103 and 128-129 (2006).

50 *See* Roger J. Goebel, *Metro II's Confirmation of the Selective Distribution Rules: Is This the End of the Road?*, 24 Common Market Law Review 605, 611 (1987). (Concluding that the ECJ's analysis of selective distribution in *Metro II* 'obviously represent[s] a 'rule of reason' approach to Article 85(1).') *But see* Barry E. Hawk, *System Failure: Vertical Restraints and EC Competition Law*, 32 Common Market Law Review 973, 987-988 (1995). (Asserting that 'there is only one set of economic principles, or to state the converse, there are not two sets of microeconomics and industrial organization theory with one operating under 85(1) and the other operating under 85(3)'. Suggesting that economic considerations should be examined under Article 101(1), while Article 101(3) should be the place for analysing non-competition policies, e.g. environmental policy, industrial policy. Criticizing the bifurcation of Article 101 analysis and submitting that "[a] more fundamental solution would be elimination of the bifurcation through amendment of the Treaty".')

51 *See* DORIS HILDEBRAND, THE ROLE OF ECONOMIC ANALYSIS IN THE EC COMPETITION RULES 235 (1998). ('The problem of a rule-of-reason in Community competition law is therefore much more *when* the overall assessment of the competition impact of an agreement should be made, than *if* this assessment is made.')

52 *See* Emmanuel P. Mastromanolis, *Insights from U.S. Antitrust Law on Exclusive and Restricted Territorial Distribution: The Creation of a New Legal Standard for European Union Competition Law*, 15 University of Pennsylvania Journal of International Business Law 559, 567-568 (1994). (Submitting that the most acknowledged hints of a rule of reason are the concept of *de minimis*, the notion of ancillary restraints and the 'judicial criteria of a "balanced" application of' Article 101(1).).

shape an idiosyncratic test of competitiveness. Third, the GC's judicial practice will be examined and criticized, which – notwithstanding the declaration that there is no rule of reason in EU competition law – was ready to examine the pros and cons of the arrangements at stake. Fourth, the concept of ancillary restraints will be considered that is, besides the concept of 'rule of reason', the only theory that attempts to give a comprehensive explanation to the judicial practice of Article 101(1) and to the fact that some 'reasonable' restraints, while formally falling foul of Article 101(1), can be justified under this provision. As regards the theory of ancillary restraints it will be demonstrated that albeit this concept may be a useful analytical tool in certain cases, it is not capable of being the overall theory of Article 101(1).

The threshold question of appreciability in EU competition law

Article 101 contains a threshold test of appreciability (concept of *de minimis* agreements/agreements of minor importance). This test is not simply the projection of the ancient principle: *de minimis non curat lex.*[53] Competition law is destined to protect competition, whatever this term means, and, hence, if a conduct has no effect on competition, no competition law intervention is required. Accordingly, the concept of appreciability is a substantive law notion in nature: it is not simply a matter of procedural convenience or efficient resource allocation. This proposition is very important, especially in the context of private enforcement, which is gaining increasing importance, as agreements considered *de minimis* do not only go unprosecuted by the competition authorities, but they are not violating Article 101 at all, and are therefore lawful.

Appreciability is examined at two different points under Article 101. The applicability of EU competition rules presupposes that a given conduct affects inter-state trade *appreciably*.[54] This is a question of jurisdiction.[55] The other point, where appreciability has a role, is the agreement's impact on competition. In the first case the question is whether the conduct at stake has an appreciable effect *on inter-state trade*, while in the second the question is whether the agreement has appreciable effect *on the market*. Initially, the two notions of appreciability were inseparably conjoined: the ECJ judgments consistently spoke about appreciable effects on inter-state trade *and* on the market and the first Commission notices

53 'The law does not concern itself with trifles' Black's Law Dictionary (8th ed. 2004).

54 This rule applies both to Article 101 and Article 102. The concept of appreciability also has a third projection: Article 101 may be declared inapplicable if the restriction itself is insignificant. *See* Joined Cases C-180/98 to C-184/98 *Pavel Pavlov and Others v Stichting Pensioenfonds Medische Specialisten* [2000] ECR I-06451; 86/507/EEC *Irish Banks' Standing Committee* OJ [1986] L 295/28, para 16; 2001/782/EC *Visa International* OJ [2001] L 293/24; 2001/478/EC *UEFA's broadcasting regulations* OJ [2001] L 171/12; 2001/696/EC *Identrus* 511 OJ [2001] L 249/12. *See also* Richard Whish, Competition law 141-142 (2009).

55 *See* Richard Whish, Competition Law 144 (2009).

on agreements of minor importance also covered both aspects of appreciability.[56] Subsequently, the two projections of appreciability pulled apart, and currently the Commission has two separate notices on *de minimis* agreements and agreements not affecting inter-state trade, respectively.[57]

The ECJ established the concept of appreciability in *Völk v Vervaecke*,[58] where it held that

> [i]f an agreement is to be capable of affecting trade between Member States it must be possible to foresee with a sufficient degree of probability on the basis of a set of objective factors of law or of fact that the agreement in question may have an influence, direct or indirect, actual or potential, on the pattern of trade between Member States in such a way that is might hinder the attainment of the objectives of a single market between states. Moreover, the prohibition in Article 85(1) is applicable only if the agreement in question also has as its object or effect the prevention, restriction or distortion of competition within the common market. Those conditions must be understood by reference to the actual circumstances of the agreement. Consequently *an agreement falls outside the prohibition in Article 85 when it has only an insignificant effect on the markets*, taking into account the weak position which the persons concerned have on the market of the product in question. *Thus an exclusive dealing agreement, even with absolute territorial protection, may*, having regard to the weak position of the persons concerned on the market in the products in question in the area covered by the absolute protection, escape the prohibition laid down in Article 85(1).[59]

In this case the supplier's market share was indeed negligible: it was 0.08 per cent on the level of the common market, 0.2 per cent in Germany (where the producer was located) and 0.6 per cent in Belgium and Luxembourg (where the distributor was located).[60]

---

56 *See Notice Concerning Agreements, Decisions and Concerted Practices in the Field of Cooperation between Enterprises* OJ [1968] C 75/3, corrected in OJ [1968] C 84/14.; *Notice on Agreements of Minor Importance Which Do Not Fall Within the Meaning of Article 85 (1) of the Treaty Establishing the European Community* OJ [1997] C 372/13.

57 *Notice on Agreements of Minor Importance Which Do Not Appreciably Restrict Competition under Article 81(1) of the Treaty Establishing the European Community (De Minimis)*. OJ [2001] C 368/13. On the 2001 *Notice on Agreements of Minor Importance see* Luc Peeperkorn, *Revision of the 1997 Notice on Agreements of Minor Importance*, 2001(2) Competition Policy Newsletter 4 (2001); Luc Peeperkorn, *New Notice on agreements of minor importance (de minimis Notice)*, 2002(1) Competition Policy Newsletter 45 (2002). *Commission Notice: Guidelines on the Effect on Trade Concept Contained in Articles 81 and 82 of the Treaty.* OJ [2004] C 101/81.

58 Case 5/69 *Franz Völk v S.P.R.L. Ets J. Vervaecke* [1969] ECR 295.

59 Paras 5-7.

60 Mario Filipponi, Luc Peeperkorn and Donncadh Woods, *Chapter 9: Vertical Agreements, in* THE EC LAW OF COMPETITION § 9.48 (Jonathan Faull and Ali Nikpay ed., 2007).

The ECJ virtually reiterated the above language in *Cadillon v Maschinenbau*.[61]

> First of all, for Article 85 of the Treaty to apply to an agreement, that agreement must be capable of affecting trade between Member States.
>
> This condition is fulfilled if the agreement, on the basis of all the objective factors of law or of fact, makes it possible to foresee with a sufficient degree of probability that it may have an influence, direct or indirect, actual or potential, on the pattern of trade between Member States in such a way that it might hinder the attainment of the objectives of a single market between states.
>
> Moreover, the prohibition in Article 85(1) is applicable only if the agreement has as its object or effect the prevention, restriction or distortion of competition within the common market.
>
> Those conditions must be understood by reference to the actual circumstances of the agreement.
>
> An exclusive dealing agreement may escape the prohibition laid down in Article 85(1) because, in view of the weak position of the parties on the market in the products in question in the territory covered by the exclusive dealing arrangement, it is not capable of hindering the attainment of the objectives of a single market between states, even if it creates absolute territorial protection.

Accordingly, the argumentation of both ECJ judgments adopts the following structure: 1. Article 101 can be applied only if inter-state trade is affected, 2. the general prohibition on restrictive agreements embedded in Article 101 is applicable to agreements that have anti-competitive object or effect, 3. agreements are to be assessed in their actual context, 4. it follows that an agreement does not come under the scope of Article 101 if it has insignificant effects on the market. Consequently, the conclusion of point 4 may refer both to premise 1 and premise 2; and most probably it refers to both of them.[62] Therewith, it cannot be disregarded that the scholarship almost uniformly shares the opinion that *Völk v Vervaecke* is the starting point of the rule on *de minimis* agreements at large, that is, it covers both prongs of the doctrine.[63]

One of the pivotal questions of the concept of appreciability is whether it applies to all types of arrangements or it covers only 'effect' type agreements, with the exclusion of agreements anti-competitive by object. The scholarship is not

61 Case 1/71 *Société anonyme Cadillon v Firma Höss, Maschinenbau KG* [1971] ECR 351, paras 5-9.

62 *See* Mario Filipponi, Luc Peeperkorn and Donncadh Woods, *Chapter 9: Vertical Agreements*, *in* THE EC LAW OF COMPETITION § 9.47 (Jonathan Faull and Ali Nikpay ed., 2007).

63 *See* ERNST-JOACHIM MESTMÄCKER AND HEIKE SCHWEITZER, EUROPÄISCHES WETTBEWERBSRECHT 291 (2004); RICHARD WHISH, COMPETITION LAW 137-138 and 141 (2009); Maija Laurila, *The De Minimis Doctrine in EEC Competition Law: Agreements of Minor Importance*, 14(3) European Competition Law Review 97, 98 (1993); VALENTINE KORAH AND DENIS O'SULLIVAN, DISTRIBUTION AGREEMENTS UNDER THE EC COMPETITION RULES 67 (2002).

uniform in this regard;[64] it is submitted that the most appropriate position seems to be that the concept of appreciability of market impact has no role regarding agreements that are anti-competitive by their object. Even though concerning absolute territorial protection it is indeed unclear whether according to the ECJ's jurisprudence the concept of *de minimis* agreements has a role, it seems that, in principle, object type agreements cannot benefit from the notion of *de minimis*, at least, as far as horizontal agreements are concerned. Initially, in *Consten v Grundig* the ECJ held that in case of agreements restrictive by object there is no need for further inquiry. The very concept of 'object' type agreements is that they can be condemned on their face, without any need to inspect the context; this convenience would be lost if the concept of *de minimis* applied to object type agreements; the definition of the relevant market, the identification of the competitors and the calculation of the market shares could not be avoided.

While the ECJ's judgment in *Völk v Vervaecke* could have been interpreted as suggesting that the *Consten v Grundig* rule is qualified (as the Court applied the appreciability doctrine to an object type agreement), subsequent jurisprudence makes it clear that agreements that are anti-competitive by object are condemned without further ado, i.e. without any inquiry into the effects.[65] For instance, the

---

64 For the proposition that object type agreements cannot avoid Article 101 condemnation even if they have no appreciable effect on the market *see* JOANNA GOYDER, EU DISTRIBUTION LAW 28 and 70 (4th ed., 2005). ('However, it should be noted that (…) [the] thresholds [of the *Notice on Agreements of Minor Importance*] do not apply to hard core restrictions such as price-fixing clauses or clauses providing for absolute territorial protection, which may infringe Article 81(1) however small the parties' market shares.') ('Similarly, if the relevant market shares are low, so that the agreement is not capable of appreciably affecting competition, EU competition rules are not infringed, unless the agreement contains hard-core restrictions such as price-fixing or absolute territorial protection.'; CSONGOR ISTVÁN NAGY, KARTELLJOGI KÉZIKÖNYV 343-344 and 346 (2008). For the proposition that both object and effect type agreements may avoid the net of Article 101 if they have no appreciable effect on the market *see* RICHARD WHISH, COMPETITION LAW 138 (2009); Ali Nikpay, Jonathan Faull and Lars Kjølbye, *Chapter 3: Article 81*, *in* THE EC LAW OF COMPETITION § 3.158 (Jonathan Faull and Ali Nikpay ed., 2007). *But see* Ali Nikpay, Jonathan Faull and Lars Kjølbye, *Chapter 3: Article 81*, *in* THE EC LAW OF COMPETITION § 3.164 (Jonathan Faull and Ali Nikpay ed., 2007). ('Thus, in summary, it would seem fair to conclude that even for companies with little market power, agreements containing restrictions by object run a very serious risk of infringing Article 81(1).'); FRANK WIJCKMANS, FILIP TUYTSCHAEVER AND ALAIN VANDERELST, VERTICAL AGREEMENTS IN EC COMPETITION LAW § 2.144 (2006).

65 *See* Maija Laurila, *The De Minimis Doctrine in EEC Competition Law: Agreements of Minor Importance*, 14(3) European Competition Law Review 97, 98 (1993) *See also* Mario Filipponi, Luc Peeperkorn and Donncadh Woods, *Chapter 9: Vertical Agreements*, *in* THE EC LAW OF COMPETITION § 9.50 (Jonathan Faull and Ali Nikpay ed., 2007). (While 'restrictions by object are subject to the appreciability doctrine, (…) [subsequent jurisprudence reveals] that the doctrine does not appear to have been consistently applied to both the restriction of competition and effect on trade criteria. In many cases the appreciability of the restriction appears to be assumed (i.e. restriction by nature), with the analysis of appreciability

GC held in *Montedipe SpA v Commission* and in *Tréfilunion SA v Commission* in the context of horizontal hard-core restrictions that these practices *per se* violate Article 101(1), a language that simply leaves no room for the application of the concept of appreciability.[66] Furthermore, whereas both *Völk v Vervaecke* and *Cadillon v Maschinenbau* seem to apply the concept of appreciability to both inter-state trade and market impact, the ECJ's subsequent jurisprudence narrowed the projection of this principle to the effect on inter-state trade; subsequent judgments simply 'forgot' to mention the term 'market' in the context of appreciability.[67] The Commission's position, as expressed in the *Notice on Agreements of Minor Importance*, seems to be clear is this regard: hardcore agreements cannot be treated as agreements of minor importance, irrespective of the parties' market share.[68] The Commission's decisional practice also follows this approach.[69] This relates, of course, only to the substantive law position of the Commission; another question is that the Commission is perfectly free not to investigate agreements of minor importance as a matter of efficient resource allocation; and in fact formal decisions

concentrating upon effect on trade between Member States.') In *Erauw-Jacquery* the ECJ seems to have applied the concept of appreciability only to the effect on inter-state trade. Case 27/87 *SPRL Louis Erauw-Jacquery v La Hesbignonne SC* [1988] ECR 01919. This case is especially revealing as AG Mischo's opinion, on the contrary, applied the foregoing test both to the effects on inter-state trade and on competition. AG Mischo's opinion in Case 27/87 *SPRL Louis Erauw-Jacquery v La Hesbignonne SC*, [1988] ECR 1919, paras 37-47. In *Parker Pen* the GC automatically condemned an export prohibition without any inquiry as to the restriction's appreciability concerning competition. Case T-77/92 *Parker Pen Ltd v Commission* [1994] ECR II-549, para 37.

66 Case T-14/89 *Montedipe SpA v Commission* [1992] ECR II-01155, para 265; Case T-148/89 *Tréfilunion SA v Commission* [1995] ECR II-1063, para 109.

67 Case 19/77 *Miller International Schallplatten GmbH v Commission* [1978] ECR 131, paras 14-15; Case C-306/96 *Javico International and Javico AG v Yves Saint Laurent Parfums SA (YSLP)* [1998] ECR I-1983, paras 15-17.

68 *Notice on Agreements of Minor Importance*, para 11. *See* Ali Nikpay, Jonathan Faull and Lars Kjølbye, *Chapter 3: Article 81*, *in* The EC Law of Competition § 3.163 (Jonathan Faull and Ali Nikpay ed., 2007). ('The approach taken by the Commission in the *Notice on agreements of minor importance* means, for instance, that the Notice would not apply to a case where market shares are akin to those in *Völk*.') This was the approach followed by the earlier Notice too. *Notice on agreements of minor importance*. OJ [1997] 372/13, para 11 ('With regard to: (a) horizontal agreements which have as their object to fix prices or to limit production or sales, or to share markets or sources of supply, (b) vertical agreements which have as their object to fix resale prices, or to confer territorial protection on the participating undertakings or third undertakings, the applicability of Article 85 (1) cannot be ruled out even where the aggregate market shares held by all of the participating undertakings remain below the thresholds mentioned in points 9 and 10.')

69 *See* 92/426/EEC *Viho/Parker Pen* OJ [1992] L 233/27; 94/987/EC *Tretorn and others* OJ [1994] L 378/45.

concerning *de minimis* agreements are very rare.[70] This issue may gain more practical significance with the development of private enforcement, as private parties do not take into account whether public interest warrants the procedure but they examine whether their interests do so.

Accordingly, the basic question is whether the concept of appreciability as established in *Völk v Vervaecke* and in *Cadillon v Maschinenbau* relates both to inter-state trade and market impact or solely to inter-state trade. More precisely, the question is what these precedents mean for the time being, taking into account subsequent judicial developments. If accepting that in subsequent jurisprudence object type agreements were condemned automatically, without any inquiry as regards appreciability, and taking into account that in *Völk v Vervaecke* and in *Cadillon v Maschinenbau* the ECJ refused to condemn such a vertical object type agreement, it could be argued that the only way to reconcile these cases is to say that appreciability in *Völk v Vervaecke* and in *Cadillon v Maschinenbau* covered only the element of inter-state trade. Nevertheless, it could also be argued that whatever the purpose of the ECJ was in *Völk v Vervaecke* and in *Cadillon v Maschinenbau*, these judgments were partially overruled by subsequent jurisprudence.[71] Even in this case it could be argued that the Court in *Völk v Vervaecke* and in *Cadillon v Maschinenbau* did not apply the concept of appreciability to all agreements, but created an exceptional rule that concerns only absolute territorial protection or by analogy vertical agreements in general, while horizontal hardcore restraints are excluded from the benefit of this case-law; or at least the holding of these cases has been confined to vertical agreements by subsequent jurisprudence.[72]

---

70 Richard Whish, Competition law 138 (2009). ('Formal decisions applying the doctrine are rare: the Commission would normally not initiate proceedings in relation to a *de minimis* agreement, and if it were to do so it would be likely to settle the case informally.') ('Of course the Commission might decide, as a matter of prosecutorial discretion, not to proceed against hard-core restrictions (…), but that is a different matter from providing such restrictions with a safe harbour.'); *Cf.* Frank Wijckmans, Filip Tuytschaever and Alain Vanderelst, Vertical Agreements in EC Competition Law § 2.145 (2006). ('On restrictions which have the restriction of competition as their object, the Commission's policy seems to be to informally apply the *De Minimis* Notice, and this is in spite of the Notice's wording, namely, that it excludes hardcore restrictions from its scope of application.')

71 *See* Mario Filipponi, Luc Peeperkorn and Donncadh Woods, *Chapter 9: Vertical Agreements*, *in* The EC Law of Competition § 9.47 (Jonathan Faull and Ali Nikpay ed., 2007). (The subsequent case-law of the EU courts suggests that 'the real litmus test for restrictions by object appears not to be one of appreciability of the restriction but rather whether it is capable of having an appreciable effect on trade between Member States').

72 *Cf.* Ali Nikpay, Jonathan Faull and Lars Kjølbye, *Chapter 3: Article 81*, *in* The EC Law of Competition 227 (Jonathan Faull and Ali Nikpay ed., 2007). ('In any event, given the general tenor of the case law on cartels, it would seem implausible that the European Courts would permit cartels to escape the Article 81 prohibition on the basis of low market shares alone.')

The elements of the reasonableness (anti-competitiveness) test under Article 101(1): the 'market context' approach and the concept of 'comparison' (counter-factual) in the judicial practice of the ECJ.

Although the ECJ has not yet taken a clear position on whether Article 101(1) contains a reasonableness ('rule of reason') standard, it did not exclude the perspective of such an interpretation. In *Montecatini*, the Court chose the more convenient way, saying that the case did not require a decision on the issue whether a rule of reason exists since the agreement at stake was a hardcore cartel, which was to be judged by its object. Nevertheless, the Court left the question explicitly open.[73]

> On this point, it need merely be stated that, even if the rule of reason did have a place in the context of Article 85(1) of the Treaty, in no event may it exclude application of that provision in the case of a restrictive arrangement involving producers accounting for almost all the Community market and concerning price targets, production limits and sharing out of the market. The Court of First Instance did not therefore commit an error of law when it considered that the clear nature of the infringement in any event precluded the application of the rule of reason.[74]

Notwithstanding this guarded wording, the ECJ, in fact, has often used a rule of reason approach. In several cases the requirement that when dealing with effect type agreements the market context and the market consequences of the arrangement are to be taken into account certainly implies that the reasonableness

73 *See* Beverley Robertson, *What is a Restriction of Competition? The Implications of the CFI's Judgment in O2 Germany and the Rule of Reason*, 28(4) European Competition Law Review 252, 257 (2007). ('The ECJ has left this issue open. In *Montecatini*, the ECJ rejected the argument that the CFI should have applied a "rule of reason" analysis (...) to an agreement with a seriously anti-competitive object, but did not rule out that a balancing exercise would ever be appropriate.') *Contra* Case T-65/98 *Van den Bergh Foods Ltd v Commission* [2003] ECR II-4653, para 107. (Referring to *Montecatini* as a buttress for the proposition that 'Article 85(3) of the Treaty would lose much of its effectiveness if such an examination had already to be carried out under Article 85(1) of the Treaty (…).') Case T-112/99 *Métropole télévision (M6), Suez-Lyonnaise des eaux, France Télécom and Télévision française 1 SA (TF1) v Commission* [2001] ECR II-2459, para 72. (Concluding from the ECJ's 'even if existed' formulation in para 133 of *Montecatini*, i.e. 'even if the rule of reason did have a place in the context of Article 85(1) of the Treaty', that the ECJ in fact questioned the existence of a rule of reason under Article 101(1): '[q]uite to the contrary, in various judgments the Court of Justice and the Court of First Instance have been at pains to indicate that the existence of a rule of reason in Community competition law is doubtful'). Case T-328/03 *O2 (Germany) GmbH and Co. OHG v Commission* [2006] ECR II-1231, para 69 (Referring to *Montecatini* in order to underpin the proposition that 'the Community judicature has not deemed [the rule of reason test] to have its place under Article 81(1) EC'.)

74 Case C-235/92 *Montecatini SpA v Commission* [1999] ECR I-4539, para 133.

(competitiveness) of the restraint is to be analysed.[75] The Court declared very early, in *Société Technique Minière*,[76] that in case of effect type agreements the arrangement's effects on competition are to be investigated taking into account the actual market context (concept of market context). The Court went even further when saying that the situations of competition with and without the agreement are to be compared (concept of comparison, or alternatively called: concept of counter-factual[77]). This comparison implies that individual anti-competitive effects are not relevant in themselves but the ultimate question is what the final effect on competition is. Namely, if an agreement, put it at simplest, gives more to competition than it takes away, at the end of the day it is pro-competitive. At the same moment, if such a comparison is not only permissible but obligatory, the concept of reasonableness (competitiveness) embedded in Article 101(1) can hardly be denied.

> The competition in question must be understood within the actual context in which it would occur in the absence of the agreement in dispute. In particular it may be doubted whether there is an interference with competition if the said agreement seems really necessary for the penetration of a new area by an undertaking. Therefore, in order to decide whether an agreement containing a clause 'granting an exclusive right of sale' is to be considered as prohibited by reason of its object or of its effect, it is appropriate to take into account in particular the nature and quantity, limited or otherwise, of the products covered by the agreement, the position and importance of the grantor and the concessionnaire on the market for the products concerned, the isolated nature of the disputed agreement or, alternatively, its position in a series of agreements, the severity of the clauses intended to protect the exclusive dealership or, alternatively, the opportunities allowed for other commercial competitors in the same products by way of parallel re-exportation and importation.[78]

---

75 *See* Doris Hildebrand, The role of economic analysis in the EC competition rules 235-236 (1998). (Characterizing the jurisprudence of the ECJ as appearing to apply a limited kind of a rule of reason.)

76 Case 56/65 *Société Technique Minière (L.T.M.) v Maschinenbau Ulm GmbH (M.B.U.)* [1966] ECR 235.

77 The comparison is accomplished through reference to the counterfactual (the would-be competitive situation). *See* Beverley Robertson, *What is a Restriction of Competition? The Implications of the CFI's Judgment in O2 Germany and the Rule of Reason*, 28(4) European Competition Law Review 252, 257 and 258 (2007); Valentine Korah, An Introductory Guide to EC Competition Law and Practice 78 (2007); *Guidelines on Article 101(3)*, para 18; Vivien Rose and Peter Roth, *Article 81(1)*, *in* Bellamy and Child's European Community Law of Competition 2.099 (Peter Roth and Vivien Rose ed., 2008).

78 Case 161/84 *Pronuptia de Paris GmbH v Pronuptia de Paris Irmgard Schillgallis* [1986] ECR 353.

The above approach was later endorsed and became the settled case-law of the Court.[79] The ECJ in fact did give the green light under Article 101(1) to arrangements that clearly restricted competition in literal sense. In *Société Technique Minière*, an exclusivity clause was accepted due to the free-rider argument.[80] In *Pronuptia*, the Court held that certain restrictions in franchising agreements are not caught by Article 101(1), presumably because they are reasonable and enhance competition.[81] In *Metro*, the same unspoken 'restricts but reasonably' logic was used for endorsing a selective distribution agreement under Article 101(1).[82] In *Nungesser*, the ECJ held that Article 101(1) is not applicable to an exclusive licence due to its being reasonably necessary for penetrating a new market.[83] In *Remia*, the ECJ did not find Article 101(1) concerns in case of a non-compete obligation attached to a sale of business contract, asserting that without this restraint 'the agreement for the transfer of the undertaking could not be given effect' and the agreements did 'contribute to the promotion of competition because they lead to an increase in the number of undertakings in the market in question'.[84] In *Gøttrup-Klim*, the ECJ declared the Article 101(1) compatibility of an agricultural cooperative's rule providing that the members of the cooperative may not have membership in another cooperative. The Court considered that the cooperative actually intensified competition in the sense of rivalry, thus, it promoted rather than hindered the

---

79 Case 42/84 *Remia BV and others v Commission* [1985] ECR 2545, para 18. ('In order to determine whether or not such clauses come within the prohibition on Article 85(1), it is necessary to examine what would be the state of competition if those clauses did not exist.') Case C-399/93 *H. G. Oude Luttikhuis and others v Verenigde Coöperatieve Melkindustrie Coberco BA* [1995] ECR I-4515, para 10. ('It is settled case-law that in defining the criteria for the application of Article 85(1) to a specific case, account should be taken of the economic context in which the undertakings operate, the products or services covered by the agreements, the structure of the market concerned and the actual conditions in which it functions.'). *See also* Case C-234/89 *Stergios Delimitis v Henninger Bräu AG* [1991] ECR I-935, paras 28 and 31; Case T-168/01 *GlaxoSmithKline Services Unlimited v Commission* [2006] ECR II-02969, para 162. (The examination of 'the actual or potential effects of the agreement on competition (…) entails a comparison of the competitive situation resulting from the agreement and the situation that would exist in its absence'); *White Paper on Modernisation of the Rules Implementing Article 85 and 86 of the EC Treaty.* Commission Programme 99/027. COM (99) 101 final. OJ [1999] C 132/1, para 57 fn 47. (Regarding *Nungesser* and *Pronuptia* as 'rule of reason' judgments.)

80 Case 56/65 *Société Technique Minière (L.T.M.) v Maschinenbau Ulm GmbH (M.B.U.)* [1966] ECR 235.

81 Case 161/84 *Pronuptia de Paris GmbH v Pronuptia de Paris Irmgard Schillgallis* [1986] ECR 353.

82 Case 26/76 *Metro SB-Großmärkte GmbH and Co. KG v Commission* [1977] ECR 1875.

83 Case 258/78 *L.C. Nungesser KG and Kurt Eisele v Commission* [1982] ECR 2015, para 57.

84 Case 42/84 *Remia BV and others v Commission* [1985] ECR 2545, paras 19-20.

competitive process.[85] All in all, the ECJ not only did establish a test where the reasonableness of the arrangement is to be evaluated from a competition point of view but it did remove certain pro-competitive restrictions from the ambit of Article 101(1).

Of course, agreements having an anti-competitive object do not merit any contextual analysis under Article 101(1) and any justification concerning such agreements can be brought up exclusively under Article 101(3), the anti-competitiveness of the arrangement being conclusively presumed under Article 101(1).[86]

The GC's fear of the rule of reason

While the ECJ, as noted above, has remained graciously silent, the GC was in fact very enthusiastic in holding that the rule of reason and its cousins are *persona non grata* in the realm of Article 101(1). Nonetheless, the GC's outright refusal against any reference to the rule of reason seems to be inconsistent with what the GC has in fact done.

In *Van den Bergh Foods*,[87] the GC held that 'the existence of (…) [the rule of reason] in Community competition law is not accepted'.[88] The GC's strongest argument was structuralist in nature: all concerns related to 'reason' belong to Article 101(3); a different interpretation would be 'difficult to reconcile with the structure of the rules prescribed by Article 85'.[89]

---

85 Case C-250/92 *Gøttrup-Klim e.a. Grovvareforeninger v Dansk Landbrugs Grovvareselskab AmbA.* [1994] ECR I-5641.

86 Joined Cases T-374/94, T-375/94, T-384/94 and T-388/94 *European Night Services Ltd (ENS) et altera v Commission* [1998] ECR II-3141, para 136. (In case of an agreement 'containing obvious restrictions of competition such as price-fixing, market-sharing or the control of outlets (…), such restrictions may be weighed against their claimed pro-competitive effects only in the context of Article 85(3) of the Treaty, with a view to granting an exemption from the prohibition in Article 85(1)'.)

87 Case T-65/98 *Van den Bergh Foods Ltd v Commission* [2003] ECR II-4653.

88 Para 106. It is noteworthy that the GC's earlier judgments neither confirmed, nor refuted the existence of rule of reason in EU competition law. *See* Case T-14/89 *Montedipe SpA v Commission* [1992] ECR II-01155, para 265. ('Furthermore, the fact that the infringement of Article 85(1) of the EEC Treaty, in particular subparagraphs (a), (b) and (c), is a clear one *precludes the application of a rule of reason*, assuming such a rule to be applicable in Community competition law, since in that case *it must be regarded as an infringement per se of the competition rules*.'); Case T-148/89 *Tréfilunion SA v Commission* [1995] ECR II-1063, para 109. ('It must be borne in mind that the Commission has established to the requisite legal standard that the object of the agreements was anti-competitive within the meaning of Article 85(1) of the Treaty. Moreover, the fact that the infringement of Article 85(1) of the Treaty, in particular subparagraphs (a) and (c), is a clear one *necessarily precludes the application of a rule of reason*, assuming such a rule to be applicable in Community competition law, since in that case it must be regarded as an *infringement per se of the competition rules* (Case T-14/89 Montedipe v Commission [1992] ECR II-1155, paragraph 265).')

89 Para 106.

> Article 85 of the Treaty expressly provides, in its third paragraph, for the exemption of agreements that restrict competition where they satisfy a number of conditions (…). It is only within the specific framework of that provision that the pro and anti-competitive aspects of a restriction may be weighed (…). Article 85(3) of the Treaty would lose much of its effectiveness if such an examination had already to be carried out under Article 85(1) of the Treaty …[90]

According to the GC, however, the foregoing stance has no bearing on the existence of the concept of market context.

> When assessing the effects of such a network of distribution agreements, it is necessary to have regard to the economic and legal context in which it operates and in which it might combine with others so as to have a cumulative effect on competition …[91]

In *Métropole*,[92] the GC was a little bit more euphemistic but came to the very same conclusion when holding that 'the existence of a rule of reason in Community competition law is doubtful'.[93] The GC based its interpretation on the same structuralist logic: if the pro- and anti-competitive aspects of a restriction were weighed under Article 101(1), Article 101(3) 'would lose much of its effectiveness'.[94] The GC perceived that there is a tension between the alleged non-existence of a 'European rule of reason' and the concept of market context, and it tried to lift it; nonetheless, rather unsuccessfully.

> It is true that in a number of judgments the Court of Justice and the Court of First Instance have favoured a more flexible interpretation of the prohibition laid down in Article 85(1) of the Treaty (…).
>
> Those judgments cannot, however, be interpreted as establishing the existence of a rule of reason in Community competition law. They are, rather, part of a broader trend in the case-law according to which it is not necessary to hold, wholly abstractly and without drawing any distinction, that any agreement

---

90 Para 107. *Contra White Paper on Modernisation of the Rules Implementing Article 85 and 86 of the EC Treaty.* Commission Programme 99/027. COM (99) 101 final. OJ [1999] C 132/1, para 57. (Expressly declaring that Article 101(1), though to a limited extent, may serve as a place for assessing pro- and anti-competitive effects. 'The Commission has already adopted this approach to a limited extent and has carried out an assessment of the pro- and anti-competitive aspects of some restrictive practices under Article 85(1).')

91 Para 109.

92 Case T-112/99 *Métropole téhlévision (M6), Suez-Lyonnaise des eaux, France Télécom and Télévision française 1 SA (TF1) v Commission* [2001] ECR II-2459.

93 Para 72. ('[I]n various judgments the Court of Justice and the Court of First Instance have been at pains to indicate that the existence of a rule of reason in Community competition law is doubtful.')

94 Para 74.

> restricting the freedom of action of one or more of the parties is necessarily caught by the prohibition laid down in Article 85(1) of the Treaty. In assessing the applicability of Article 85(1) to an agreement, account should be taken of the actual conditions in which it functions, in particular the economic context in which the undertakings operate, the products or services covered by the agreement and the actual structure of the market concerned (…).
>
> That interpretation, while observing the substantive scheme of Article 85 of the Treaty and, in particular, preserving the effectiveness of Article 85(3), makes it possible to prevent the prohibition in Article 85(1) from extending wholly abstractly and without distinction to all agreements whose effect is to restrict the freedom of action of one or more of the parties. It must, however, be emphasised that such an approach does not mean that it is necessary to weigh the pro and anti-competitive effects of an agreement when determining whether the prohibition laid down in Article 85(1) of the Treaty applies.[95]

The foregoing construction is far from convincing and falls foul of the settled case-law. The GC essentially considered that the concrete effects of the agreement are to be analysed in order to ascertain whether it is anti-competitive, but no pro-competitive effects may be taken into account.[96] Nonetheless, since theoretically all self-restraints on an undertaking's freedom of action restrain competition,[97]

95 Paras 75-77.

96 The GC's stance is followed by the Commission. Para 11 of the *Guidelines on Article 101(3)* provides as follows. 'The assessment under Article 81 thus consists of two parts. The first step is to assess whether an agreement between undertakings, which is capable of affecting trade between Member States, has an anti-competitive object or actual or potential anti-competitive effects. The second step, which only becomes relevant when an agreement is found to be restrictive of competition, is to determine the pro-competitive benefits produced by that agreement and to assess whether these pro-competitive effects outweigh the anti-competitive effects. The balancing of anti-competitive and pro-competitive effects is conducted exclusively within the framework laid down by Article 81(3).' The footnote attached to the *Guidelines*' foregoing statement expressly refers to *Van den Bergh Foods* and *Métropole*.

97 The starting point of this approach is that theoretically all restraints on one's freedom of action raise competition law concerns, however, not all such restraints are actually caught in the net of Article 101(1), as account must be taken also of the market context. Case C-309/99 *J. C. J. Wouters, J. W. Savelbergh and Price Waterhouse Belastingadviseurs BV v Algemene Raad van de Nederlandse Orde van Advocaten, intervener: Raad van de Balies van de Europese Gemeenschap* [2002] ECR I-01577, para 97. ('However, *not every agreement* between undertakings or every decision of an association of undertakings *which restricts the freedom of action of the parties or of one of them* necessarily falls within the prohibition laid down in Article 85(1) of the Treaty. For the purposes of application of that provision to a particular case, *account must first of all be taken of the overall context* in which the decision of the association of undertakings was taken or produces its effects.'); Case C-209/07 *Competition Authority v Beef Industry Development Society Ltd and Barry Brothers (Carrigmore) Meats Ltd* [2008] ECR I-8637,

the GC's approach would, in effect, seem to turn the concept of 'market context' into a 'market power' test. Since all voluntarily assumed restraints on one's freedom of action restrict competition, abstractly, or at least embody a potential for restriction, the only chance for the parties is to argue that the restriction is not palpable, i.e. competition is restricted only abstractly. As according to the above construction only those effects of the agreement are to be taken into account that are detrimental to competition,[98] the ones that are beneficial being left to Article 101(3), the defendant may escape competition law condemnation only if demonstrating that the *in abstracto* dangers did not became a reality *in concreto*. This is, however, a *de minimis* logic; if redeeming virtue is not taken into account, Article 101(1) essentially becomes a big *de minimis*/market power analysis: the parties may succeed only if lack of market power is proved.[99] Nevertheless, the concept of comparison suggests that this is not the case; the absence of market power is only one of the ways to escape Article 101(1). What is more, an effect test based solely on market power is incompatible with the

para 34 ('That type of arrangement conflicts patently with the concept inherent in the EC Treaty provisions relating to competition, according to which *each economic operator must determine independently the policy which it intends to adopt* on the common market. Article 81(1) EC is intended to prohibit any form of coordination which deliberately substitutes practical cooperation between undertakings for the risks of competition.') *Cf. Board of Trade of City of Chicago v U.S.*, 246 U.S. 231, 238 (1918). ('But the legality of an agreement or regulation cannot be determined by so simple a test, as whether it restrains competition. Every agreement concerning trade, every regulation of trade, restrains. To bind, to restrain, is of their very essence.')

98 *See* Beverley Robertson, *What Is a Restriction of Competition? The Implications of the CFI's Judgment in O2 Germany and the Rule of Reason*, 28(4) European Competition Law Review 252, 257 (2007) ('It seems that balancing can only be avoided altogether if it is argued that just one potentially anti-competitive effect is sufficient for an agreement to be caught by Art.81(1). Agreements with both anti and pro-competitive effects will always therefore be caught.') *Cf.* Vincent Verouden, *Vertical Agreements and Article 81(1) EC: The Evolving Role of the Economic Analysis*, 71 Antitrust Law Journal 525, 563-564 (2003). ('From an economist's point of view, this approach is somewhat difficult to follow. It certainly does not correspond to the way many economists would assess whether a certain agreement "restricts competition". It entails an incomplete analysis of competition in the sense that, when examining whether or not an agreement restricts competition, the Court does not consider the economic context in order to determine the net effect on competition, but rather considers it only to verify the existence of possible anticompetitive effects.')

99 *Cf. Guidelines on Article 101(3)*, para 24. (Suggesting that in case of effect type agreements it is the weight, i.e. the 'extent' and the appreciability, of the arrangement's effects that is relevant. 'For an agreement to be restrictive by effect it must affect actual or potential competition to such an extent that on the relevant market negative effects on prices, output, innovation or the variety or quality of goods and services can be expected with a reasonable degree of probability. Such negative effects must be appreciable. The prohibition rule of Article 81(1) does not apply when the identified anti-competitive effects are insignificant.')

ECJ's case-law, which declared the inapplicability of Article 101(1) to certain restraints – e.g. territorial exclusivity, franchising, selective distribution – due to pro-competitive justifications.[100]

The terminological rigidity of the GC was especially blatant in *O2 (Germany) GmbH & Co. OHG*[101] where the GC held that even though the agreement concerned had considerable anti-competitive effects, its overall effect was pro-competitive, i.e. it enhanced competition. The interest of the case is that the determination of the legal test under Article 101(1) had conclusive bearing on the merits of the case: the Commission's decision was condemned for not having analysed certain pro-competitive justifications under Article 101(1) and for having left them to Article 101(3).

Besides the 'market context' theory, the GC also stressed the significance of the 'comparison' theory, admitting that these two concepts are 'intrinsically linked';[102] in fact, it was the latter that revealed the flaw in the Commission's approach.

> [T]he effects of the agreement should be considered and for it to be caught by the prohibition it is necessary to find that those factors are present which show that competition has in fact been prevented or restricted or distorted to an appreciable extent. The competition in question must be understood within the actual context in which it would occur in the absence of the agreement in dispute; the interference with competition may in particular be doubted if the agreement seems really necessary for the penetration of a new area by an undertaking.[103]

At the very same moment the GC made a row against the concept of rule of reason in terms of weighing the anti- and pro-competitive effects of the arrangement concerned.

> Such a method of analysis, as regards in particular the taking into account of the competition situation that would exist in the absence of the agreement, does not amount to carrying out an assessment of the pro- and anti-competitive effects of the agreement and thus to applying a rule of reason, which the Community judicature has not deemed to have its place under Article 81(1) EC (…).
>
> In this respect, to submit, as the applicant does, that the Commission failed to carry out a full analysis by not examining what the competitive situation would have been in the absence of the agreement does not mean that an assessment

100 *See* Ali Nikpay, Jonathan Faull and Lars Kjølbye, *Chapter 3: Article 81*, *in* The EC Law of Competition § 3.249 (Jonathan Faull and Ali Nikpay ed., 2007). (Opining that a certain degree of balancing of the pro- and anti-competitive effects is inherent in the above approach.)

101 Case T-328/03 *O2 (Germany) GmbH and Co. OHG v Commission* [2006] ECR II-1231.

102 Para 71.

103 Para 68.

> of the positive and negative effects of the agreement from the point of view of competition must be carried out at the stage of Article 81(1) EC. Contrary to the defendant's interpretation of the applicant's arguments, the applicant relies only on the method of analysis required by settled case-law.
>
> The examination required in the light of Article 81(1) EC consists essentially in taking account of the impact of the agreement on existing and potential competition (…) and the competition situation in the absence of the agreement (…), those two factors being intrinsically linked.[104]

The GC's above reasoning seems to be odd. The 'comparison' method is equivalent to the balancing of the pro- and anti-competitive effects, since both scrutinize the net effect on competition, whatever this term may mean. It seems to be self-contradictory to make the comparing of the situations with and without the agreement mandatory, while interdicting the exploration of the individual elements that make the situations before and after the agreement different. Especially as in several cases the situation after the agreement may not have materialized at the time of adjudication: e.g. the Commission may claim that the agreement, once implemented, *would* lead to the deterioration of competition. In such a scenario no comparison can be made, but the elements that can be scrutinized are the ones that build up the situation of competition after the agreement has been duly implemented. Finally, the existence of Article 101(3) does not entail that no 'reasonableness' analysis could take place under Article 101(1);[105] it simply means that the two substantive analyses should have different focuses.

The blind alley of Article 101(1): the European concept of ancillarity

Besides reasonableness (competitiveness), the fingerprints of another concept are also perceivable in the judicial practice; this is the doctrine of 'ancillary restraints'. The parallelism to US antitrust law's early dichotomy of naked and ancillary restraints is salient. The structure of the European concept of 'ancillary restraints' follows essentially the same scheme. The restraint is acceptable if it is reasonably related, i.e. ancillary, to a legitimate transaction ('main transaction').

The European concept of ancillarity has two subcategories. The first case is when the 'main transaction' pursues a legitimate economic or commercial purpose (commercial or economic ancillarity). This is the traditional and conventional meaning of the term 'ancillary restraints'. This section deals with economic ancillarity. The second subcategory is the emerging field of public interest or regulatory ancillarity, where it is a legitimate public interest or regulatory purpose that justifies the ancillary restraints. This notion was developed by the ECJ

104 Paras 69-71.

105 *See* René Joliet, The Rule of Reason in Antitrust Law; American, German and Common Market Laws in Comparative Perspective 5 (1967). (Contending that it is a misconception that Article 101(3) is 'nothing more than the codification of the American rule of reason'.)

only in 2002 (*Wouters*) and is examined below in the section on public interest reasonableness. Accordingly, the methodological criticism demonstrated in this section relates solely to economic ancillarity.[106]

In *Remia*, the ECJ found that the transfer of a business (main transaction) enhanced competition because it increased the number of market operators, while the insertion of a non-compete clause into the contract was necessary (ancillary restraint), as otherwise the seller, having profound information and experience in the market concerned, could easily frustrate the legitimate expectations of the purchaser, who, therefore, would not be inclined to enter into such a transaction.[107]

In *Métropole*,[108] the GC also followed an 'ancillarity' logic and relied heavily on the merger control concept of ancillary restraints. The GC put the sign of equality between the latter and the notion of Article 101(1), thus, making the whole 'ancillary restraints' analysis flawed: namely, in case of mergers the legitimate end is given, i.e. a concentration that is in conformity with competition law, whereas concerning Article 101(1) the fundamental question is whether there is a legitimate end at all. Citing both *Remia* and the provisions of the then-effective EU merger control regulation,[109] the GC concluded that '[i]n Community competition law the concept of "ancillary restriction" covers any restriction which is directly

106 *See* Richard Whish, Competition law 126 (2009). (Distinguishing between commercial and regulatory ancillarity); Edith Loozen, *Professional ethics and restraints of competition*, 31(1) European Law Review 28 (2006). (Explaining *Wouters* with the concept of 'deontological ancillary'.)

107 Case 42/84 *Remia BV and others v Commission* [1985] ECR 2545, paras 19-20. ('If that were the case, and should the vendor and the purchaser remain competitors after the transfer, it is clear that the agreement for the transfer of the undertaking could not be given effect. The vendor, with his particularly detailed knowledge of the transferred undertaking, would still be in a position to win back his former customers immediately after the transfer and thereby drive the undertaking out of business. Against that background non-competition clauses incorporated in an agreement for the transfer of an undertaking in principle have the merit of ensuring that the transfer has the effect intended. By virtue of that very fact they contribute to the promotion of competition because the lead to an increase in the number of undertakings in the market in question. Nevertheless, in order to have that beneficial effect on competition, such clauses must be necessary to the transfer of the undertaking concerned and their duration and scope must be strictly limited to that purpose. The Commission was therefore right in holding that where those conditions are satisfied such clauses are free of the prohibition laid down in Article 85(1).')

108 Case T-112/99 *Métropole télévision (M6), Suez-Lyonnaise des eaux, France Télécom and Télévision française 1 SA (TF1) v Commission* [2001] ECR II-2459.

109 Paras 104-106. Article 8(2) of the then-effective merger control regulation provided that '[t]he decision declaring the concentration compatible shall also cover restrictions directly related and necessary to the implementation of the concentration'. Regulation 4064/89 OJ [1989] L 395/1; amended by Regulation 1310/97 OJ [1997] L 180/1. Essentially, the same language is used by the currently effective merger control regulation: '[a] decision declaring a concentration compatible shall be deemed to cover restrictions

related and necessary to the implementation of a main operation'.[110] A restriction is directly related if it 'is subordinate to the implementation of that operation and (...) has an evident link with it',[111] while the requirement of necessity implies that 'the restriction is objectively necessary for the implementation of the main operation and (...) it is proportionate to it'.[112] The examination of the issue of objective necessity is relatively abstract.[113] Nonetheless, the GC also established that the concept of ancillary restraints cannot be used to weigh the pro- and anti-competitive effects and to bring back the concept of rule of reason through the backdoor.[114] The doctrine of ancillary restraints simply embraces an *accessorium sequitur principale* logic, i.e. the accessory follows its principal. Accordingly, the accessory restraint shares the fate of the main transaction: if the main operation is in conformity with Article 101(1), so would be the ancillary restraint.[115]

Although EU courts used the term 'ancillary restraints' scarcely (see the above cases), according to the scholarship the doctrine was allegedly used in *Nungesser*,[116]

---

directly related and necessary to the implementation of the concentration', Article 6(1)(a) of Regulation 139/2004 OJ [2004] L 24/1.

110 Para 104.

111 Para 105.

112 Para 106.

113 Para 109. ('It is not a question of analysing whether, in the light of the competitive situation on the relevant market, the restriction is indispensable to the commercial success of the main operation but of determining whether, in the specific context of the main operation, the restriction is necessary to implement that operation. If, without the restriction, the main operation is difficult or even impossible to implement, the restriction may be regarded as objectively necessary for its implementation.')

114 Paras 107-108. ('[I]t would be wrong, when classifying ancillary restrictions, to interpret the requirement for objective necessity as implying a need to weigh the pro and anti-competitive effects of an agreement. Such an analysis can take place only in the specific framework of Article 85(3) of the Treaty. That approach is justified not merely so as to preserve the effectiveness of Article 85(3) of the Treaty, but also on grounds of consistency. As Article 85(1) of the Treaty does not require an analysis of the positive and negative effects on competition of a principal restriction, the same finding is necessary with regard to the analysis of accompanying restrictions.')

115 Paras 115-116. ('If it is established that a restriction is directly related and necessary to achieving a main operation, the compatibility of that restriction with the competition rules must be examined with that of the main operation, para 116. Thus, if the main operation does not fall within the scope of the prohibition laid down in Article 85(1) of the Treaty, the same holds for the restrictions directly related and necessary for that operation (...). If, on the other hand, the main operation is a restriction within the meaning of Article 85(1) but benefits from an exemption under Article 85(3) of the Treaty, that exemption also covers those ancillary restrictions.')

116 Paras 56-58.

Coditel II[117] and *Pronuptia*[118, 119] which might at the same time also be regarded as reasonableness or 'rule of reason' cases as well. In *Nungesser* and *Coditel II*, the Court used the following argumentation: transfer of technology is good, so are all restraints attached to it pardoned. As a matter of fact, the parallelism between technology transfer and the sale of business seems to be plausible. Nevertheless, the resemblance is fairly far-fetched in case of franchising (see *Pronuptia*); and this is *a fortiori* true regarding selective distribution agreements (see *AEG-Telefunken*,[120] *L'Oréal*[121]).[122]

While it is obviously true that benefits to competition may justify the tolerance of the detriments to it, this is the very issue that is analysed by the concept of rule of reason. Designating the benefits as 'main operation' and blandishing the detriments as 'ancillary restraints' seems to be spurious. The impact on competition should be established rather by weighing the pro- and the anti-competitive effects, i.e. inquiring the net effects of the arrangement. It is a rather imbalanced approach if solely the benefits are taken into account when determining the fate of the arrangement (main transaction), while awarding the main operation's fate to the detriments automatically.

Accordingly, the foregoing jurisprudence leaves open the question as to what the purview of the concept of ancillary restraints is. Put at its most abstract, the concept of ancillary restraints covers all cases where there is a legitimate end and where different restraints are directly related to and necessary for the attainment of that purpose. In this case, the question emerges automatically: which main transactions are sufficiently legitimate to justify the restriction of competition? Once these legitimate ends are defined, the subsequent issue is the 'ancillary nature' of the restraint itself: does it mean that there must be no less restrictive alternative, or it is a requirement to balance the restriction triggered with the legitimate end served?

---

117 Case 262/81 *Coditel SA, Compagnie générale pour la diffusion de la télévision, and others v Ciné-Vog Films SA and others* [1982] ECR 3381, paras 15-20. (The owner of the copyright in a film granted exclusive licence regarding a Member State. The ECJ held that the mere fact of such an exclusive license is not contrary to Article 101(1).)

118 Case 161/84 *Pronuptia de Paris GmbH v Pronuptia de Paris Irmgard Schillgallis* [1986] ECR 353.

119 *See* F. Enrique Gonzalez Diaz, *The Notion of Ancillary Restraints under EC Competition Law*, 19 Fordham International Law Journal 951 (1996); Joanna Goyder, EU Distribution Law 28 (4th ed., 2005); Valentine Korah, An Introductory Guide to EC Competition Law and Practice 80-83 (2007).

120 Case 107/82 *Allgemeine Elektrizitäts-Gesellschaft AEG-Telefunken AG v Commission* [1983] ECR 3151.

121 Case 31/80 *NV L'Oréal and SA L'Oréal v PVBA 'De Nieuwe AMCK'* [1980] ECR 3775.

122 *Cf.* F. Enrique Gonzalez Diaz, *The Notion of Ancillary Restraints under EC Competition Law*, 19 Fordham International Law Journal 951, 992 (1996).

A less ambitious grasp of the ancillary restraints doctrine is to view it as applicable to situations where preservation or transfer of value is involved in the transaction and this calls for the restriction of competition.[123] The 'preservation or transfer of value' label may cover a very wide category of cases: transfers of undertakings, joint ventures, technology transfer agreements, trademark licensing agreements, franchising agreements, exclusive and selective distribution agreements.[124]

Nevertheless, it is submitted that the above logic of the doctrine, irrespective of whether a general or a more restricted grasp is followed, seems to be seriously flawed.[125]

First, in case the legitimate end is grasped generally, the competitiveness of the main transaction is to be defined anyway, thus, the doctrine leads back to the problem of rule of reason/reasonableness (threshold problem): is franchising, selective distribution etc. pro-competitive?[126] The 'preservation or transfer of value' theory certainly has an apparent merit: since the concept of reasonableness of Article 101(1) has not been settled yet, and there is no legal test giving a comprehensive explanation about which agreements fall in and out of the general prohibition on restrictive agreements, this theory singles out one subset of contractual clauses and tries to give a clear guidance concerning them; nevertheless, this guidance is less clear than it may seem to be. Even the restrictive theory is at fault for the answer of how the notion of 'preservation or transfer of value' is to be defined and why these fact patterns should be immune from Article 101(1). Albeit this theory confines the application of the ancillary restraints doctrine to cases involving preservation or transfer of value, it does not say anything about the competition law acceptability of this preservation or transfer; certainly, not all preservations or transfers of value are in conformity with Article 101(1). The Article 101(1) assessment of the main operation cannot

123 F. Enrique Gonzalez Diaz, *The Notion of Ancillary Restraints under EC Competition Law*, 19 Fordham International Law Journal 951 (1996). *See* Valentine Korah, An Introductory Guide to EC Competition Law and Practice 101 (2007).

124 F. Enrique Gonzalez Diaz, *The Notion of Ancillary Restraints under EC Competition Law*, 19 Fordham International Law Journal 951, 958-996 (1996).

125 The European concept of ancillarity also has shortcomings as regards clarity and certainty. Ali Nikpay, Jonathan Faull and Lars Kjølbye, *Chapter 3: Article 81*, *in* The EC Law of Competition 242 (Jonathan Faull and Ali Nikpay ed., 2007). ('[I]t is clear that the concept [of ancillarity] still raises more questions than it answers. It is very difficult, if not impossible, to identify in the abstract whether a particular restraint will be treated as ancillary to a particular type of agreement.')

126 *See* Ali Nikpay, Jonathan Faull and Lars Kjølbye, *Chapter 3: Article 81*, *in* The EC Law of Competition 252 (Jonathan Faull and Ali Nikpay ed., 2007). ('[T]he very finding that a particular activity is legitimate implies a value judgment; in a commercial ancillarity case this will inevitably involve an assessment of whether the main agreement "taken as a whole (...) is capable of encouraging competition on the market" or is, at least neutral in competitive terms.')

be avoided even in this case either and the concept of ancillary restraints leads back to the issue of rule of reason (reasonableness). A preservation or transfer of value is not obviously immune from Article 101(1), so it is to be defined which preservations or transfers of value should merit such a treatment.

Second, independently of the theory pursued, it seems to be an over-complication of the problem if legitimacy is examined only regarding the main but not the entire operation, though the assessment of the former may at the same time ensure the green light for the entire transaction (fragmentation of the assessment). Although it is true that the legal assessment of the 'main transaction' is normally decisive for the whole agreement, it is still problematic from a methodological point of view if not the entire agreement's reasonableness (competitiveness) but only that of the 'main transaction' is analysed, while automatically awarding the same fate to all related restraints. This theoretical problem may, nevertheless, be overridden by the practical need for a rule of thumb. It seems to be reasonable to argue, as a rule of thumb, that if the establishment of a joint venture is pro-competitive, all non-compete and exclusivity clauses directly related to and necessary for the establishment of this joint venture should be presumed to be pro-competitive as well.

Third, the requirement of proportionality seems to be inconsistent too. The main transaction gets a green light due to its competitive nature and the allegedly ancillary restraint partakes of this benefit only if the restriction it causes is proportionate to the legitimate end. Such a necessary/proportionate test may generally be used in situations where the purpose served by the legitimate end, which the ancillary restraint is directly related to, and the disadvantage caused are not congenial, e.g. free movement of goods versus public interest. On the other hand, it seems to be over-elaborate to say that the legitimate end is contribution to the promotion of competition, while the restriction of competition caused by the restraints directly related to the legitimate end of promoting competition should be proportionate to the benefit caused to competition.

All in all, the ancillary restraints doctrine under Article 101(1) has serious theoretical shortcomings; nevertheless, it may have a useful role as a rule of thumb. In practical terms, it is reasonable to assert that if the main operation does not fall foul of Article 101(1), the ancillary restraints would very likely not turn the scale. Nonetheless, the efforts to distinguish between operations in compliance and in non-compliance with Article 101(1) cannot be saved. Accordingly, the concept of ancillary restraints may have only a subordinated role to the concept of reasonableness (competitiveness), increasing legal certainty for one subset of competition cases. Nevertheless, the doctrine of ancillary restraints is not capable of being a general, embracing theory under Article 101(1) and, thus, of standing as a pretender for the crown against the concept of reasonableness (competitiveness).

Summary on the reasonableness ('rule of reason') test of Article 101(1)

It is a difficult task to decide which is more authoritative: what EU courts, especially the GC, say or what they, in fact, do. Indisputably, Article 101(1) cannot serve as a floor for a comprehensive analysis, simply because of the very existence of Article 101(3). Nevertheless, it is also undeniable that some justifications can also be raised under Article 101(1) thanks to the market context theory and the concept of comparison, which are theorems endorsed by the ECJ. The employment of the term 'rule of reason' might raise needless terminological controversies, since it is reminiscent of the American antirust concept, which is obviously not applicable on European soil.[127] Saying that the 'rule of reason' is not applicable on this side of the Atlantic is plausible and simply raises the question of denomination: how should the European counterpart of 'rule of reason' be called? Nonetheless, the GC went further and grasped the problem not only as a terminological but also as a substantive issue when saying that under Article 101(1) the anti- and pro-competitive justifications cannot be weighed; at the same moment, the GC did not remain constant to its principles when applying the concept of comparison and contrasting the competitive situations with and without the agreement.

All rival theories of the 'rule of reason' approach fail at some points. The concept of appreciability is only a minimum standard of reasonableness and is not envisaged as being a general theory of Article 101(1). The concept of ancillarity is a blind alley; although this concept can be very useful in certain matters, it certainly cannot serve as a comprehensive theory: according to this theorem all restraints that are ancillary to a legitimate end (main transaction) are in accord with Article 101(1); nevertheless, this theorem fails to give a test on how to define these legitimate ends. The question whether an end is legitimate leads back to our starting-point: how to define arrangements that are legitimate under Article 101(1).

All in all, the 'rule of reason' method, based on the principles of market context and comparison, is the only approach that is capable of giving an overall explanation about Article 101(1) and about the cases analysed under this provision. Accordingly, when applying Article 101(1), in word or in thought, the anti- and pro-competitive impacts of the arrangement are to be contrasted and balanced. Nonetheless, it is a reasonable requirement that Article 101(1) must share Article 101 with Article 101(3). So, the next question is: what is the balancer in Article 101(1) and how is it to be distinguished from Article 101(3)?

Public interest reasonableness

Before examining the different focuses of Article 101(1) and 101(3), it is worthwhile touching upon the question of whether public interest has a place in Article 101(1). Namely, although Article 101(1) centres around competition – implying that non-competition values, in principle, cannot have a say – the effects-

---

127 *See* Richard Whish, Competition Law 131-132 (2009).

analysis may exceptionally take into account public interest (or self-regulatory) arguments.[128] This concept of 'public interest reasonableness'[129] has not been part of EU competition law for long, and it was only the start of 2002 (*Wouters*) that saw the emergence of this ECJ jurisprudence. Since then, this concept was endorsed in *Meca-Medina and Majcen*.

In *Wouters*[130] the Dutch Bar forbade multi-disciplinary partnerships between lawyers and auditors, i.e. lawyers and auditors were prevented from establishing joint partnerships. The reason for this prohibition was that lawyers and auditors may have conflicting roles: lawyers have to act for the interests of the principal and preserve its secrets, while auditors have to give an objective assessment of the books and financial status of the company. According to the Bar, the preservation of these conflicting roles would be jeopardized if the same organization provided legal and auditing services.[131]

The ECJ first established that the above ethical norm is competition restrictive. Afterwards, the Court dealt with the Bar's argument that it may be pro-competitive: the Bar argued that since the auditor market is concentrated, multi-disciplinary partnerships would entail concentration also on the legal market. The Court refused to accept this position establishing that 'the preservation of a sufficient degree of competition on the market in legal services could be guaranteed by less extreme

128 *See* Philip Andrews, *Self-regulation by professions – the approach under E.U. and U.S. competition rules*, 23(6) European Competition Law Review 281 (2002). (Arguing that *Wouters* implies a 'rule of reason' approach and comparing *Wouters* with *California Dental Ass'n v FTC*, 526 U.S. 756, 772-773 (1999).) *Cf.* Edith Loozen, *Professional ethics and restraints of competition*, 31(1) European Law Review 28 (2006). (Contending that Article 101(1) implies no public interest rule of reason, arguing that such a concept would run counter to the function of this provision. Introducing the concept of 'deontological ancillary' for designating restraints that 'are necessary to ensure the compliance with the fundamental principles of a particular profession'.)

129 *See* Csongor István Nagy, Kartelljogi kézikönyv 423-427 (2008).

130 Case C-309/99 *J. C. J. Wouters, J. W. Savelbergh and Price Waterhouse Belastingadviseurs BV v Algemene Raad van de Nederlandse Orde van Advocaten, intervener: Raad van de Balies van de Europese Gemeenschap* [2002] ECR I-01577. For notes on the case *see* Daniel Denman, *Case Comment, European Court of Justice: anticompetitive agreements – professional rules – Netherlands Bar*, 23 European Competition Law Review N73 (2002); Elspeth Deards, *Case Comment, Closed shop versus one stop shop: the battle goes on*, 27 European Law Review 618 (2002); Deirdre Ahern, *Case Comment, Hemat v The Medical Council: the Wouters Legacy revisited*, 28 European Competition Law Review 366 (2007).

131 Interestingly, the English version of the judgment employs misleading language, when using the term 'accountants' instead of 'auditors'. The German version is clearer and uses the term 'Wirtschaftsprüfer' and not 'Buchhalter', which is the equivalent of accountant. The same holds true for the Dutch version. Probably, the latter is echoed in the English version. The Dutch version uses the term 'accountant', which stands for auditor; while the Dutch term for accountant is 'boekhouder'. The French version uses the term 'expert-comptable'.

measures'.[132] According to the traditional concept of economic reasonableness this would have closed the analysis: the Court established that the arrangement had restrictive, i.e. anti-competitive, instincts and had no substantial pro-competitive virtue, hence, overall it was anti-competitive. Nevertheless, in the third step, the ECJ was ready to take into account that the arrangement was justified by the public interest: the non-competition value of professional ethics was considered to be susceptible of justifying such a restrictive measure. Essentially, the Court declared that not all restrictions on one's freedom of action violates Article 101(1) but only the illegitimate (or unreasonable) ones. Restrictions ancillary to a legitimate public interest are not illegitimate.

> However, not every agreement between undertakings or every decision of an association of undertakings which restricts the freedom of action of the parties or of one of them necessarily falls within the prohibition laid down in Article 85(1) of the Treaty. For the purposes of application of that provision to a particular case, account must first of all be taken of the overall context in which the decision of the association of undertakings was taken or produces its effects. More particularly, account must be taken of its objectives, which are here connected with the need to make rules relating to organisation, qualifications, professional ethics, supervision and liability, in order to ensure that the ultimate consumers of legal services and the sound administration of justice are provided with the necessary guarantees in relation to integrity and experience (see, to that effect, Case C-3/95 Reisebüro Broede [1996] ECR I-6511, paragraph 38). It has then to be considered whether the consequential effects restrictive of competition are inherent in the pursuit of those objectives.[133]

The Court, on the basis of the above analysis, came to the conclusion that the provisions concerned 'could (...) reasonably be considered to be necessary in order to ensure the proper practice of the legal profession, as it is organised in the Member State concerned'.[134] The language of the judgment – e.g. 'could (...) reasonably be considered ...', the Bar 'was entitled to consider ...'[135] – suggests that the self-regulatory body has a certain margin of appreciation.

After *Wouters* it was not clear whether the concept of 'public interest reasonableness' applies only to professional services or it has a wider application. In *Meca-Medina and Majcen*[136] the ECJ revealed that this concept has a general

132 Para 94.

133 Para 97. In paras 98-104 the ECJ enumerated those aspects of the case that are to be taken into account as part of the overall context.

134 Para 107.

135 Para 105.

136 C-519/04 P. *David Meca-Medina and Igor Majcen v Commission* [2006] ECR I-6991. *See* Erika Szyszczak, *Competition and Sport*, 32(1) European Law Review 95, 101 and 104 (2007). (Analysing the ECJ's ruling in *Meca-Medina and Majcen* in the

purview.[137] In this case the International Swimming Federation's anti-doping rules were subjected to public interest reasonableness analysis. The ECJ repeated the language of *Wouters*, refining it by expressly mentioning the requirement of proportionality. In *Wouters*, it was held that '[i]t has then to be considered whether the consequential effects restrictive of competition are inherent in the pursuit of (...) [the public interest] objectives (*Wouters and Others*, paragraph 97)';[138] in *Meca-Medina and Majcen* the Court added that these restrictive effects must also be proportionate to these objectives;[139] a requirement arguably implied in *Wouters*. The ECJ held that unwarranted rules, i.e. unreasonable conditions for establishing doping, and excessively severe penalties would not meet the requirement of proportionality.[140, 141]

Interestingly, *Wouters* could also have possibly been situated in the area of economic reasonableness. The independence of lawyers, the protection of the rights of their clients and the preservation of the impartiality of the auditors also has an economic value (e.g. it may tackle the principal-agent problem or the problem of moral hazards), apart from the obvious ethical aspects. On the other hand, regarding *Meca-Medina and Majcen* this is less clear. Namely, from an economic point of view what matters is that the rules of the game are settled and equally applied to all participants.

On the basis of the above it seems that public interest is not exiled from Article 101(1) and in limited cases such arguments can be raised. It is important to stress the peculiar methodological aspect of the 'public interest reasonableness' concept. As regards economic reasonableness it was submitted that the concept of ancillarity is a blind alley and cannot serve as an embracing theory of Article 101(1). The reason is that legitimate economic purposes and the side-effects pardoned are not congenial phenomena, and hence it seems to be illogical to establish first whether a particular economic end (main transaction) is pro-competitive and then to exonerate all related restrictions (ancillary restraints). Instead, it would be more reasonable to evaluate the arrangement as

---

context of the EU law on sport.) *See also* Stefaan Van den Bogaert and An Vermeersch, *Sport and the EC Treaty: a tale of uneasy bedfellows*, 31(6) European Law Review 821, 833-835 (2006).

137 In this case the Court, when considering the overall context of the rules, identified the following public interest objectives: 'to combat doping in order for competitive sport to be conducted fairly and that it included the need to safeguard equal chances for athletes, athletes' health, the integrity and objectivity of competitive sport and ethical values in sport'. Para 43.

138 Para 97.

139 Para 42.

140 Paras 47-48.

141 The next public interest reasonableness case could have been Case C-243/06 *SA Sporting du Pays de Charleroi and Groupement des Clubs de football europeens* (*Oulmers* case), which was, however, removed from the Court's register. 2009/C 69/56, OJ [2009] 69/30.

a whole, i.e. the main transaction and the restrictions related to it. Nonetheless, the situation is completely different in case of public interest reasonableness, as here the legitimate end (public interest) and the ancillary restraints (restriction of competition) are not congenial at all.

The balancers of Article 101 or conceptualizing the inconsistent: proposal for a workable analytical framework

The jurisprudence of the EU courts seems to suggest that Article 101(1) is the proper place for certain justifications for voluntary self-restraints on one's freedom of action, without giving any coherent guidance on how to distinguish Article 101(1) defences from Article 101(3) justifications.[142]

The Commission's *Guidelines on Article 101(3)* try to give some hints, though with limited success. From the point of view of Article 101(1), it is the 'negative effects on prices, output, innovation or the variety or quality of goods and services' that are relevant.[143] On the other hand, Article 101(3) centres around efficiency, which lowers production costs, improves quality and accelerates the creation of new products. If the conditions of Article 101(3) are met, these efficiencies have positive effects 'on prices, output, innovation or the variety or quality of goods and services'.[144] *Ergo*, it is visible that the *Guidelines'* attempt is a vicious

142 AG Léger in his Opinion delivered in *Wouters*, while acknowledging that there are 'learned disputes concerning the definition of (…) [the concept of rule of reason] or the advisability of its introduction into Community law', found that the jurisprudence of the ECJ 'made limited application of the rule of reason in some judgments'. As examples for such limited application, the opinion lists selective distribution systems, open exclusive licences envisaged disseminating new agricultural products, contracts for the transfer of an undertaking and related non-competition clauses, franchise agreements, and statutes of cooperative purchasing associations 'forbidding its members to participate in other forms of organised cooperation which are in direct competition with it'. AG Léger's opinion in *J. C. J. Wouters, J. W. Savelbergh and Price Waterhouse Belastingadviseurs BV v Algemene Raad van de Nederlandse Orde van Advocaten, intervener: Raad van de Balies van de Europese Gemeenschap* [2002] ECR I-1577, para 103.

143 *Guidelines on Article 101(3)*, para 24 ('For an agreement to be restrictive by effect it must affect actual or potential competition to such an extent that on the relevant market negative effects on prices, output, innovation or the variety or quality of goods and services can be expected with a reasonable degree of probability. Such negative effects must be appreciable.')

144 *Guidelines on Article 101(3)*, para 33. ('Agreements that restrict competition may at the same time have pro-competitive effects by way of efficiency gains. Efficiencies may create additional value by lowering the cost of producing an output, improving the quality of the product or creating a new product. When the pro-competitive effects of an agreement outweigh its anti-competitive effects the agreement is on balance pro-competitive and compatible with the objectives of the Community competition rules. The net effect of such agreements is to promote the very essence of the competitive process, namely to win customers by offering better products or better prices than those offered

circle:[145] an agreement is caught by Article 101(1) if it is detrimental to price, output, quality, variety or innovation but it may be exempted if it is beneficial to price, output, quality, variety or innovation. Now, if an agreement does have such positive effects, then why is it caught by Article 101(1) and how does it come that it reaches Article 101(3) at all?

The very concept of 'effect type' agreements, i.e. the fact that there are agreements that are to be judged according to their impact on competition, implies that there is some sort of a reasonableness (competitiveness) standard enshrined in Article 101(1). Consequently, if assuming that the two prongs of Article 101 do not contain unnecessary duplications, Article 101 must contain two canons of legality; this raises the question: what is the difference as regards the focuses of the two provisions? Below, it will be argued that while under Article 101(1) the question is (or ought to be) whether the agreement reduces, enhances or is neutral to the intensity of competition (rivalry), Article 101(3) deals with efficiency.[146] Of course, 'a restriction of rivalry is not, in and of itself, sufficient for the application of Article 81(1): agreements must be assessed in their specific market context'.[147]

When proposing a workable analytical framework, it is not inevitable to criticize the prevailing mainstream approach since there is no ossified case-law in this regard, although some mosaics of the puzzle have already been laid down. As no firm position has been taken, yet, there is a perspective to propose mosaics for the empty places, notwithstanding the GC's inconsistency when refusing to

---

by rivals. This analytical framework is reflected in Article 81(1) and Article 81(3). The latter provision expressly acknowledges that restrictive agreements may generate objective economic benefits so as to outweigh the negative effects of the restriction of competition.')

145 *See* Beverley Robertson, *What Is a Restriction of Competition? The Implications of the CFI's Judgment in O2 Germany and the Rule of Reason*, 28(4) European Competition Law Review 252, 258 (2007).

146 *See* VALENTINE KORAH AND DENIS O'SULLIVAN, DISTRIBUTION AGREEMENTS UNDER THE EC COMPETITION RULES 65 (2002). ('Article 81(3) permits non-competitive considerations to be brought in, but Article 81(1) forbids only agreements that have the object or effect of *restricting competition*. For the agreement to be forbidden, the object or effect must be to restrict competition and *not merely conduct*.')

147 Ali Nikpay, Jonathan Faull and Lars Kjølbye, *Chapter 3: Article 81*, *in* THE EC LAW OF COMPETITION § 3.248 (Jonathan Faull and Ali Nikpay ed., 2007). *See* VALENTINE KORAH AND DENIS O'SULLIVAN, DISTRIBUTION AGREEMENTS UNDER THE EC COMPETITION RULES 65 (2002). ('Article 81(1) forbids only agreements that have the object or effect of *restricting competition*. For the agreement to be forbidden, the object or effect must be to restrict competition and *not merely conduct*.') The Commission's initial practice was to treat restraints on one's freedom of action as normally anti-competitive. However, in the '90s economic analysis gradually gained ground in the decisional practice of Article 101(1). *See* VALENTINE KORAH AND DENIS O'SULLIVAN, DISTRIBUTION AGREEMENTS UNDER THE EC COMPETITION RULES 78 (2002).

contrast the anti- and pro-competitive effects, while admitting the existence of the 'comparison' theory.[148]

As a workable analytical framework, it is submitted that the economic justifications are to be grouped into two categories: competitive (rivalry) and (productive) efficiency arguments. Article 101(1) covers competitive concerns: here, the question is whether the arrangement's overall effects result in more or less competition in the sense of rivalry. On the other hand, Article 101(3) deals with efficiency justifications: notwithstanding the decrease in the intensity of competition (rivalry), an agreement may entail, for instance, significant cost savings, which make both producers and consumers better off. The fundamental of Article 101 is that competition (rivalry) is the optimal and most efficient structure of the market, whereas in exceptional cases cooperation can be more efficient than competition.[149] Accordingly, the parties bear the burden of proof only if they argue that in the given case cooperation is more beneficial to the society than competition.[150] This is in conformity with conventional wisdom: rivalry is the most efficient structure of the market, but cooperation might be more useful under certain circumstances.[151]

---

148 *See* Beverley Robertson, *What Is a Restriction of Competition? The Implications of the CFI's Judgment in O2 Germany and the Rule of Reason*, 28(4) European Competition Law Review 252, 260 (2007). ('[T]he requirement to balance pro and anti-competitive effects under Art. 81(1) flows necessarily from the Court's ruling in *Société Technique Minière* and *O2 Germany*. Specifically, it is a consequence of the requirement that the competitive situation which results from the agreement must be compared to that which is expected to prevail without it.')

149 *See* René Joliet, The Rule of Reason in Antitrust Law; American, German and Common Market Laws in Comparative Perspective 60 (1967). (Stating that in European competition laws 'competition is not necessarily the ultimate panacea: in some circumstances, it may be creative of efficiency, while in others destructive of investments'.)

150 Regulation 1/2003/EC, Article 2. *See* Case T-29/92 *Vereniging van Samenwerkende Prijsregelende Organisaties in de Bouwnijverheid and others v Commission* [1995] ECR II-289, paras 262. ('It is settled law that it is for undertakings seeking an exemption under Article 85(3) to establish, on the basis of documentary evidence, that an exemption is justified. Accordingly, the Commission cannot be criticized for failing to put forward alternative solutions or to indicate in what respects it would regard the grant of an exemption as justified (…). In applying the competition rules, all that is incumbent upon the Commission, by virtue of its obligation to state reasons, is to mention the matters of fact and of law and the considerations which prompted it to take a decision rejecting the application for exemption, and the applicants may not require it to discuss all the matters of fact and law raised by them in the administrative procedure.')

151 *Cf.* René Joliet, The Rule of Reason in Antitrust Law; American, German and Common Market Laws in Comparative Perspective 184 (1967) (Submitting that Article 101(1) demands a rule of reason analysis in the sense of the American one, while Article 101(3) contains values that are not present in US antitrust, *see ibid.* at 59-60. Note that in the relevant period the American rule of reason centred around competition in the sense of rivalry or competitive process, *see ibid.* at 59-60.)

Obviously, in its widest sense the term 'competition' embraces both rivalry and efficiency justifications and focuses on social or consumer welfare. The ultimate question of competition law should be: what is the arrangement's effect on prices, output, quality etc., albeit such questions can rarely be answered precisely. At least this is the meaning attributed to 'competition' by the Commission documents[152] and the ECJ judgments. Curiously, the term 'competition' is equally used when exempting agreements that notwithstanding their unquestionable merits in terms of productive efficiency do exclude rivalry: these are the cases where cooperation is considered to be more efficient than competition.[153] Nonetheless, this all-embracing definition of competition is misleading: it is odd to argue that if undertakings cooperate to develop a new technology jointly, in order to avoid unnecessary cost duplications, the arrangement is pro-competitive simply because it saves costs. In this case, the arrangement is certainly efficient, though not pro-competitive. The intermingling of competition and cooperative efficiency is salient.

In *Bayer/Gist-Brocades* the Commission gave a concise summary of this approach.

> For the agreements to contribute to the improvement of production or distribution, or to promote technical or economic progress, they must objectively constitute an improvement on the situation that would otherwise exist. The fundamental principle in this respect, established at the time the common market was formed, lays down that fair and undistorted competition is the best guarantee of regular supply on the best terms. *Thus the question of a contribution to economic progress within the meaning of Article 85(3) can only arise in those exceptional cases where the free play of competition is unable to produce the best result economically speaking.*[154]

The above division is underpinned by language, structural and economic arguments.

First, there is a solid textual argument for the above distinction: Article 101(1) speaks about competition, while Article 101(3) centres around the improving of production or distribution of goods and the promotion of technical or economic progress.

Second, the structure of Article 101 – i.e. a general rule and an exception – also suggests that there are two sets of justifications in EU competition law; otherwise

---

152 *See Guidelines on Article 101(3)*, para 16.; *Guidelines on Horizontal Cooperation Agreements*, paras 20, 48 and 183.

153 *See Guidelines on Article 101(3)*, paras 11 and 30.

154 76/172/EEC *Bayer/Gist-Brocades* OJ [1976] L 30/13, point III/1.

there would be no point in having two tests.[155] In *Van den Bergh Foods*,[156] the GC's strongest argument against the rule of reason was that its existence would be 'difficult to reconcile with the structure of the rules prescribed by Article 85'[157] and 'Article 85(3) of the Treaty would lose much of its effectiveness if such an examination had already to be carried out under Article 85(1) of the Treaty.'[158] Nevertheless, the structure of Article 101 suggests quite the contrary. Article 101(3) would not lose much of its effectiveness if some parts (or rather some aspects) of the competition law examination had to be carried out under Article 101(1). The analysis under Article 101(1) would be senseless if it were deprived of all reason. Furthermore, Article 101 mentions competition twice: in Article 101(1), when interdicting all agreements that prevent, restrict or distort *competition*, and in Article 101(3)(b), which provides that no individual exemption is granted if the agreement affords the 'undertakings the possibility of eliminating *competition* in respect of a substantial part of the products in question'. This circumstance suggests three propositions: Article 101(1) and Article 101(3) must have different focuses (a conclusion already drawn); Article 101(3) does not centre around competition; and the restriction (prevention, distortion) of competition is a matter of degree: Article 101 tolerates some deceleration of competition if that is necessary for the sake of efficiency, but it does not tolerate its complete elimination irrespective of whether efficiency is enhanced or not.[159]

---

155 *Cf. White Paper on Modernisation of the Rules Implementing Article 85 and 86 of the EC Treaty.* Commission Programme 99/027. COM (99) 101 final. OJ [1999] C 132/1, para 57. (Considering the implications of Article 101's bifurcation. 'The Commission has already adopted this approach to a limited extent and has carried out an assessment of the pro- and anti-competitive aspects of some restrictive practices under Article 85(1). This approach has been endorsed by the Court of Justice. However, the structure of Article 85 is such as to prevent greater use being made of this approach: if more systematic use were made under Article 85(1) of an analysis of the pro and anti-competitive aspects of a restrictive agreement, Article 85(3) would be cast aside, whereas any such change could be made only through revision of the Treaty. It would at the very least be paradoxical to cast aside Article 85(3) when that provision in fact contains all the elements of a "rule of reason". It would moreover be dangerous if modernisation of the competition rules were to be based on developments in decision-making practice, subject to such developments being upheld by the Community Courts. Any such approach would mean that modernisation was contingent upon the cases submitted to the Commission and could take many years. Lastly, this option would run the risk of diverting Article 85(3) from its purpose, which is to provide a legal framework for the economic assessment of restrictive practices and not to allow application of the competition rules to be set aside because of political considerations.')

156 Case T-65/98 *Van den Bergh Foods Ltd v Commission* [2003] ECR II-4653.

157 Para 106.

158 Para 107.

159 Matthew Bennett and A. Jorge Padilla, *Article 81 EC Revisited: Deciphering European Commission Antitrust Goals and Rules*, *in* COMPETITION POLICY IN THE EU 63 (Xavier Vives ed., 2009). (Interpreting the term 'competition' in Article 101(3)(b) as rivalry or competitive process.)

Third, economic common sense and intuition suggests that economic competition (rivalry) is the most efficient market structure, and supports the view that the plaintiff, including the competition authority, has to prove merely that there is a real restriction of competition in order to trigger the assumption that social welfare is being endangered. Since competition in the sense of rivalry is presumed to be the most efficient structure of the market, the burden of proof shifts to the defendant only if it intends to come up with justifications based on cooperative efficiency (i.e. efficiency arising from cooperation), which, as both conventional wisdom and intuition suggest, triumphs over competitive efficiency only exceptionally.

It is admitted that the above classification may not use the terms of mainstream economic theory and in several cases competition and cooperative efficiency may hardly be distinguished. Nevertheless, in real world cases equations rarely furnish the answer. Due to the permanent lack of adequate market data, the fundamental role of abstract economic theory is to serve as an analytical tool. Consumer welfare may hardly be quantified, instead, indices are used. Economic theory helps to grasp the consequences of different market practices abstractly, but real life cases rarely go hand in hand with empirical data enabling numerical conclusions, and can hardly be reduced to an equation where most variables are known.

All forms of cooperation that recreate one of the otherwise missing preconditions of perfect competition, or increase the intensity of rivalry, are pro-competitive. If an arrangement lowers transaction costs, especially the consumers' search costs, it deserves being rated as pro-competitive. For instance, certain ways of cooperation make the goods more comparable by standardization and increase the transparency of the market thus intensifying competition. Other arrangements create incentives for distributors to invest in promotion, thus, ensuring that consumers learn about the merchandise and thus they have a real choice. Lowering entry barriers also enhances rivalry.[160] Roughly speaking, most arrangements contributing to allocative efficiency are pro-competitive in the sense that they promote rivalry and strengthen the competitive pressure on market operators.[161] On the other hand, most enhancements of productive efficiency are not pro-competitive but deserve attention under Article 101(3). Arrangements reaping the benefits of economies of scale or economies of scope should certainly be analysed under Article 101(3). Similarly, all ways of cooperation eliminating the unnecessary duplications of R&D expenses enhance efficiency in this sense. Nevertheless, these arrangements are far from being pro-competitive: they are efficient because they replace competition (rivalry) with co-operation.

---

160 *See* Case T-328/03 *O2 (Germany) GmbH and Co. OHG v Commission* [2006] ECR II-1231.

161 *Cf.* Okeoghene Odudu, The Boundaries of EC Competition Law 98, 103 and 128-129 (2006). (Arguing that Article 101(1) deals with allocative efficiency, while Article 101(3) deals with productive efficiency.)

Accordingly, EU competition law admits that competition (rivalry) is not always the most efficient arrangement. Hence, it contains a safeguard also for agreements that restrict the competitive process. Article 101(3) contains four conditions that are to be met for benefiting from an exemption. Nonetheless, as the four conditions are very vague, EU competition law developed a system of block exemption regulations. The gist of the latter is that there are certain agreements and restraints that would always (or almost always) meet the conditions of Article 101(3), thus, being exempted, and, hence, procedural economy and legal certainty justify that such agreements and restraints are to be defined in concrete terms, more clearly than the conditions of individual exemption. Put it simple, the block exemption regulations define those categories of agreements that fulfil the requirements of Article 101(3) with sufficient certainty and, thus, it is reasonable to fetch them off from the group of agreements of concern and to drive them into a safe harbour. Accordingly, only those agreements remain in the 'swamp' of Article 101(3) that are, to some extent, dubious.

Even though in practice the checklist starts with the block exemption regulations, and the analysis of Article 101(3) comes up only if no block exemption regulation is applicable, theoretically speaking, the conceptual logic starts with the individual exemption followed by the block exemption regulations, the latter being the concretizations of the former.

Article 101(3) of the TFEU provides that the general prohibition on restrictive agreements as embedded in Article 101(1):

> may (...) be declared inapplicable in the case of any agreement or category of agreements between undertakings, any decision or category of decisions by associations of undertakings, any concerted practice or category of concerted practices, which contributes to improving the production or distribution of goods or to promoting technical or economic progress, while allowing consumers a fair share of the resulting benefit, and which does not: (a) impose on the undertakings concerned restrictions which are not indispensable to the attainment of these objectives; (b) afford such undertakings the possibility of eliminating competition in respect of a substantial part of the products in question.

Apparently, the applicability of individual exemption centres around the concept of efficiency, i.e. improvement of production or distribution or promotion of technical or economic progress.[162] All the other pre-conditions are mainly accessory: fair

162 *Guidelines on Article 101(3)*, para 48. *See* Christopher Thomas, *Article 81(3)*, *in* Bellamy and Child's European Community Law of Competition 3.021 (Peter Roth and Vivien Rose ed., 2008). ('[T]he Commission equates "improving the production or distribution of goods" and "promoting technical or economic progress" with "efficiency gains", and exclusively uses the language of "efficiencies" when referring to the benefits that might justify the application of Article 81(3).'); *White Paper on Modernisation of*

share to the consumers, proportionality, no elimination of competition. Once the efficiency entailed by the agreement outweighs the loss in efficacy caused by the reduction in competition (rivalry), it is a real case of individual exemption. Thereafter, only the scope and modus of cooperation are to be shaped in a way that conforms to the last three conditions.

Nevertheless, the interpretation of efficiency under Article 101(3) has not always been consistent: numerous judgments of the EU courts and decisions of the Commission took into account potential benefits, which were not productive but which had the tendency of contributing to the increase of the intensity of competition in the market. In *Pronuptia*, the ECJ held that the consideration that in the absence of certain restrictions franchisees would not take the risk and invest in becoming part of the franchise system is to be examined under Article 101(3).[163] The Commission established in several decisions that exclusive distribution arrangements can contribute to technical and economic progress by improving the distribution of goods due to the fact that they enable distributors to concentrate on their respective territory of responsibility, reduce transaction costs as the producer has to deal only with one distributor and can overcome

---

the rules implementing Articles 85 and 86 of the EC Treaty. Commission programme No 99/027, para 57. (The purpose of Article 101(3), formerly 85(3), 'is to provide a legal framework for the economic assessment of restrictive practices and not to allow application of the competition rules to be set aside because of political considerations'.) Nevertheless, it cannot be disregarded that the Commission occasionally did take non-efficiency goals into account when applying Article 101(3), though these cases are rather rare and seem to be outdated. *See* James S. Venit, *Brave New World: the Modernization and Decentralization of Enforcement under Articles 81 and 82 of the EC Treaty*, 545, 579 (2003); Rein Wesseling, *The Commission White Paper on Modernisation of E.C. Antitrust Law: Unspoken Consequences and Incomplete Treatment of Alternative Options*, 20(8) European Competition Law Review 420, 422-423 (1999). (Advocating that non-economic values can be taken into account under Article 101(3), like, for instance, environment protection, employment, industrial policy.) Lennart Ritter and W. David Braun, European Competition Law: a Practitioner's Guide 148 (3d ed., 2005). (Giving examples for cases where the maintenance of employment and environment protection were taken into account under Article 101(3).); Joanna Goyder, EU Distribution Law 30-31 (4th ed., 2005); *Cf.* Claus Dieter Ehlermann, *The Modernization of EC Antitrust Policy: a Legal and Cultural Revolution*, 37 Common Market Law Review 537, 549 (2000) (Taking the position that 'non-competition-oriented political considerations should not determine the assessment under Article 81(3)'.)

163 Case 161/84 *Pronuptia de Paris GmbH v Pronuptia de Paris Irmgard Schillgallis* [1986] ECR 353, para 24. ('It is of course possible that a prospective franchisee would not take the risk of becoming part of the chain, investing his own money, paying a relatively high entry fee and undertaking to pay a substantial annual royalty, unless he could hope, thanks to a degree of protection against competition on the part of the franchisor and other franchisees, that his business would be profitable. That consideration, however, is relevant only to an examination of the agreement in the light of the conditions laid down in Article 85(3).')

distribution difficulties of international trade that result from linguistic, legal and other difference.[164] The Commission also established that exclusivity ensures 'an adequate level of quality in the provisions of additional support services' and stimulates inter-brand competition.[165] As regards selective distribution based on qualitative selection criteria the Commission established that these criteria ensure that the 'products are distributed only by dealers having adequate facilities and staff, which makes the distribution of (…) [the] products more rational and more efficient. The requirements imposed on dealers regarding stocks and the carrying of the complete (…) [product] range ensure that (…) [the producer] can rely on a comprehensive network of selected dealers who are prepared to make a particular effort to distribute (…) [the producer's] products, thus promoting sales.'[166] In a decision concerning technology-transfer the Commission, in the context of Article 101(3), found that the prohibition on export 'facilitates the dissemination of new varieties in Member States (…) by encouraging undertakings in those Member States to accept the risks involved in producing and/or marketing new varieties'.[167] The Commission also found that common tariff structures increase market transparency by facilitating the comparability of the routes and enhance competition.[168] '[I]nforming consumers about as complete a range as possible of products available on the market' was considered to be 'aimed at improving the distribution of paper goods and promoting economic progress.'[169] All these examples show that both EU courts and the Commission occasionally refused to assess arguments related to the promotion of competition under Article 101(1), and were ready to deal with them only under Article 101(3).

Another fundamental question is the relationship between the concept of hardcore restrictions and Article 101(3). While in principle all agreements have the chance to meet the requirements of Article 101(3) and it cannot be said that a particular type of agreement is automatically excluded from the perspective of exemption,[170] it is very unlikely that a hardcore agreement could fulfil these conditions.[171] In this sense the analysis under Article 101(1) and that under Article

164 *See* 97/123/EC *Novalliance/Systemform* OJ [1997] L 47/11, para 70; 97/780/EC *Unisource* OJ [1997] L 318/1, para 89; 97/781/EC *Uniworld* OJ [1997] L 318/24, para 75; 1999/230/EC *Whitbread* OJ [1999] L 88/26, para 151; 1999/473/EC *Bass* OJ [1999] L 186/1, para 169; 1999/474/EC *Scottish and Newcastle* OJ [1999] L 186/28, para 138.

165 1999/573/EC *Cégétel + 4* OJ [1999] L 218/14, para 58.

166 94/29/EC *Grundig's EC distribution system* OJ [1994] L 20/15, para 36.

167 1999/6/EC *Sicasov* OJ [1999] L 4/27, para 74.

168 93/174/EEC *Tariff structures in the combined transport of goods* OJ [1993] L 73/38, paras 50 and 53.

169 91/128/EEC *Sippa* OJ [1991] L 60/19, para 18.

170 Case T-17/93 *Matra Hachette SA v Commission* [1994] ECR II-595, para 85; Case T-168/01 *GlaxoSmithKline Services Unlimited v Commission* [2006] ECR II-2969, para 233.

171 Frank Wijckmans, Filip Tuytschaever and Alain Vanderelst, Vertical Agreements in EC Competition Law § 2.134 (2006) ('[H]ardcore restrictions (…) are

101(3) converge as far as quick condemnation is concerned. Restrictions by object and restrictions that are by their very nature anti-competitive are two designations for the same group of agreements and are part of the terminology of Article 101(1).[172] On the other hand, the concept of hardcore restrictions, even though it designates the very same species of agreements, has a much broader application as it is a notion used both under Article 101(1) and Article 101(3) (see Figure 4.1).[173]

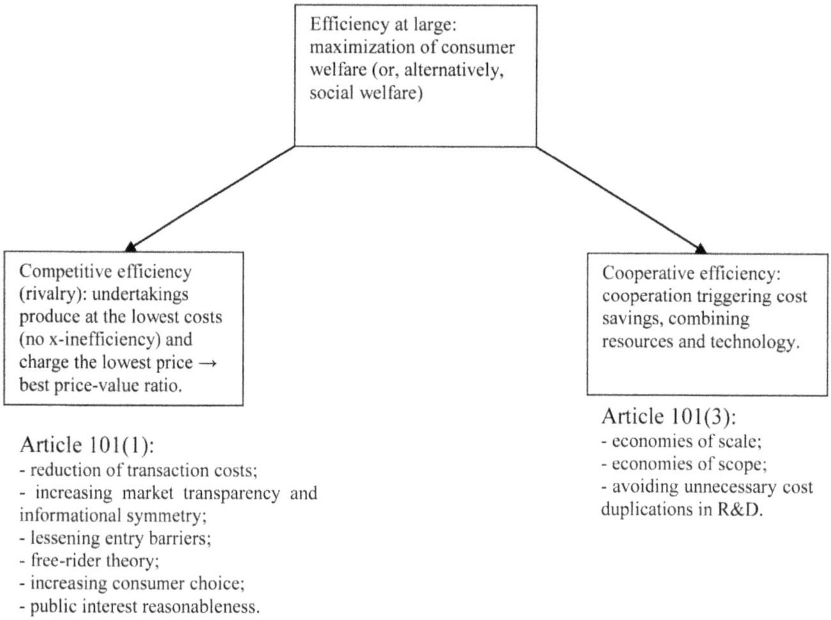

Figure 4.1

almost by way of definition banned by EC competition law.'); Ali Nikpay, Jonathan Faull and Lars Kjølbye, *Chapter 3: Article 81*, *in* THE EC LAW OF COMPETITION § 3.405 (Jonathan Faull and Ali Nikpay ed., 2007). ('Article 81 does not contain a *per se* rule. However, this fact is not as significant as it might seem: restrictions of competition that can be qualified as "hardcore" are very unlikely to fulfil the conditions of Article 81(3).'). *See also* Case 28/77 *Tepea BV v Commission* [1978] ECR 1391, para 57; Case 35/83 *BAT Cigaretten-Fabriken GmbH v Commission* [1985] ECR 363, para 41.

172 *See* Case C-306/96 *Javico International and Javico AG v Yves Saint Laurent Parfums SA (YSLP)* [1998] ECR I-1983, paras 14 and 20-21.

173 *See Guidelines on Article 101(3)*, para 23; Mario Filipponi, Luc Peeperkorn and Donncadh Woods, *Chapter 9: Vertical Agreements*, *in* THE EC LAW OF COMPETITION § 9.41 (Jonathan Faull and Ali Nikpay ed., 2007). Alternatively, it could be argued that all restraints enumerated in Article 4 of the BER are anti-competitive by object, but only the first two are hardcore, i.e. fixing the minimal or concrete resale price and absolute territorial protection.

An expressive example of an Article 101(1) case is the free-rider theory of territorial exclusivity. When a producer enters a new geographic market, it usually appoints an exclusive distributor. By granting the privilege to the dealer that nobody else would sell the brand concerned in the territory in question the producer reduces competition in some respect: intra-brand competition is certainly reduced if the brand is marketed by an exclusive distributor. However, the small loss sustained by the competitive process is abundantly made up by the pro-competitive effects of the arrangement. Namely, the exclusive distributor will be interested in fiercely promoting the brand, thus, reducing the search costs of the consumers, who will learn about the brand and have more real alternatives; in turn, consumer choice will increase competitive pressure. In the absence of exclusivity, the distributor would probably not invest in promoting the brand due to the risk that other non-investing dealers could reap the benefits of the consumers' increased attention. In short, some reduction in intra-brand competition may lead to a much more significant increase in inter-brand competition since one more virtual alternative would be at the consumers' disposal. Thus, taking everything into account, the foregoing arrangement does not set back but enhances competition. There is no need to apply Article 101(3) as the agreement is not anti-competitive and, accordingly, is not caught by Article 101(1).

An example of an Article 101(3) case is the treasure-island parable. Assume that there are five treasure-hunter teams searching for a treasure valued at 500 euros hidden on an island. The adventure has considerable expenses: the search costs them equally 500 euros. It is also assumed that they have equal chances to find the treasure. Since only one can succeed and the expenditures of those who fail are wasted, it is more efficient not to compete but to cooperate. The society would be better off if the treasure-hunters cooperated, since the parties could share the costs while the benefit of the adventure to the society would remain the same, i.e. 5000 euros. If the hunters are working on a competitive basis, the costs of finding the treasure would amount to 2500 euros altogether (5 x 500 euros). If they cooperate, they can share the costs (500 euros/five teams) and the income. The parties will cooperate since it is reasonable for them to combine: the cooperation not only eliminates the risk of failure but it also improves the balance between the costs and the expected value due to cost saving. In case of competition, the expected value of the independent adventure is 1000 euros (the value of the treasure is 5000 euros and there are five teams having equal chances: 5000 euros x 1/5), while the cost is 500 euros; accordingly, the balance is 500 euros. If the parties co-operate, the expected value is 1000 euros per member, which will be earned with 100 per cent certainty. The costs are, however, not the same: the expenditure of 500 euros would be shared equally by the parties; thus, the cost per hunter would be 100 euros; and the balance of the common adventure would be 900 euros. Accordingly, the net profit of the common adventure is higher by 400 euros than the balance of the independent treasure-hunting, and the society also save 2000 euros. There remains nothing more than to substitute the treasure with a new patentable technology and the question as to why cooperation in R&D is efficient is answered, notwithstanding its obvious anti-competitive nature.

Theoretically, all restrictions on an undertaking's independent market behaviour are caught in the net of Article 101(1) as suspect. Market operators are expected to determine their behaviour independently.[174] Nonetheless, the general prohibition of restrictive agreements has its immanent limitations, since cooperation is sometimes inevitable even in the sphere of rivalry. This is the case especially in vertical relations where the standing relationship between the parties and the need to reduce transaction costs in themselves necessitate the fixing of a framework for the individual transactions. What is more, some cooperative arrangements have both anti- and pro-competitive effects that may not be severable. An agreement is anti-competitive only if it takes away more from competition than it adds. Accordingly, the pro and anti-competitive elements of the agreement are to be contrasted in order to evaluate it. If the pro-competitive elements are predominant, the agreement escapes. Otherwise, it comes within the purview of the prohibition and its last hope is to somehow fulfil the conditions of Article 101(3), directly or through a block exemption regulation.

As described above, the essential difference between the competitiveness test embedded in Article 101(1) and the notion of exemption embedded in Article 101(3) is that the latter gives safeguard to cooperative arrangements that despite reducing the level of rivalry increase efficiency. Article 101(3) is not meant to exempt agreements that increase competition, since such arrangements are given the green light already under Article 101(1).

Having said the foregoing, it is to be admitted that in practice it is not easy to do the above classification. In several cases, it is easier to establish the economic or efficiency value of a particular arrangement, while it is blurred whether it is an Article 101(1) or an Article 101(3) case. Sometimes, economic analysis cannot be broken on the wheel and be forced into pre-determined legal boxes and, hence, it might be easier to state that Article 101 does not forbid a particular conduct. Still, the conceptualization of Article 101 is very important also from a practical point of view. According to Article 2 of Regulation 1/2003,[175] while the burden of proof regarding Article 101(3) rests on the undertaking raising it, the burden of proof concerning the pre-conditions of Article 101(1) is borne by the party alleging the infringement, including the competition authority.

> In any national or Community proceedings for the application of Articles 81 and 82 of the Treaty, the burden of proving an infringement of Article 81(1) or of Article 82 of the Treaty shall rest on the party or the authority alleging the infringement. The undertaking or association of undertakings claiming the

---

174 *Guidelines on Article 101(3)*, para 14. ('A general principle underlying Article 81(1) which is expressed in the case law of the Community Courts is that each economic operator must determine independently the policy, which he intends to adopt on the market.') *See* Vivien Rose and Peter Roth, *Article 81(1)*, *in* BELLAMY AND CHILD'S EUROPEAN COMMUNITY LAW OF COMPETITION § 2.095 (Peter Roth and Vivien Rose ed., 2008).

175 Regulation 1/2003 OJ [2003] L 1/1.

> benefit of Article 81(3) of the Treaty shall bear the burden of proving that the conditions of that paragraph are fulfilled.[176]

Accordingly, it is far from irrelevant whether the justification for the agreement is based on a competition (rivalry) or an efficiency enhancing theory. The relevance of the foregoing differentiation was certainly reduced by the elimination of the notification system. Until 1 May 2004 the exemption under Article 101(3) was not automatic but granted by individual administrative decision upon request.[177] The Commission had exclusive jurisdiction to grant exemptions under Article 101(3), while only Article 101(1) had direct effect. The exemption procedure was lengthy, burdensome and expensive. The consequences of the classification were enormous.[178] An agreement in accord with Article 101(1) was automatically lawful and convenient for the undertaking's competition lawyer, while seeking individual exemption under Article 101(3) amounted to a torture. Regulation 1/2003 replaced this scheme

> by a directly applicable exception system in which the competition authorities and courts of the Member States have the power to apply not only Article 81(1) and Article 82 of the Treaty, which have direct applicability by virtue of the case-law of the Court of Justice of the European Communities, but also Article 101(3) of the Treaty.[179]

Article 1 of Regulation 1/2003 provides as follows

> Agreements, decisions and concerted practices caught by Article 81(1) of the Treaty which do not satisfy the conditions of Article 101(3) of the Treaty shall be prohibited, no prior decision to that effect being required. Agreements, decisions and concerted practices caught by Article 101(1) of the Treaty which satisfy the conditions of Article 101(3) of the Treaty shall not be prohibited, no prior decision to that effect being required.

---

176 Nevertheless, if the defendant produces arguments that seem to be plausible, the Commission is obliged to give explanation for non-acceptance. Case T-168/01 *GlaxoSmithKline Services Unlimited v Commission* [2006] ECR II-2969, para 236. ('The Commission, for its part, must adequately examine those arguments and that evidence (...), that is to say, it must determine whether they demonstrate that the conditions for the application of Article 81(3) EC are satisfied. In certain cases, those arguments and that evidence may be of such a kind as to require the Commission to provide an explanation or justification, failing which it is permissible to conclude that the burden of proof borne by the person who relies on Article 81(3) EC has been discharged (…). As the Commission agrees in its written submissions, in such a case it must refute those arguments and that evidence.'). *See* VALENTINE KORAH, AN INTRODUCTORY GUIDE TO EC COMPETITION LAW AND PRACTICE 78 (2007).

177 Regulation 17, Article 9(1).

178 Pietro Manzini, *The European Rule of Reason – Crossing the Sea of Doubt*, 23 European Competition Law Review 392, 393-394 (2002).

179 Regulation 1/2003/EC, Recital 4.

The amalgamation of competition (rivalry) and co-operative efficiency is perceivable in the block exemption regulations. Since both types of efficiency involve a considerable amount of uncertainty, the block exemption regulations make a general declaration about the competition law conformity of certain kinds of agreements: they are not prohibited under Article 101 at large. Simply put, even if the agreement were caught by Article 101(1) it would certainly benefit from Article 101(3). Nonetheless, this amalgamation does not question the difference between the foregoing types of efficiencies.

As noted above, the concept of individual exemption is elastic but vague. The interests of legal certainty and predictability demanded the introduction of a system that is concrete, though inelastic; this is the system of block exemption regulations, which identify and exempt restraints that meet the requirement of Article 101(3) in general. Article 103 TFEU authorizes the Council to issue block exemption regulations in consultation procedure.[180] The Council, however, delegated some parts of this legislative power to the Commission through regulations, which authorize the latter to issue block exemption regulations in specific fields. The authorizing regulations determine the subject matter of the delegation and establish certain provisions regarding the structure and content of the block exemption regulation in question.[181]

In the domain of distribution there are two regimes: the general (umbrella) block exemption regulation (BER)[182] and the motor vehicle block exemption

180 According to Article 103(1), '[t]he appropriate regulations or directives to give effect to the principles set out in Articles 101 and 102 shall be laid down by the Council, on a proposal from the Commission and after consulting the European Parliament'. Article 103(2)(b) expressly mentions the issue of exemption: '[t]he regulations or directives referred to in paragraph 1 shall be designed in particular (...) to lay down detailed rules for the application of Article 101(3), taking into account the need to ensure effective supervision on the one hand, and to simplify administration to the greatest possible extent on the other'.

181 The Council adopted the following authorizing regulations. For horizontal agreements: Regulation 2821/71 OJ [1971] L 285/46, amended by Regulation 2743/72 OJ [1972] L 291/144 and Regulation 1/2003/EC OJ [2003] L 1/1. For vertical agreements: Regulation 19/65/EEC OJ [1965] 36/533, amended by Regulation 1215/1999 OJ [1999] L 148/1 and Regulation 1/2003 OJ [2003] L 1/1. For specific sectors: Regulation 3976/87 OJ [1987] L 374/9, amended by Regulation 2344/90 OJ [1990] L 217/15, Regulation 2411/92 OJ [1992] L 240/19, Regulation 1/2003 OJ [2002] L 1/1, Regulation 411/2004 OJ [2004] L 68/1; Regulation 1534/91 OJ [1991] L 143/1, amended by Regulation 1/2003 OJ [2002] L 1/1; Regulation 479/92 OJ [1992] L 55/3, amended by Regulation 1/2003 OJ [2002] L 1/1.

182 Regulation 330/2010 OJ [2010] L 102/1. For overviews on the BER, *see* Richard Whish and David Bailey, *Regulation 330/2010: The Commission's new block exemption for vertical agreements*, 47(6) Common Market Law Review 1757 (2010); Louis Vogel, *EU Competition Law Applicable to Distribution Agreements: Review of 2010 and Outlook for 2011*, 2(3) Journal of European Competition Law and Practice 245 (2011). For overviews on the Old BER, *see* Mark Griffiths, *A Glorification of De Minimis – The Regulation on Vertical Agreements*, 21(5) European Competition Law Review 241 (2000); Richard

regulations (MVBER and New MVBER).[183] While the first establishes rules that are generally applicable to all distribution agreements, the MVBER and the New MVBER govern distribution activity specifically in the motor-vehicle sector. Nonetheless, the motor vehicle industry's special regime is destined to melt into the general regime. The New MVBER extends the scope of the BER to distribution agreements relating to the motor vehicle industry in two steps. On the one hand, as from 1 June 2010, vertical agreements relating to the motor vehicle aftermarket (purchase, sale or resale of spare parts for motor vehicles, provision of repair and maintenance services for motor vehicles) are block-exempted if they meet the conditions of the BER and do not contain any of the hardcore restrictions listed in Article 5 of the New MVBER. On the other hand, the BER applies to vertical agreements relating to the purchase, sale or resale of new motor vehicles with effect from 1 June 2013 (until then the MVBER is to be applied).

Furthermore, the technology transfer regulation (TTBER)[184] is to be mentioned too, which governs certain vertical relations and, thus, it may serve as a useful point of reference for the regulation of the distribution sector. The block exemption regulations governing vertical agreements employ basically the same structure. In the first step, they exempt all agreements under a certain market share, and in the second step, they pull out certain hardcore and blacklisted agreements from the benefit of the block exemption.

US antitrust law

Contrary to Article 101, in US antitrust law the statutory language of Section 1 seems to contain a substantive test of a one-step analysis; the judicial practice elaborated, however, a structured pattern of analysis. For the sake of judicial convenience and legal certainty, inherently anti-competitive agreements with no perspective of redeeming virtue are presumed to be anti-competitive and hence illegal conclusively. Other agreements are to be examined under the rule of reason, taking into account their pros and cons. The central element of the rule of reason method is the balancer that is used for measuring the reasonableness of the restraint at stake. This balancer, in fact, combines the focuses of Article 101(1) and 101(3). Recently, a new method of analysis evolved in the courtrooms: 'quick look' or truncated rule of reason. While its purview is rather ambiguous, if applicable, it enables the full-blown rule of reason analysis of agreements formally belonging to one of the *per se* categories, provided that the justifications offered by the defendant are facially capable of being accepted as legitimate.

Whish, *Regulation 2790/99: the Commission's 'New Style' Block Exemption for Vertical Agreements*, 37 Common Market Law Review 887 (2000).

183 *See* Regulation 1400/2002 OJ [2002] L 203/30 and Regulation 461/2010 OJ [2010] OJ L 129/52.

184 Regulation 772/2004 OJ [2004] L 123/11.

The above three concepts, i.e. *per se* illegality, rule of reason and quick look, will be analysed in chronological order: in the first step, the *per se* versus rule of reason dichotomy will be considered, followed by a detailed analysis of the rule of reason (structure, balancer); in the third step, the quick look rule will be examined. The latter's most important consequence is that it pulls out some agreements from the realm of *per se* illegality and gives them a very limited opportunity of self-defence. Nevertheless, not only historical reasons justify that quick look should be analysed separately from *per se* illegality: the basic tension lies between the two elements of the traditional dichotomy and this is the fundamental playing field the quick look analysis intruded in.

Per se *and rule of reason agreements*

Section 1 of the Sherman Act makes no reference to any classification of agreements; likewise, it simply prohibits restraints of trade or commerce with no mention of whether the concept of restraint implies inherent limitations or not. However, in practice, it turned out very early that there are some types of arrangements that never escape Section 1 condemnation, while in most cases the context of the agreement is to be examined in order to give a valid answer. Agreements that embrace the very evils of antitrust are *per se* illegal; there is no chance to plead the effects and the context of the arrangement. The jurisprudence of the Supreme Court worked out certain categories of *per se* illegality. Here, the defendant's only chance is to argue that the agreement at stake cannot be brought under the alleged *per se* heading;[185] this was supplemented by the concept of quick look. If the agreement's ship does not wreck on the rock of *per se* illegality, its context is to be analysed, i.e. market power, effects etc.[186]

---

185 *Cf.* Donald L. Beschle, *What, Never? Well, Hardly Ever': Strict Antitrust Scrutiny as an Alternative to Per Se Antitrust Illegality*, 38 Hastings Law Journal 471, 472-473 (1987). ('[The *per se*] rule condemning all acts belonging to a certain class does not eliminate the need for analysis. It merely shifts the crucial point in the analysis to the decision whether the specific act in question belongs to the illegal class.') *Id.* at 477. ('The proposition that horizontal price fixing is *per se* illegal remains the law. But our understanding of that statement has undergone serious change in the last decade. It is now more clear than ever that the process of categorizing conduct as price fixing may allow defendants to raise arguments which cannot be raised to justify a practice already characterized as price fixing.')

186 In the early days of antitrust, the theory of '*per se* v rule of reason' dichotomy had a very significant competitor. The dichotomy of naked and ancillary restraints was also a strong candidate for being the law of the land. *See U.S. v Addyston Pipe and Steel Co.*, 85 F. 271 (1898). Finally, the Supreme Court in *Standard Oil* adopted the rule of reason standard. Nevertheless, the conceptual dichotomy of naked/ancillary restraints still has a considerable role in antitrust analysis, the two theories being to some extent parallel anyway.

After a short wavering in *Trans-Missouri Freight Ass'n*[187] and *Joint-Traffic Ass'n*,[188] the Supreme Court established in *Standard Oil*[189] that the term 'restraint' actually implies 'undue or unreasonable restraints'[190] and the general principle is the rule of reason.[191] Nevertheless, the Court also sowed the seed of *per se* illegality

---

187 *U.S. v Trans-Missouri Freight Ass'n*, 166 U.S. 290 (1897). In *Trans-Missouri* the Court seems to have held that all naked agreements are anti-competitive. The Court also stated that the term 'restraint of trade or commerce' embraces all agreements that operate to restrain trade or commerce, whether legal or illegal under common law, and irrespective of whether the restraint is reasonable or unreasonable. According to the Supreme Court, the language of the statute was plain. ('In other words, we are asked to read into the act, by way of judicial legislation an exception that is not placed there by the lawmaking branch of the government, and this is to be done upon the theory that the impolicy of such legislation is so clear that it cannot be supposed congress intended the natural import of the language it used. This we cannot and ought not to do. (…) The conclusion which we have drawn from the examination above made into the question before us is that the anti-trust act (…) renders illegal all agreements which are in restraint of trade or commerce, as we have above defined that expression, and the question then arises whether the agreement before us is of that nature.') *Id.* at 327-341.

188 *U.S. v Joint-Traffic Ass'n*, 171 U.S. 505 (1898).

189 *Standard Oil Co. of New Jersey v U.S.*, 221 U.S. 1 (1911).

190 In *Standard Oil* the Supreme Court refused to give a literal meaning to the term 'restraint of trade'. The government argued 'that the language of the statute embraces every contract, combination, etc., in restraint of trade, and hence its text leaves no room for the exercise of judgment, but simply imposes the plain duty of applying its prohibitions to every case within its literal language'. However, the Court dismissed this position, holding that 'to hold to the contrary would require the conclusion either that every contract, act, or combination of any kind or nature, whether it operated a restraint on trade or not, was within the statute, and thus the statute would be destructive of all right to contract or agree combine in any respect whatever as to subjects embraced in interstate trade or commerce, or, if this conclusion were not reached, then the contention would require it to be held that, as the statute did not define the things to which it related, and excluded resort to the only means by which the acts to which it relates could be ascertained – the light of reason – the enforcement of the statute was impossible because of its uncertainty'. *Id.* at 63.

191 'The statute under this view evidenced the intent not to restrain the right to make and enforce contracts, whether resulting from combinations or otherwise, which did not unduly restrain interstate or foreign commerce, but to protect that commerce from being restrained by methods, whether old or new, which would constitute an interference – that is, an undue restraint. (…) Thus not specifying, but indubitably contemplating and requiring a standard, it follows that it was intended that the standard of reason which had been applied at the common law and in this country in dealing with subjects of the character embraced by the statute was intended to be the measure used for the purpose of determining whether, in a given case, a particular act had or had not brought about the wrong against which the statute provided.' *Id.* at 60. *See Northern Pac. Ry. Co. v U.S.*, 356 U.S. 1, 5 (1958). ('Although this prohibition is literally all-encompassing, the courts have construed it as precluding only those contracts or combinations which "unreasonably" restrain competition.')

in the ground of antitrust[192] when distinguishing and endorsing *Trans-Missouri Freight Ass'n* and *Joint-Traffic Ass'n*, holding that the 'nature and character' of the agreement may create a 'conclusive presumption' of illegality.[193] Proceeding from this point, the jurisprudence of the federal courts worked out the concepts of *per se* illegality and rule of reason. However, the two concepts are the two weapons of the very same antitrust warrior:[194] both of them target unreasonable restraints of trade, albeit in case of an agreement in one of the *per se* categories the 'unreasonably restrictive' character is presumed conclusively.

> *Per se* rules are invoked when surrounding circumstances make the likelihood of anticompetitive conduct so great as to render unjustified further examination of the challenged conduct. But whether the ultimate finding is the product of a presumption or actual market analysis, the essential inquiry remains the same whether or not the challenged restraint enhances competition.[195]

There are certain arrangements that always or almost always entail anti-competitive results[196] without any reasonable chance for redeeming virtue. Procedural convenience[197] and legal certainty justify that such agreements should not be analysed in detail each time they come up but they can be condemned automatically based on past experience.[198] Nevertheless, the standard approach is rule of reason

192 *See U.S. v Trenton Potteries Co.*, 273 U.S. 392, 399 (1927). ('That the opinions in the *Standard Oil* and *Tobacco* Cases were not intended to affect this view of the illegality of price-fixing agreements affirmatively appears from the opinion in the *Standard Oil* Case.') The term '*per se*' was first used in 1940 in *United States v Socony-Vacuum Oil Co.*, 310 U.S. 150 (1940). *See* Donald L. Beschle, *What, Never? 'Well, Hardly Ever': Strict Antitrust Scrutiny as an Alternative to Per Se Antitrust Illegality*, 38 Hastings Law Journal 471, 477 (1987).

193 '[T]he cases but decided that the nature and character of the contracts, creating, as they did, a conclusive presumption which brought them within the statute, such result was not to be disregarded by the substitution of a judicial appreciation of what the law ought to be for the plain judicial duty of enforcing the law as it was made.' *Standard Oil Co. of New Jersey v U.S.*, 221 U.S. 1, 65 (1911).

194 *Cf.* Alan J. Meese, *Price Theory, Competition, and the Rule of Reason*, 2003 University of Illinois Law Review 77, 93 (2003). ('While courts refer to this second step as a Rule of Reason analysis, both steps of the process attempt to answer the question put by Standard Oil, viz., is a restraint "unreasonably restrictive of competitive conditions".')

195 *National Collegiate Athletic Ass'n v Board of Regents of University of Oklahoma*, 468 U.S. 85, 103-104 (1984).

196 *See Broadcast Music, Inc. v Columbia Broadcasting System, Inc.*, 441 U.S. 1, 19-20 (1979).

197 *U.S. v Topco Associates, Inc.*, 405 U.S. 596, 609-610 (1972).; *Arizona v Maricopa County Medical Soc.*, 457 U.S. 332, 343-344 (1982).; *Northwest Wholesale Stationers, Inc. v Pacific Stationery and Printing Co.*, 472 U.S. 284 (1985).; *Arizona v Maricopa County Medical Soc.*, 457 U.S. 332, 343 (1982).

198 Oliver Black, *Per Se Rules and Rules of Reason: What Are They?*, 18(3) European Competition Law Review 145, 151-152 (1997). (Summarizing the arguments for *per se*

analysis,[199] and the doctrine of *per se* illegality applies only to arrangements that were specifically classified as such.[200] Furthermore, *per se* illegality should not serve the purpose of convenience but it covers only agreements of which the anti-competitive nature is evident. '*Per se* rules of illegality are appropriate only when they relate to conduct that is manifestly anticompetitive.'[201] In the *per se* 'category are those agreements whose nature and necessary effect are so plainly anticompetitive that no elaborate study of the industry is needed to establish their illegality – they are "illegal *per se*"'.[202]

The courts have treated certain types of agreements since the early days of the Sherman Act not only as being presumably anti-competitive but they also refused to hear any justification by the defendant (price fixing,[203] division of markets,[204] group boycotts[205] or tying arrangements[206]). The *per se* illegality approach had, however, not been conceptualized for a long time. Perhaps, one of the first comprehensive explanations is the Supreme Court's reasoning in *Northern Pacific*.[207]

> [T]here are certain agreements or practices which because of their pernicious effect on competition and lack of any redeeming virtue are conclusively presumed to be unreasonable and therefore illegal without elaborate inquiry as to the precise harm they have caused or the business excuse for their use. This principle of *per se* unreasonableness not only makes the type of restraints which are proscribed by the Sherman Act more certain to the benefit of everyone

---

rules as follows: first, 'efficiency of administration, litigation and adjudication', reducing 'the need for continuous supervision of business practices and the need for courts to make economic judgments'; second, 'certainty, clarity and simplicity'; third, 'predictability and deterrence'; fourth, 'if *per se* rules are in place, enforcement of section 1 is less likely to be arbitrary, irrational, erroneous, prejudiced or unfair; *per se* rules thus promote the rule of law'; fifth, 'they prevent any bias towards defendants in judgments under section 1'; sixth, 'they are dynamically stabilising in the sense that, even if at first their application produces some undesirable decisions in borderline cases, people learn to adjust their behaviour to avoid such results'.)

199 In *Sylvania*, the Supreme Court, with reference to *Standard Oil*, held that 'since the early years of this century a judicial gloss on this statutory language has established the "rule of reason" as the prevailing standard of analysis.' *Continental T. V., Inc. v GTE Sylvania Inc.*, 433 U.S. 36, 49 (1977).

200 *Northwest Wholesale Stationers, Inc. v Pacific Stationery and Printing Co.*, 472 U.S. 284, 289 (1985).

201 *Continental T. V., Inc. v GTE Sylvania Inc.*, 433 U.S. 36, 49-50 (1977).

202 *National Soc. of Professional Engineers v U. S.*, 435 U.S. 679, 692 (1978).

203 *U.S. v Trenton Potteries Co.*, 273 U.S. 392, 400 (1927), *United States v Socony-Vacuum Oil Co.*, 310 U.S. 150 (1940).

204 *U.S. v Addyston Pipe and Steel Co.*, 175 U.S. 211 (1899).

205 *Fashion Originators' Guild of America v Federal Trade Commission*, 312 U.S. 457 (1941).

206 *International Salt Co. v U.S.*, 332 U.S. 392 (1947).

207 *Northern Pac. Ry. Co. v U.S.*, 356 U.S. 1 (1958).

> concerned, but it also avoids the necessity for an incredibly complicated and prolonged economic investigation into the entire history of the industry involved, as well as related industries, in an effort to determine at large whether a particular restraint has been unreasonable – an inquiry so often wholly fruitless when undertaken.[208]

The *per se* approach is exceptional[209] and 'there is a presumption in favour of a rule-of-reason standard; departure from that standard must be justified by demonstrable economic effect (...) rather than formalistic distinctions'.[210] While clear-cut rules have their inherent merits (e.g. legal certainty, judicial convenience, deterrence), these obvious benefits do not justify the extensive use of the *per se* approach. *Per se* illegality is not a question of trade-off between the judicial costs of the rule of reason analysis and the chances that agreements of a particular kind may escape Section 1 scrutiny based on reasonable arguments. The only reason to pronounce a particular group of arrangements to be *per se* illegal is that they have manifest anti-competitive effects with no or negligible chance for any pro-competitive value.[211] This was made clear by the Supreme Court, *inter alia*, in *Sylvania*.

---

208 *Id.* at 5. *See Broadcast Music, Inc. v Columbia Broadcasting System, Inc.*, 441 U.S. 1, 19-20 (1979). ('[I]n characterizing (...) [a] conduct under the *per se* rule, our inquiry must focus on whether the effect and, here because it tends to show effect (...), the purpose of the practice are to threaten the proper operation of our predominantly free-market economy – that is, whether the practice facially appears to be one that would always or almost always tend to restrict competition and decrease output, and in what portion of the market, or instead one designed to "increase economic efficiency and render markets more, rather than less, competitive".') *National Collegiate Athletic Ass'n v Board of Regents of University of Oklahoma*, 468 U.S. 85, 103-104 (1984). ('*Per se* rules are invoked when surrounding circumstances make the likelihood of anticompetitive conduct so great as to render unjustified further examination of the challenged conduct.')

209 *See Northwest Wholesale Stationers, Inc. v Pacific Stationery and Printing Co.*, 472 U.S. 284, 289-291 (1985).; *Business Electronics Corp. v Sharp Electronics Corp.*, 485 U.S. 717, 723-724 (1988).; *FTC v Indiana Federation of Dentists*, 476 U.S. 447, 458-459 (1986). ('[W]e have been slow to extend *per se* analysis to restraints imposed in the context of business relationships where the economic impact of certain practices is not immediately obvious.'); *National Collegiate Athletic Ass'n v Board of Regents of University of Oklahoma*, 468 U.S. 85, 103-104 (1984). ('*Per se* rules are invoked when surrounding circumstances make the likelihood of anticompetitive conduct so great as to render unjustified further examination of the challenged conduct.'); *National Soc. of Professional Engineers v U.S.*, 435 U.S. 679, 692 (1978). ('There are, thus, two complementary categories of antitrust analysis. In the first category are agreements whose nature and necessary effect are so plainly anticompetitive that no elaborate study of the industry is needed to establish their illegality-they are 'illegal *per se*".')

210 *Business Electronics Corp. v Sharp Electronics Corp.*, 485 U.S. 717, 726 (1988).

211 *Cf.* LAWRENCE A. SULLIVAN AND WARREN S. GRIMES, THE LAW OF ANTITRUST: AN INTEGRATED HANDBOOK 203 (2000). ('[F]or an offense like price fixing there is little if any social cost to balance against this enhanced deterrence. As a generalization, price-fixing

> *Per se* rules thus require the Court to make broad generalizations about the social utility of particular commercial practices. The probability that anticompetitive consequences will result from a practice and the severity of those consequences must be balanced against its pro-competitive consequences. Cases that do not fit the generalization may arise, but a *per se* rule reflects the judgment that such cases are not sufficiently common or important to justify the time and expense necessary to identify them. Once established, *per se* rules tend to provide guidance to the business community and to minimize the burdens on litigants and the judicial system of the more complex rule-of-reason trials (…) but those advantages are not sufficient in themselves to justify the creation of *per se* rules. If it were otherwise, all of antitrust law would be reduced to *per se* rules, thus introducing an unintended and undesirable rigidity in the law.[212]

Antitrust law's commitment in favour of the rule of reason approach entails that the creation of a *per se* illegality category requires long-standing judicial experience. The mechanism is the following. Courts should not make quick judgments regarding particular types of restraints but they are expected to carry out a detailed analysis without begrudging the judicial resources. Nevertheless, if the multitude of benevolent antitrust analyses of a particular type of arrangement coherently leads to condemnation, such an experience may justify the judicial reflex of outright prohibition. 'Once experience with a particular kind of restraint enables the Court to predict with confidence that the rule of reason will condemn it, it has applied a conclusive presumption that the restraint is unreasonable.'[213] Accordingly, the Supreme Court is 'slow (…) to extend *per se* analysis to restraints imposed in the context of business relationships where the economic impact of certain practices is not immediately obvious'.[214]

---

does not become socially beneficial when power is lacking; it simply becomes ineffective. (…) [E]ven if this leads to overenforcement (…), the "overenforcement" would not inhibit any socially valuable conduct; it merely inhibits ineffective attempts to do something both harmful and unlawful.')

212 *Continental T. V., Inc. v GTE Sylvania Inc.*, 433 U.S. 36, 50 fn 16 (1977). *See also Arizona v Maricopa County Medical Soc.*, 457 U.S. 332, 344 (1982). ('Once experience with a particular kind of restraint enables the Court to predict with confidence that the rule of reason will condemn it, it has applied a conclusive presumption that the restraint is unreasonable. As in every rule of general application, the match between the presumed and the actual is imperfect. For the sake of business certainty and litigation efficiency, we have tolerated the invalidation of some agreements that a fullblown inquiry might have proved to be reasonable.'); *Leegin Creative Leather Products, Inc. v PSKS, Inc.*, 127 S.Ct. 2705, 2718 (2007). (Emphasizing that administrative convenience is, in itself, not sufficient to justify the creation of a *per se* rule.)

213 *Arizona v Maricopa County Medical Soc.*, 457 U.S. 332, 344 fn 14 (1982).

214 *FTC v Indiana Federation of Dentists*, 476 U.S. 447, 458-459 (1986).

The rule of reason analysis

In *Board of Trade of City of Chicago,*[215] the Supreme Court – reversing the *per se* approach followed by the District Court – gave a profound amplification of the rule of reason, which, over time, has become a classic formulation.[216]

> But the legality of an agreement or regulation cannot be determined by so simple a test, as whether it restrains competition. Every agreement concerning trade, every regulation of trade, restrains. To bind, to restrain, is of their very essence. The true test of legality is whether the restraint imposed is such as merely regulates and perhaps thereby promotes competition or whether it is such as may suppress or even destroy competition. To determine that question the court must ordinarily consider the facts peculiar to the business to which the restraint is applied; its condition before and after the restraint was imposed; the nature of the restraint and its effect, actual or probable. The history of the restraint, the evil believed to exist, the reason for adopting the particular remedy, the purpose or end sought to be attained, are all relevant facts. This is not because a good intention will save an otherwise objectionable regulation or the reverse; but because knowledge of intent may help the court to interpret facts and to predict consequences.[217]

All in all, the rule of reason analysis is nothing else but a rather speculative[218] balancing of the anti-competitive effects and the reasonable justifications where 'everything goes into the blender'[219] and where 'everything is relevant, nothing is dispositive'.[220] 'Under this rule, the factfinder weighs all of the circumstances of

215 *Board of Trade of City of Chicago v U.S.*, 246 U.S. 231 (1918).

216 *See* Thomas A. Piraino, *Reconciling the Per Se and Rule of Reason Approached to Antitrust Analysis*, 64 Southern California Law Review 685, 689 (1991).

217 *Board of Trade of City of Chicago v U.S.*, 246 U.S. 231, 238-239 (1918).

218 Thomas C. Arthur, *A Workable Rule of Reason: a Less Ambitious Antitrust Role for the Federal Courts*, 68 Antitrust Law Journal 337, 338 (2000). ('This uncertainty is not likely to go away. Clarity in antitrust law is not possible under the current conception of the Sherman Act as a standardless delegation to the federal courts to engage in microeconomic regulation.') *See* Thomas C. Arthur, *Farewell to the Sea of Doubt: Jettisoning the Constitutional Sherman Act*, 74 California Law Review 263 (1986); Thomas C. Arthur, *Workable Antitrust Law: the Statutory Approach to Antitrust*, 62 Tulane Law Review 1163 (1988).

219 Terry Calvani, *Some Thoughts on the Rule of Reason*, 22(6) European Competition Law Review 201, 201 (2001).

220 Frank H. Easterbrook, *The Limits of Antitrust*, 63 Texas Law Review 1, 12 (1984). *See* Thomas C. Arthur, *A Workable Rule of Reason: a Less Ambitious Antitrust Role for the Federal Courts*, 68 Antitrust Law Journal 337, 346-347 (2000). ('Justice Brandeis's opinion in *Chicago Board of Trade* made things worse. (…) [H]is famous restatement of the rule of reason required a trial court to consider *all* the surrounding facts before reaching judgment, but gave no indication of the relative significance of any particular inquiry. [Brandeis's approach] reintroduced the English/American minority rule's concern for producer welfare

a case in deciding whether a restrictive practice should be prohibited as imposing an unreasonable restraint on competition.'[221] Not surprisingly, the ambiguity and the all-in character of the rule of reason analysis shifted antitrust litigation towards *per se* cases.[222]

The structure of the rule of reason analysis

The rule of reason consists of a three-step analysis: proof of anti-competitive effects by the plaintiff (showing a *prima facie* case), proof of pro-competitive justifications by the defendant and balancing by the court. First, one must enquire whether the agreement at stake has substantial anti-competitive consequences; an issue in relation to which the burden of proof rests on the shoulders of the plaintiff. If such effects are proved, then secondly, the defendant has the chance to show objective justifications, arguing that the agreement produces pro-competitive effects or is efficient. If substantial pro-competitive effects are proved by the defendant, who bears the burden in this regard, the third step calls for a balancing; an exercise to be done by the court.

Accordingly, in the first step the plaintiff has to present a *prima facie* case. Showing market power is a customary way of meeting the plaintiff's burden of proof, albeit in *F.T.C. v Indiana Federation of Dentists*[223] the Supreme Court held

---

and self-interested private regulation back into the rule of reason, at least for difficult cases, and suggested that industry members might regulate competition among themselves for any non-productive purpose a judge might deem reasonable.')

221 *Continental T. V., Inc. v GTE Sylvania Inc.*, 433 U.S. 36, 49 (1977). *See* Phillip Areeda, *The Rule of Reason – A Catechism on Competition*, 55 Antitrust Law Journal 571, 572-573 and 582 (1986); Phillip Areeda, *A Second Century of the Rule of Reason*, 59 Antitrust Law Journal 143, 149-150 (1990). ('When courts find that both detriment and redeeming virtue are present in more-or-less significant degree, I predict that the redeeming virtue will come increasingly to trump the detriment.')

222 Thomas C. Arthur, *A Workable Rule of Reason: a Less Ambitious Antitrust Role for the Federal Courts*, 68 Antitrust Law Journal 337, 349-350 (2000). ('[T]he *Chicago Board of Trade/Appalachian Coals* rule of reason was little more than "a euphemism for an endless economic inquiry resulting in a defense verdict". (...) Both *Chicago Board of Trade* and *Appalachian Coals* had spoken approvingly of private regulation to eliminate "competitive evils" that made life harder on producers. Neither case limited defendants to efficiency defenses. (…) Not surprisingly, plaintiffs, especially private ones, sought to force their claims into the *per se* pigeonholes. If they succeeded, they won; if not, in most cases they gave up. As a result, the *per se* rules dominated antitrust litigation for over three decades and almost completely eclipsed the rule of reason.')

223 The roots of this proposition may be found in *National Collegiate Athletic Ass'n v Board of Regents of the University of Oklahoma*, 468 U.S. 85, 109 (1984); nevertheless, this case concerned a naked restraint, and it was highly questionable whether the proposition can have a more general application. ('As a matter of law, the absence of proof of market power does not justify a naked restriction on price or output. To the contrary, when there is an agreement not to compete in terms of price or output, "no elaborate industry analysis is required to demonstrate the anticompetitive character of such an agreement".')

that market power is not a necessary pre-requisite of establishing anti-competitive effects.[224] Instead, the real test is actual anti-competitive effect ('competitive harm') demonstrated empirically, and the market power test can only serve as a surrogate for this;[225] a very useful one, though, 'due to the difficulty of isolating the market effects of challenged conduct',[226] which is in practice 'an integral part of showing anti-competitiveness in traditional rule of reason cases'.[227] Accordingly, the market power filter is not necessary but it is sufficient for establishing a *prima facie* case for the plaintiff.

While the defendant is completely free to proffer evidence refuting the stance that anti-competitive effects were actually entailed, if the plaintiff meets his burden of proof, it is up to the defendant to come up with pro-competitive arguments, i.e. he can (and should) argue that despite its restrictive effects on inter-firm rivalry the agreement is featured by pro-competitive justifications, mainly in the form of efficiency benefits.[228] These justifications are to be proved. If the defendant proves that such pro-competitive benefits are present, the plaintiff can produce the defence that the arrangement at stake is not the least restrictive alternative, i.e. the same pro-competitive benefits could have been achieved with means that are substantially less restrictive to competition and that are still reasonably capable of achieving the same legitimate end. Nonetheless, courts tend to show some

224 It could be argued that the fact pattern concerned a horizontal agreement and, hence, the above proposition is not applicable to vertical cases; however, the judgment's language suggests the contrary. *See* Alan J. Meese, *Price Theory, Competition, and the Rule of Reason*, 2003 University of Illinois Law Review 77, 103-104 (2003).

225 *FTC v Indiana Federation of Dentists*, 476 U.S. 447 (1986). ('Since the purpose of the inquiries into market definition and market power is to determine whether an arrangement has the potential for genuine adverse effects on competition, "proof of actual detrimental effects, such as a reduction of output', can obviate the need for an inquiry into market power, which is but a "surrogate for detrimental effects".'). *But see* Mark R. Patterson, *The Market Power Requirement in Antitrust Rule of Reason Cases: a Rhetorical History*, 37 San Diego Law Review 1, 8 (2000).

226 *U.S. v Brown University in Providence in State of R.I.*, 5 F.3d 658, 668 (1993). ('Such proof is often impossible to make, however, due to the difficulty of isolating the market effects of challenged conduct. (…) Accordingly, courts typically allow proof of the defendant's "market power" instead.')

227 Marina Lao, *Comment: the Rule of Reason and Horizontal Restraints Involving Professionals*, 68 Antitrust Law Journal 499, 504 (2000).

228 *FTC and DOJ Guidelines for Collaborations Among Competitors*, April 2000, 23. (Introducing pro-competitive benefits as follows. 'Competition usually spurs firms to achieve efficiencies internally. Nevertheless, as explained above, competitor collaborations have the potential to generate significant efficiencies that benefit consumers in a variety of ways. For example, a competitor collaboration may enable firms to offer goods or services that are cheaper, more valuable to consumers, or brought to market faster than would otherwise be possible. Efficiency gains from competitor collaborations often stem from combinations of different capabilities or resources. (…) Indeed, the primary benefit of competitor collaborations to the economy is their potential to generate such efficiencies.')

deference to the sound business decisions of the market, when enquiring whether 'reasonable alternatives' exist.[229]

If the defendant does not meet his burden of proof, a decision is made for the plaintiff; if he does, the case reaches the third analytical phase: the court has to balance the anti- and pro-competitive effects in order to ascertain the net effects. Nevertheless, '[w]hen courts are truly troubled by a restraint, but they see that it has both pro- and anticompetitive incidents that are non-trivial, they tend to find for the defendant. In other words, presence of a significant benefit is often determinative.'[230] One of the reasons may be that 90 per cent of the antitrust cases in the US is brought to court by private plaintiffs and is tried in civil procedure,[231] where the usual standard of proof is preponderance of evidence (balance of probabilities). Accordingly, a circumstance is proved if it is more likely than not (or it is 'more probable than not'[232]), that it is true.

The balancer in the rule of reason analysis

The pivotal question of the rule of reason test is the balancer, which is closely connected to the ultimate purpose of antitrust law.[233] The first scale holds the anti-competitive effects, which are responsible for arousing the antitrust lion and which are to be counterbalanced. Nonetheless, it is far from clear which are the values that are capable of having a counter-balancing function and which could be laid on the second scale. Section 1 is silent in this regard. Moreover, different concurring

---

229 Phillip Areeda, *The Rule of Reason – a Catechism on Competition*, 55 Antitrust Law Journal 571, 582 (1986); *FTC and DOJ Guidelines for Collaborations Among Competitors*, April 2000, 24. ('The Agencies consider only those efficiencies for which the relevant agreement is reasonably necessary. An agreement may be "reasonably necessary" without being essential. However, if the participants could have achieved or could achieve similar efficiencies by practical, significantly less restrictive means, then the Agencies conclude that the relevant agreement is not reasonably necessary to their achievement. *In making this assessment, the Agencies consider only alternatives that are practical in the business situation faced by the participants; the Agencies do not search for a theoretically less restrictive alternative that is not realistic given business realities.*').

230 Phillip Areeda, *The Rule of Reason – A Catechism on Competition*, 55 Antitrust Law Journal 571, 582 (1986).

231 *See* Clifford A. Jones, Private enforcement of antitrust law in the EU, UK and USA 16 (1999); Jonathan Sinclair, *Damages in private antitrust actions in Europe*, 14 Loyola Consumer Law Review 547 (2002); Katherine Holmes, *Public enforcement or private enforcement? Enforcement of competition law in the EC and UK*, 25(1) European Competition Law Review 25, 31 (2004).

232 *See* Lord Denning's famous definition in *Miller v. Minister of Pensions* [1947] 2 All ER 372. ('It must carry a reasonable degree of probability, not so high as is required in a criminal case. If the evidence is such that the tribunal can say: "we think it more probable than not", the burden is discharged, but if the probabilities are equal it is not.')

233 *See* Phillip Areeda, *The Rule of Reason – A Catechism on Competition*, 55 Antitrust Law Journal 571, 572 (1986).

policy goals pop up in the legislative history of the Sherman Act (efficiency, consumer welfare and the protection of 'small dealers and worthy men'), without any indication on how to rank them.[234]

Although the jurisprudence of the courts has always been very ambiguous regarding the identity of the balancer, note the 'everything goes into the blender'[235] approach described above, the mainstream approach had been a 'fight fire with fire' logic for a long time.[236] The foregoing implied the paradigm of atomistic competition and was heavily based on the process of rivalry.[237] The concept of atomistic competition[238] centres around the independent behaviour of the market operators and the lack of any voluntarily assumed self-restraint of action.[239] In *Standard Oil of Cal. v United States*, the Supreme Court condemned an exclusive dealing arrangement that bound only 6.7 per cent of the dealers in the given region. The Court held that 'in view of the widespread adoption of such contracts by Standard's competitors and the availability of alternative ways of obtaining an assured market, evidence that competitive activity has not actually declined is inconclusive. Standard's use of the contracts creates just such a potential clog on competition as it was the purpose of s

---

234 *See* Jennifer E. Gladieux, *Towards a Single Standard for Antitrust: the Federal Trade Commission's Evolving Rule of Reason*, 5 George Mason Law Review 471, 475-476 (1997). ('Congress passed the Sherman Act in 1890. The 51st Congress believed that the Sherman Act furthered competition by protecting consumers from monopolies and cartels, and by protecting competitors from predatory conduct. However, an examination of the legislative history reveals testimonial support from the drafters for almost any policy goal, from the promotion of "small dealers and worthy men" to an overriding emphasis on the maximization of efficiency and consumer welfare.'); RUDOLPH J. R. PERITZ, COMPETITION POLICY IN AMERICA 1888-1992 (1996); SANDRA MARCO COLINO, VERTICAL AGREEMENTS AND COMPETITION LAW: A COMPARATIVE STUDY OF THE EU AND US REGIMES 47-50 (2010).

235 Frank H. Easterbrook, *The Limits of Antitrust*, 63 Texas Law Review 1, 12 (1984).

236 Oliver Black, *Per Se Rules and Rules of Reason: What Are They?*, 18(3) European Competition Law Review 145, 146 (1997) ('The dominant tradition has it that the purpose of section 1 is solely to promote competition, and it therefore views the reasonableness or unreasonableness of a restraint, for the purposes of the section, as solely a matter of the restraint's effect on competition. This view is indeterminate because "competition" has various meanings.')

237 Alan J. Meese, *Price Theory, Competition and the Rule of Reason*, 2003 University of Illinois Law Review 77, 86 (2003). ('Such an analysis did not involve implementation of any abstract, technical conception of competition. Unlike modern economists, who view competition as a technical term of art, functionally linked to the efficient allocation of resources, the Standard Oil Court, like classical economists, equated competition with rivalry, the struggle between several firms to realize economic opportunities.')

238 *See* Frank H. Easterbrook, *Workable Antitrust Policy*, 84 Michigan Law Review 1696, 1696 (1986). *See also* Eleanor M. Fox and Lawrence A. Sullivan, *Antitrust-Retrospective and Prospective: Where are We Coming from? Where are We Going?*, 62 New York University Law Review 936, 942-944 (1987).

239 *See* Frank H. Easterbrook, *Workable Antitrust Policy*, 84 Michigan Law Review 1696, 1696-1697 (1986).

3 to remove wherever.'[240] In *United States v Richfield Oil Corp.*, the Court held, in the context of an exclusive dealing arrangement covering a trivial part of the market, that 'effective competition required that traders have large freedom of action when conducting their own affairs'.[241] In *Dictograph Prods., Inc. v FTC*, it was held that '[i]t is the policy of the Congress that [the defendant's] merchandise must stand on its own feet in the open market (...) without the competitive advantage to be obtained by the use of prohibited exclusionary agreements'.[242] In *FTC v Brown Shoe Co.*, the Court held, in the context of an exclusive dealing arrangement covering a trivial part of the market, that it 'obviously conflicts with the central policy of both s 1 of the Sherman Act and s 3 of the Clayton Act against contracts which take away freedom of purchasers to buy in an open market'.[243] In the *Albrecht v Herald Co.* judgment (later overruled), the Supreme Court justified the *per se* illegality of vertical maximum price-fixing with the fact that it eliminated the dealers' unrestrained freedom of action: 'schemes to fix maximum prices, by substituting the perhaps erroneous judgment of a seller for the forces of the competitive market, may severely intrude upon the ability of buyers to compete and survive in that market'.[244] In *Times-Picayune Pub. Co. v U.S.*, the Supreme Court held that '[t]ying arrangements, we may readily agree, flout the Sherman Act's policy that competition rule the marts of trade. Basic to the faith that a free economy best promotes the public weal is that goods must stand the cold test of competition; that the public, acting through the market's impersonal judgment, shall allocate the Nation's resources and thus direct the course its economic development will take.'[245]

The concept of atomistic competition has a strong 'liberty' background as well: 'courts treated "liberty from contract" and "trader freedom" as values of independent significance under the antitrust laws, treating contractual restrictions on such freedom as a "harm" for purposes of applying the *per se* rule'.[246] In *Kiefer-Stewart Co. v Joseph Seagram & Sons, Inc.*, the Supreme Court stated that the problem with vertical maximum price fixing agreements is that they 'cripple the freedom of traders and thereby restrain their ability to sell in accordance with their own judgment'.[247] In *N. Pac. Ry. Co. v United States*, the Supreme Court held that

---

240 *See Standard Oil of Cal. v United States*, 337 U.S. 293, 314 (1949).

241 *United States v Richfield Oil Corp.*, 99 F. Supp. 280, 293 (1951), affirmed 343 U.S. 922 (1952). (The Court held, in the context of an exclusive dealing arrangement covering a trivial part of the market, that 'effective competition required that traders have large freedom of action when conducting their own affairs.')

242 *Dictograph Prods., Inc. v FTC*, 217 F.2d 821, 828 (1954).

243 *FTC v Brown Shoe Co.*, 384 U.S. 316, 21 (1966).

244 *Albrecht v Herald Co.*, 390 U.S. 145, 152 (1968). The *per se* illegality of maximum resale price fixing was overruled in *State Oil Co. v Khan*, 118 S.Ct. 275 (1997).

245 *Times-Picayune Pub. Co. v U.S.*, 345 U.S. 594, 605 (1953).

246 Alan J. Meese, *Farewell to the Quick Look: Redefining the Scope and Content of the Rule of Reason*, 68 Antitrust Law Journal 461, 467 (2000).

247 *Kiefer-Stewart Co. v Joseph Seagram and Sons, Inc.*, 340 U.S. 211, 213 (1951).

> The Sherman Act was designed to be a comprehensive charter of economic liberty aimed at preserving free and unfettered competition as the rule of trade. It rests on the premise that the unrestrained interaction of competitive forces will yield the best allocation of our economic resources, the lowest prices, the highest quality and the greatest material progress, while at the same time providing an environment conductive to the preservation of our democratic political and social institutions.[248]

A similarly elevated language appears in *U.S. v Topco Associates, Inc.*

> Antitrust laws in general, and the Sherman Act in particular, are the Magna Carta of free enterprise. They are as important to the preservation of economic freedom and our free-enterprise system as the Bill of Rights is to the protection of our fundamental personal freedoms. And the freedom guaranteed each and every business, no matter how small, is the freedom to compete-to assert with vigor, imagination, devotion, and ingenuity whatever economic muscle it can muster. Implicit in such freedom is the notion that it cannot be foreclosed with respect to one sector of the economy because certain private citizens or groups believe that such foreclosure might promote greater competition in a more important sector of the economy.[249]

Co-operative efficiency does not really fit this picture. The traditional approach admitted that the restraint's reasonableness is to be measured according to its effects on competition, i.e. if the final effect of the restraint is positive it is irrelevant whether the arrangement also has anti-competitive effects besides the pro-competitive ones, since the latter out-weigh the former; competition was equated with rivalry. Nevertheless, only those competition-enhancing implications could be taken into account, which accelerated, for instance, the scope or intensity of rivalry: 'the Standard Oil Court, like classical economists, equated competition with rivalry, the struggle between several firms to realize economic opportunities'.[250] Non-competition (i.e. non-rivalry) values were, in principle, irrelevant. This was made clear by the Supreme Court in *National Society of Professional Engineers*.[251]

> In the (…) [rule of reason] category are agreements whose competitive effect can only be evaluated by analyzing the facts peculiar to the business, the history

248 *Northern Pac. Ry. Co. v U.S.*, 356 U.S. 1 (1958).

249 *U.S. v Topco Associates, Inc.*, 405 U.S. 596, 610-611 (1972).

250 Alan J. Meese, *Price Theory, Competition, and the Rule of Reason*, 2003 University of Illinois Law Review 77, 86 (2003). *See* René Joliet, The Rule of Reason in Antitrust Law; American, German and Common Market Laws in Comparative Perspective 59-60 (1967). (Stating in 1967 that 'American Antitrust Law is built upon absolute faith in the values of competition'.)

251 *National Soc. of Professional Engineers v U. S.*, 435 U.S. 679 (1978).

> of the restraint, and the reasons why it was imposed. In either event, the purpose of the analysis is to form a judgment about the competitive significance of the restraint; it is not to decide whether a policy favoring competition is in the public interest, or in the interest of the members of an industry. Subject to exceptions defined by statute, that policy decision has been made by the Congress.[252]

Notwithstanding the above grasp of competition, which, interestingly, resembles pretty much the paradigm of ordoliberalism, courts gradually converted competition into consumer welfare,[253] thus, letting co-operative efficiency justifications in the club.[254] For the time being, consumer welfare is the established primary, though not sole, purpose of antitrust law.[255] In *National Collegiate Athletic Ass'n v Board*

---

252 *National Soc. of Professional Engineers v U. S.*, 435 U.S. 679, 692 (1978). *See U.S. v National Lead Co.*, 63 F.Supp. 513, 525 (1945). ('Indeed, the major premise of the Sherman Act is that the suppression of competition (...) is in and of itself a public injury; or at any rate, that such suppression is a greater price than we want to pay for the benefits it sometimes secures. (...) Anyone is free to speculate whether, in the absence of the arrangement, the stimulus of competition might not have produced far greater strides in these beneficial directions. The economic theory underlying the Sherman Act is that, in the long run, competition is a more effective prod to production and a more trustworthy regulator of prices than even an enlightened combination.') *Contra* Phillip Areeda, *The Rule of Reason – A Catechism on Competition*, 55 Antitrust Law Journal 571, 579-580 (1986). ('In *Professional Engineers* (…) [t]he Supreme Court characterized this defense as a generalized appeal to the public interest and rejected it. The Court seemed to say that only competition counted and that it would listen only to the argument that a restraint, which superficially restrains competition, doesn't really do so when closely examined. I doubt that *Professional Engineers* will be applied so absolutely. In some cases, "public interest" justifications will be considered where they are powerful and the restraint is minor.')

253 Robert H. Bork, The Antitrust Paradox 107-115, 405-407 (1978); Phillip Areeda, *The Rule of Reason – A Catechism on Competition*, 55 Antitrust Law Journal 571, 572 (1986). Russell Pitman, *Consumer Surplus as the Appropriate Standard for Antitrust Enforcement*, 3(2) Competition Policy International 205 (2007). *Cf.* Richard A. Posner, Antitrust Law. An economic perspective 4 (1976). (Stressing antitrust's efficiency goal.).

254 David A. Ettinger and Gerard Mantese, *The Rule of Reason*, 64 Michigan Bar Journal 36, 40 (1985) ('[T]he defense that a practice improves efficiency has traditionally been rejected by the courts on the ground that the only issue is whether the practice enhances competition. (…) Later on, however, the courts have given indications that the economies or efficiencies resulting from a practice will be considered in determining whether a practice is unlawful. In doing so the courts have equated economies with pro-competitive effects, though whether a practice enhances efficiency need have no relation to its impact on the degree of competition in the market.')

255 *See* David A. Ettinger and Gerard Mantese, *The Rule of Reason*, 64 Michigan Bar Journal 36, 40 (1985); Phillip Areeda, *The Rule of Reason – A Catechism on Competition*, 55 Antitrust Law Journal 571, 572 (1986). ('Whether or not such consumer welfare is the exclusive objective of the antitrust laws, the Supreme Court has made clear that consumer welfare is the *prima facie* standard by which reasonableness is to be assessed.'); Frank H.

of Regents of University of Oklahoma,[256] the Supreme Court explicitly declared that the final purpose of the Sherman Act is consumer welfare.

> The anticompetitive consequences of this arrangement are apparent. Individual competitors lose their freedom to compete. Price is higher and output lower than they would otherwise be, and both are unresponsive to consumer preference. This latter point is perhaps the most significant, since 'Congress designed the Sherman Act as a *consumer welfare prescription*.'[257]

In *Broadcast Music, Inc. v Columbia Broadcasting System, Inc.*, the Supreme Court held that efficiency arguments may serve as valid justifications for an agreement.[258] Accordingly, 'competition' and 'pro-competitive' embrace all practices having an efficiency and welfare enhancing character.[259]

Easterbrook, *Workable Antitrust Policy*, 84 Michigan Law Review 1696, 1698 (1986). *Cf.* Herbert Hovenkamp, *Distributive Justice and the Antitrust Laws*, 51 George Washington Law Review 1 (1982). *See also FTC and DOJ Guidelines for Collaborations Among Competitors*, April 2000, 5-6; Robert H. Bork, The Antitrust Paradox 107-115, 405-407 (1978).

256 *National Collegiate Athletic Ass'n v Board of Regents of University of Oklahoma*, 468 U.S. 85 (1984).

257 *Id.* at 107. *See White and White, Inc. v American Hosp. Supply Corp.* 723 F.2d 495, 509 (1983). ('[E]xpensive medical technologies, a progressively aging population, the strain on public and private payment plans, and competition from franchised for-profit hospital chains, forced non-profit hospitals to realize that they cannot continue business as usual, but must demand new, more cost-effective, products and services. One approach has been to purchase supplies in volume as a member of a group. AHSC, recognizing, as the district court also found, that local suppliers will decline as the market so reforms itself, sought to prepare itself for the future. This Court cannot, like King Canute, employ the antitrust laws to hold back the tides that threaten these plaintiffs.')

258 *Broadcast Music, Inc. v Columbia Broadcasting System, Inc.*, 441 U.S. 1, 19-20 (1979). ('More generally, in characterizing this conduct under the *per se* rule, our inquiry must focus on whether the effect and, here because it tends to show effect, (...) the purpose of the practice are to threaten the proper operation of our predominantly free-market economy – that is, whether the practice facially appears to be one that would always or almost always tend to restrict competition and decrease output, and in what portion of the market, or instead one designed to "increase economic efficiency and render markets more, rather than less, competitive".') *Cf.* Timothy J. Muris, *The New Rule of Reason*, 57 Antitrust Law Journal 859, 861-862 (1989). ('If the conduct is inherently suspect, then the issue becomes the existence of efficiency justifications.'); Thomas C. Arthur, *A Workable Rule of Reason: a Less Ambitious Antitrust Role for the Federal Courts*, 68 Antitrust Law Journal 337, 363 (2000). ('There is no dispute that restraints can be justified as procompetitive if they produce productive efficiencies.') *See also* Lawrence A. Sullivan and Warren S. Grimes, The Law of Antitrust: an Integrated Handbook 205 (2000).

259 Alan J. Meese, *Price Theory, Competition, and the Rule of Reason*, 2003 University of Illinois Law Review 77, 78-79, 97 (2003). ('If society defines as competitive all marketplace activity that enhances its welfare, then many forms of cooperation, even

The proposition that the final effect on welfare should be identified also appears in the FTC's and DOJ's *Antitrust Guidelines for Collaborations among Competitors*, providing that the price, output, quality, service and innovation with the agreement are to be compared with the price, output, quality, service and innovation without the agreement.

> Rule of reason analysis focuses on the state of competition with, as compared to without, the relevant agreement. The central question is whether the agreement likely harms competition by increasing the ability or incentive profitably to raise price above or reduce output, quality, service or innovation below what would prevail in the absence of the relevant agreement.[260]

The above applies only with the proviso that this is only the mainstream approach, and there are several examples where courts, either explicitly or implicitly, have also taken balancers into consideration that were not related to the enhancement of competition.[261] For instance, the protection of small and medium-size enterprises' freedom of action played a central role in condemning RPM. Furthermore, it is also ambiguous what is meant by pro-competitive effects. May 'competition' be equated with the concept of 'social surplus'?[262] Is consumer surplus (welfare) that is indeed relevant and in fact meant by pro-competitive effects?[263]

---

those that eliminate competition between cooperating parties, are competitive in the sense that is relevant for antitrust purposes.') ('Put another way, a restraint is procompetitive if it affects productive activity in a manner that enhances the welfare of consumers.') *See* *Continental T.V., Inc. v GTE Sylvania Inc.*, 433 U.S. 36, 54-55 (1977), where the Court, while overruling the *per se* condemnation of vertical non-price restrictions, made a laconic reference to efficiency. ('Vertical restrictions promote interbrand competition by allowing the manufacturer to achieve certain efficiencies in the distribution of his products. These "redeeming virtues" are implicit in every decision sustaining vertical restrictions under the rule of reason. Economists have identified a number of ways in which manufacturers can use such restrictions to compete more effectively against other manufacturers.')

260 *FTC and DOJ Guidelines for Collaborations Among Competitors*, April 2000, 4.

261 Oliver Black, *Per Se Rules and Rules of Reason: What Are They?*, 18(3) European Competition Law Review 145, 148 (1997). ('Although the dominant tradition regards the purpose of section 1 as being solely to promote competition, the section does not mention competition. The other tradition in the case law, which may be called the recessive tradition, includes the promotion of competition among a broad and open-ended range of purposes which it attributes to section 1.')

262 For the stance that it is overall social (consumer plus producer) surplus that is relevant, *see* Robert H. Bork, The Antitrust Paradox 107-112 (1978); Wesley J. Liebeler, *Intrabrand 'Cartels' under GTE Sylvania*, 30 University of California at Los Angeles Law Review 1, 13-16 (1982); Oliver E. Williamson, *Economies as an Antitrust Defense Revisited*, 125 University of Pennsylvania Law Review 699, 703-713 (1977).

263 For the stance that it is consumer surplus or welfare that is relevant, *see* Lawrence A. Sullivan and Warren S. Grimes, The Law of Antitrust: an Integrated Handbook

The picture would not be complete without mentioning antitrust law's slightly different flavour in respect of self-regulation in 'learned professions'. The roots of the more compassive approach to professional self-regulation are to be found in *Goldfarb v Virginia State Bar*.[264] Although condemning the horizontal price-fixing committed by the bar as *per se* illegal, the Supreme Court dropped some hints in one of the judgment's footnotes indicating that professions might enjoy a more relaxed treatment in case of less blatant restraints of trade. While emphasizing that 'it is no disparagement of the practice of law as a profession to acknowledge that it has this business aspect, and [Section 1] of the Sherman Act "(o)n its face (…) shows a carefully studied attempt to bring within the Act every person engaged in business whose activities might restrain or monopolize commercial intercourse among the states"', the Court made a hidden guarded remark in footnote 17:

> The fact that a restraint operates upon a profession as distinguished from a business is, of course, relevant in determining whether that particular restraint violates the Sherman Act. It would be unrealistic to view the practice of professions as interchangeable with other business activities, and automatically to apply to the professions antitrust concepts which originated in other areas. The public service aspect, and other features of the professions, may require that a particular practice, which could properly be viewed as a violation of the Sherman Act in another context, be treated differently. We intimate no view on any other situation than the one with which we are confronted today.[265]

Notwithstanding the above declaration, it is very ambiguous how the balancing in respect of professions may be different from the one accomplished in case of 'ordinary' business activity.[266] The Supreme Court is 'slow to condemn rules

---

12-13 (2000); *FTC and DOJ Guidelines for Collaborations Among Competitors*, April 2000, 24-25; Stephen F. Ross, *Principles of Antitrust Law* 9-11 (1993).

264 421 U.S. 773 (1975).

265 *Id.* at 787-788. The above *obiter dicta* might be traced back to *Klor's, Inc. v Broadway-Hale Stores, Inc.*, where the Supreme Court – referring to *Apex Hosiery Co. v Leader et al.*, 310 U.S. 469 (1940) – indicated in footnote 7 'that the Act is aimed primarily at combinations having commercial objectives and is applied only to a very limited extent to organizations, like labor unions, which normally have other objectives.' 359 U.S. 207, 214 (1959). *Cf. National Soc. of Professional Engineers v U. S.*, 435 U.S. 679, 696 (1978) ('[T]he cautionary footnote in Goldfarb (…) cannot be read as fashioning a broad exemption under the Rule of Reason for learned professions.')

266 Marina Lao, Comment, *The Rule of Reason and Horizontal Restraints Involving Professionals*, 68 Antitrust Law Journal 499, 512 (2000) ('Despite the Supreme Court's frequent acknowledgement of the special characteristics of the professions, it had never, in reality, accorded preferential treatment to professionals until *CDA*, [*California Dental Association* in 1999,] at least not in horizontal restraint cases involving self-interested professionals.')

adopted by professional associations as unreasonable *per se*'.[267] It would not amount to an exaggeration to contend that '[e]thical norms may serve to regulate and promote (…) competition, and thus fall within the Rule of Reason'[268] and that in case of 'learned' professions courts are inclined to show more willingness to hear all the explanations proffered in order to justify the restraint at stake.[269]

The public interest character of the self-regulation also played a central role in the antitrust analysis in *U.S. v Brown University in Providence in State of R.I.*[270] Schools created a mechanism for collectively determining the amount of financial assistance given to students admitted to more than one of the schools and agreed that the financial assistance should be rendered only in case of need. The schools exchanged information concerning students and created a uniform formula for examining need. After concluding that 'providing financial assistance solely to needy students [is] a selective reduction or "discount" from the full tuition amount' and not a charitable gift, and as such the 'financial assistance to students is part and parcel of the process of setting tuition and thus a commercial transaction',[271] the Court of Appeals considered that 'the nature of higher education, and the asserted pro-competitive and pro-consumer features of the (…) [scheme], convince us that a full rule of reason analysis is in order here',[272] contrary to the district court's applying 'quick look'. The court of appeals intimated that the fact that in the case at stake, 'the quest for economic self-interest is professed to be absent'[273] played an important role in convincing the Court about the public interest objective of the restraint at stake.[274] It seems to be rather clear that without the recognition of

267 *FTC v Indiana Federation of Dentists*, 476 U.S. 447, 458-459 (1986). (Quoting the foregoing statement of *U.S. v Socony-Vacuum Oil Co.*, 310 U.S. 150 (1940).)

268 *National Soc. of Professional Engineers v U. S.*, 435 U.S. 679, 696 (1978).

269 *See American Medical Association*, 455 U.S. 676 (1982); *Matter of Massachusetts Board of Registration in Optometry*, 110 F.T.C. 549 (1988); *California Dental Ass'n v FTC*, 526 U.S. 756, 772-773 (1999). *See also* David A. Clanton, *The FTC and the Professions*, 52 Antitrust Law Journal 209 (1983); Kenneth G. Starling, *Antitrust Defenses in Physician Peer Review Cases*, 63 Antitrust Law Journal 399 (1995); John E. Kwoka, *The Federal Trade Commission and the Professions: a Quarter Century of Accomplishment and Some New Challenges*, 72 Antitrust Law Journal 997 (2005). Obviously, *per se* rules do apply to professions. *Arizona v Maricopa County Medical Soc.*, 457 U.S. 332 (1982). *Cf.* Marina Lao, *Comment, the Rule of Reason and Horizontal Restraints Involving Professionals*, 68 Antitrust Law Journal 499, 520 (2000). ('Despite frequent citations to this footnote in subsequent cases, the Supreme Court has never relied on *Goldfarb*'s public service distinction to justify treating horizontal restraints among members of a profession differently than similar restraints among non-professionals, as it should not.')

270 5 F.3d 658 (1993).

271 *Id.* at 666 and 668.

272 *Id.* at 678.

273 *Id.* at 678.

274 *See* the Court's analysis of *Professional Engineers* and *Indiana Dentists* at *id.* at 677.

the public interest objective of the scheme, the Court would have applied 'quick look', at least, and in case of 'ordinary' business a *per se* approach would have been warranted.[275]

Quick look

Since 1911 there had been no pretenders in the empire of antitrust to claim the dethronement of the *per se*/rule of reason dichotomy. However, in 1984, in *National Collegiate Athletic Association v Board of Regents of the University of Oklahoma* the Supreme Court rendered a judgment that simply did not fit the dualistic world: the Court gave consideration to an agreement fulfilling the requirements of one of the *per se* categories and gave a chance, though a limited one, to the defendant to protect himself.[276] Although the case had a very special fact pattern, with a set of unique characteristics, the judgment entailed a virtual antitrust creed generalizing the statements of the Court and prophesying a completely new antitrust world, where there is no firm *per se* rule of reason dichotomy.[277] Nonetheless, these prophecies turned out to be wrong: although the Supreme Court created a very narrow exception for *per se* illegality or, in order to be precise, a very limited relaxation of its rigidity: the whole concept seems to be applicable only to professional services and it is probably the consequence of the overly wide definition of the individual categories of *per se* illegal agreements.[278]

275 *See* Thomas C. Arthur, *A Workable Rule of Reason: a Less Ambitious Antitrust Role for the Federal Courts*, 68 Antitrust Law Journal 337, 364 (2000). (Characterizing the arrangement as naked price-fixing.) Interestingly, *U.S. v Brown University in Providence in State of R.I.* raises another issue: the economic nature of education. While the court had no problems with bringing it under the purview of the Sherman Act, in Europe this economic characteristic is far from accepted. This could be due to the differences as to the system and organization of education, the different role of state institutions and financing by the state.

276 The notion that the dichotomy of antitrust should be made up by a third pattern of analysis is not unprecedented. In *U.S. v Realty Multi-List, Inc.*, 629 F.2d 1351, 1369-1387 (1980), the Fifth Circuit introduced the concept of 'facial unreasonableness', according to which once plaintiff proved that the arrangement at stake amounts to a significant restriction affecting competition and that defendant has market power, the burden of proof shifts and the defendant has to come up with justifications. *See National Bancard Corp. (NaBanco) v VISA U.S.A.*, Inc., 596 F.Supp. 1231, 1250-1251 (1984). Nevertheless, the 'facial unreasonableness' concept cannot be regarded as the predecessor of the 'quick look' approach, as the former simplified the adjudication of some rule of reason agreements, in favour of the plaintiff, while the latter establishes an escape-hatch for agreements that, otherwise, would qualify as *per se* illegal.

277 *See* Thomas A. Piraino, *Reconciling the Harvard and Chicago Schools: A New Antitrust Approach for the 21st Century*, 82 Indiana Law Journal 345, 366-371 (2007).

278 In *U.S. v Socony-Vacuum Oil Co*, the Supreme Court held that all arrangements tampering with price structures amount to *per se* illegal price-fixing. *U.S. v Socony-Vacuum Oil Co.*, 310 U.S. 150 (1940). ('Any combination which tampers with price structures is engaged in an unlawful activity. Even though the members of the price-fixing group were

For the time being, the gist of the whole 'quick look' (or 'truncated/abbreviated rule of reason') seems to have crystallized out. While it is still ambiguous under which circumstances it is necessary to have a quick look into the context of the agreement, it seems to be clear that the concept is applicable only to agreements that are, or would be, otherwise *per se* illegal. Accordingly, 'quick look' carves out no territory from the realm of rule of reason. On the contrary, it occupies some of the areas of *per se* illegality.

The roots of 'quick look' are said to go back to *Broadcast Music, Inc. v Columbia Broadcasting System, Inc.*,[279] where the Supreme Court applied the rule of reason to an allegedly *per se* price-fixing scheme. While it could be argued that the Court's judgment narrowed the definition of *per se* price-fixing,[280] it seems that the case did not involve the endorsement of a naked *per se* price-fixing scheme, but an ancillary restraint, where the uniform prices were ancillary to a joint venture. The dispute centred around a collective management scheme of certain intellectual property rights, which issued 'blanket licences'. Individual licences could be purchased from the members directly. Accordingly, the entire scheme was a 'joint venture', which obviously entailed the need of indirectly fixing the price of the blanket licence. *Ergo*, the arrangement was not a naked price-fixing but the uniform price was simply the natural consequence of creating and marketing the blanket licence jointly. The Supreme Court expressed this in a very clear manner when saying that 'a bulk license of some type is a necessary consequence of the integration necessary to achieve these efficiencies, and a necessary consequence of an aggregate license is that its price must be established'.[281] Thus, the decision of the Supreme Court may be easily explained with the limits of the notion of *per se* price-fixing, since the agreement did not concern prices directly: the members established the organization managing their rights collectively, while this clearly efficiency-enhancing joint venture entailed a uniform price.

In *National Collegiate Athletic Association v Board of Regents of the University of Oklahoma*, the Supreme Court encountered an arrangement involving naked *per se* illegal price-fixing and output-limitation. According to the facts of the case,

---

in no position to control the market, to the extent that they raised, lowered, or stabilized prices they would be directly interfering with the free play of market forces.'). In *U.S. v Topco Associates, Inc.*, the Supreme Court condemned an essentially joint purchasing and marketing arrangement as *per se* illegal market division. The members of the agreement were small grocery stores, who had established Topco, a cooperative association. Topco served as a purchasing agent for the members. Most of the procured items were distributed under brand names owned by Topco. Notwithstanding the foregoing circumstance, the clause of the agreement allocating exclusive marketing territories to the members was condemned as *per se* illegal (naked) market division. *U.S. v Topco Associates, Inc.*, 405 U.S. 596 (1972).

279 *Broadcast Music, Inc. v Columbia Broadcasting System, Inc.*, 441 U.S. 1 (1979).

280 The Supreme Court stressed that '[n]ot all arrangements among actual or potential competitors that have an impact on price are *per se* violations of the Sherman Act or even unreasonable restraints.' *Id.* at 23.

281 *Id.* at 21.

NCAA was the professional organization of amateur collegiate sport, heavily regulating the selling of the telecast rights for football games.[282] The NCAA fixed (recommended) the price of the telecasts and, *inter alia*, limited the number of telecasts per member institution. The arguments proffered for justifying the restrictions related to the promotion of game attendance and the preservation of the amateur character of the tournament. Nonetheless, since the measures of the NCAA fulfilled, as indicated by the Court, the conditions of two *per se* illegal categories, *viz.* price-fixing and limitation of output, the proffered justifications should not have been heard at all according to the traditional notion. The Supreme Court's judgment deduced this conclusion from the case-law very unequivocally. Nevertheless, with a sudden about-face, the Supreme Court 'decided that it would be inappropriate to apply a *per se* rule to this case'.[283] At the same time, however, the Court also refused to analyse the restraints under the rule of reason. Instead, the Court showed readiness to take a quick look at the justifications proffered by the NCAA, albeit the time spent on this investigation enabled only the examination of the question whether the arguments were facially plausible, i.e. theoretically acceptable. With this approach the Supreme Court created a third concept for antitrust analysis, subsequently denominated as 'quick look'. The phrase 'truncated/abbreviated rule of reason' is also used for this concept. Nevertheless, it is to be emphasized that 'quick look' is a threshold analysis for the application of the rule of reason. If the quick look taken at the restraint reveals facially plausible justifications, the court is supposed to go with a full-blown rule of reason. In this sense, the doctrine of 'quick look' is a way of transposing a *per se* illegal agreement into the rule of reason box but it is not capable of enabling the final assessment of the agreement.

Accordingly, in *National Collegiate Athletic Association v Board of Regents of the University of Oklahoma* the arrangement at stake was 'less ancillary', or rather, could be easily classified as naked *per se* illegal price-fixing and output-limitation, contrary to *Broadcast Music, Inc. v Columbia Broadcasting System, Inc.*, where the justifications proffered by the defendant concerned the collective marketing scheme, i.e. the blanket licence, and not the fixing of the price, which was a side-effect. Since the collective marketing turned out to be efficient, it served as a pardon for the uniform price as well; i.e. it was the blanket licence that cried for mercy and not the price-fixing, which was somehow ancillary to the former. On the other hand, in *National Collegiate Athletic Association v Board of Regents of the University of Oklahoma*, it was the price-fixing and the limitation of the output themselves that asked for quarter, although they emerged in the context of a genuine 'joint venture'.

---

282 Besides football, the NCAA had not regulated the telecasting of other athletic events. *National Collegiate Athletic Association v Board of Regents of the University of Oklahoma,* 468 U.S. 85, 88-89 (1984).

283 *National Collegiate Athletic Association v Board of Regents of the University of Oklahoma,* 468 U.S. 85, 100 (1984).

At the same time, it is to be emphasized that the Supreme Court, when examining whether the agreement at stake met the conditions of *per se* illegality, mingled the general theorem of *per se* illegality with the notion of *per se* illegal price-fixing. The Court did not start with saying that this is the definition of *per se* illegal price-fixing and let us see whether the agreement at bench fits this box but it went behind the veil of the *per se* category concerned and tried to make the characterization on the basis of the fundamental definition of *per se* illegality. The question according to the Court was not whether the agreement concerned price-fixing but whether it is, or rather should be, *per se* illegal, because it is always or almost always harmful to competition without any realistic chance for redeeming virtue.

> More generally, in characterizing this conduct under the *per se* rule, our inquiry must focus on whether the effect and, here because it tends to show effect, (…) the purpose of the practice are to threaten the proper operation of our predominantly free-market economy – that is, whether the practice facially appears to be one that would always or almost always tend to restrict competition and decrease output, and in what portion of the market, or instead one designed to 'increase economic efficiency and render markets more, rather than less, competitive'.[284]

While the incriminated restrictions maintained by the National Collegiate Athletic Association (NCAA) could have been classified as ancillary to a legitimate end, for they appeared in the context of a joint venture and of several other genuine ancillary restraints (rules of the game),[285] the Court seems to have been convinced that they were naked:[286] hence, the defendant had the headache-producing task of

284 *Id.* at 19-20.

285 *See* Alan J. Meese, *Farewell to the Quick Look: Redefining the Scope and Content of the Rule of Reason*, 68 Antitrust Law Journal 461 (2000). ('The restraints did not stand alone, however, but were instead ancillary to a joint venture that produced college football.'); Lawrence A. Sullivan and Warren S. Grimes, The Law of Antitrust: an Integrated Handbook 211 (2000). ('The Court's refusal to apply a *per se* rule to joint pricing was anything but revolutionary. The record showed no conventional price fixing agreement; the NCAA is no conventional cartel. Some integration had taken place – integration of a fairly complex kind.')

286 The Court rejected NCAA's reference to lack of market power by explaining that 'as a matter of law, the absence of proof of market power does not justify a naked restriction on price or output'. *National Collegiate Athletic Association v Board of Regents of the University of Oklahoma,* 468 U.S. 85, 86 (1984). The Court, later on, reiterated this proposition, referring to the arrangement at stake as a naked agreement: 'as a matter of law, the absence of proof of market power does not justify a naked restriction on price or output. To the contrary, when there is an agreement not to compete in terms of price or output, 'no elaborate industry analysis is required to demonstrate the anticompetitive character of such an agreement'. (…) We have never required proof of market power in such a case. *This naked restraint* on price and output requires some competitive justification even in the absence of a detailed market analysis.') Emphasis added. *Id.* at 109-110. *Cf.* William

demonstrating that price-fixing and limitation of output themselves were reasonable in the industry concerned, i.e. competition in terms of price and quality would be ruinous, taking into account the joint provision of the service. Nevertheless, in fact, it was the latter circumstance that featured an ancillary flavour to the otherwise *per se* practices: it could have been argued that the service at stake is basically not the individual matches but the tournament at large, since the meaning and the value of the individual matches could be interpreted only in the context of the entire tournament. Therewith, the situation was complicated also by the Supreme Court's judgments in *U.S. v Socony-Vacuum Oil Co.* and in *Arizona v Maricopa County Medical Soc.*, which established that naked price-fixing may never escape *per se* condemnation, irrespective of the industry concerned.[287]

While the Court gave indications about what the substance of the 'quick look' approach is, the question was still left open under which circumstances the concept is to be applied. Namely, after considering the concept of *per se* illegality, the Court suddenly and surprisingly held that 'it would be inappropriate to apply a

---

E. Cohen, *Per Se Illegality and Truncated Rule of Reason: the Search for a Foreshortened Antitrust Analysis* III. 2. (1997), http://www.ftc.gov/opp/jointvent/-persepap.shtm. ('The Court has not been entirely clear in defining the circumstances under which truncation is appropriate. Confusion may have resulted from its use of language focused on whether a practice is sufficiently 'naked'. The Court could not have been using the term 'naked' in its commonly employed sense of lacking a relationship to procompetitive benefits or to some other integration or agreement involving the same parties. If that were the intended meaning, *NCAA* and *Indiana Federation of Dentists* would entail serious internal contradictions.'); Eric D. Daniels, *Did the Supreme Court Fumble?: the Supreme Court's Failure to Endorse a Market Power Threshold to the Application of the Rule of Reason for Cases under Section 1 of the Sherman Act in NCAA v Board or Regent*, 27 Boston College Law Review 579, 601-602 (1986). ('If this case involved a naked restriction, which is one that is inherently likely to enhance price or restrict output while offering no competitive benefits, it would have been proper to condemn the NCAA's practices under the *per se* doctrine. (…) In its decision to apply the rule of reason to review the legality of the NCAA's practices, the Court implied that the NCAA's practices were not a naked restriction on price or output'.). Stephen Calkins, *California Dental Association: Not a Quick Look but not the Full Monty*, 67 Antitrust Law Journal 495, 543 (2000). ('Given *NCAA*'s association with the 'quick look', this has led to the suggestion that the 'quick look' is available only for 'naked restraints', with all other restraints being analysed under the full-blown rule of reason. Of course parties to what is truly a naked restraint on price and output should be subjected to the *per se* rule, because the arrangement would 'always or almost always tend to restrict competition and reduce output'. The only way to read *NCAA* sensibly is to presume that the Court actually was referring to arrangements that are perilously close to ones that are *per se* illegal.')

287 *U.S. v Socony-Vacuum Oil Co.*, 310 U.S. 150, 222 (1940). ('Whatever may be its peculiar problems and characteristics, the Sherman Act, so far as price-fixing agreements are concerned, establishes one uniform rule applicable to all industries alike.'); *Arizona v Maricopa County Medical Soc.*, 457 U.S. 332, 346 (1982).

per se rule to this case',[288] without giving any clear indication about the motives of its about-face. Therefore, the pivotal question is when the court should look at the context of the agreement. Failing a clarification regarding the purview of 'quick look', the analysis is to proceed from the reasons that put the Court off applying the outright prohibition embedded in *per se* illegality. The Court established that

> [t]his decision is not based on a lack of judicial experience with this type of arrangement, on the fact that the NCAA is organized as a nonprofit entity, or on our respect for the NCAA's historic role in the preservation and encouragement of intercollegiate amateur athletics. Rather, what is critical is that this case involves an industry in which horizontal restraints on competition are essential if the product is to be available at all.[289]

Accordingly, professional self-regulation was not only traditional in the market concerned but it was essential for its operation.

> Our decision not to apply a *per se* rule to this case rests in large part on our recognition that a certain degree of cooperation is necessary if the type of competition that petitioner and its member institutions seek to market is to be preserved. It is reasonable to assume that most of the regulatory controls of the NCAA are justifiable means of fostering competition among amateur athletic teams and therefore procompetitive because they enhance public interest in intercollegiate athletics. The specific restraints on football telecasts that are challenged in this case do not, however, fit into the same mold as do rules defining the conditions of the contest, the eligibility of participants, or the manner in which members of a joint enterprise shall share the responsibilities and the benefits of the total venture.[290]

---

288 *Id.* at 100.

289 *Id.* at 100-101. *Cf. California Dental Ass'n v FTC*, 526 U.S. 756, 780-781 (1999), where the Supreme Court shed more light on the purview of 'quick look', making certain that some, though rather modest, enquiry in the context of the agreement cannot be spared in order to ascertain whether 'quick look' is applicable. ('[T]here is generally no categorical line to be drawn between restraints that give rise to an intuitively obvious inference of anticompetitive effect and those that call for more detailed treatment. What is required, rather, is an enquiry meet for the case, looking to the circumstances, details, and logic of a restraint. The object is to see whether the experience of the market has been so clear, or necessarily will be, that a confident conclusion about the principal tendency of a restriction will follow from a quick (or at least quicker) look, in place of a more sedulous one. And of course what we see may vary over time, if rule-of-reason analyses in case after case reach identical conclusions.')

290 *National Collegiate Athletic Association v Board of Regents of the University of Oklahoma*, 468 U.S. 85, 117 (1984).

While the foregoing excerpt automatically raises the question that if the restrictions on telecasting at stake do not belong to the nucleus of the regulation envisaged to be tolerated, why did the Court still apply a more tolerant approach towards them? The quick answer may be that the Court was influenced by the very same circumstances that were said not to be relevant: the non-profit character of the NCAA and its prestige. At the same moment, the Supreme Court seemed to refuse to accept non-economic considerations as justification for the restraint on competition, and considered that the justifications brought up by NCAA were not plausible on the face of it.[291] Probably, the Court – notwithstanding the *per se* characterization of the conduct at stake – may subconsciously not have been able to dismiss the idea from its thoughts that the restraint in question might not have been a naked one but theoretically it could be ancillary to the joint venture of producing football, i.e. without some analysis it cannot be established with the sufficient degree of certainty that it is unrelated to the joint venture.

National Collegiate Athletic Association v Board of Regents of the University of Oklahoma was certainly a remarkable departure from settled case-law and it caused considerable excitement in the scholarship. Though later on it turned out that 'quick look' analysis is heavily limited in its scope, several scholars viewed 'quick look' as the long awaited Messiah of antitrust, which would fundamentally remake the structure of antitrust analysis. Basically, two lines of interpretation emerged.[292]

The first school argued that 'quick look' absorbed *per se* illegality: in practical terms, there is hardly any agreement without the theoretical chance of proffering justifications.[293] Albeit *per se* illegality might still be applicable to 'smoke-filled

291 Contrary to the dissent of Justice White and Justice Rehnquist, who considered the restraint to be reasonable due to fostering the non-economic goal of amateurism. *Id.* at 134-135.

292 *Cf.* Terry Calvani, *Some Thoughts on the Application of the Rule of Reason and the Per Se Rule* SH064 ALI-ABA 27, 44. (2003). ('If the abbreviated rule is applied only when the anticompetitive effects are so obvious that "an observer with even a rudimentary understanding of economics could conclude that the agreement in question would have an anticompetitive effect on customers and markets", what is left of the *per se* rule? There are a couple of possible answers. Application of the *per se* and abbreviated rules involve restraints that are inherently anticompetitive. Although the traditional wisdom barred defendants from proffering efficiency justifications for *per se* offenses, one reading of *California Dental* suggests that a court ought to consider such justifications. While the Court did not specifically address "plausibility", perhaps the efficiency justifications must be "plausible" before they can be considered. This would not leave much to the *per se* rule as it has been traditionally interpreted. A second approach would be suggest that there is still a core of *per se* offenses, but that it is limited to the classic price-fixing, bid-rigging, market allocation schemes associated with cigar smoke-filled hotel rooms. The problem with this approach is that divination of the classic price-fixing case is easier said than done. Indeed, some sought to characterize *BMI* as just such a case.')

293 William E. Cohen, *Per Se Illegality and Truncated Rule of Reason: the Search for a Foreshortened Antitrust Analysis* III. 3. (1997), http://www.ftc.gov/opp/jointvent/

hotel room' cartels, cases reaching the bench are rarely of such nature. The advocates of the foregoing interpretation submitted that *per se* illegality is dead, or at least it is dying, the only antitrust analysis being the rule of reason, which, on the other hand, might be fragmented according to a sliding scale approach, i.e. the strictness of the scrutiny might vary according to the restraint involved.[294] Interestingly, this approach was supported by the FTC as well.[295] Nevertheless, subsequent Supreme Court judgments revealed that *per se* illegality is enjoying good health:[296] in *FTC v Superior Court Trial Lawyers Association*,[297] *Palmer v BRG of Georgia, Inc.*,[298] *Northwest Wholesale Stationers, Inc. v Pacific Stationery & Printing Co.*,[299] and *Jefferson Parish Hosp. Dist. No. 2 v Hyde*[300] the Court showed no hesitation when *per se* condemning naked restraints.[301]

The second school saw 'quick look' as a wedge to be driven between the two traditional pigeonholes, which embraced the agreements on the edges of the two

---

persepap.shtm. (Arguing that basically all *per se* illegal arrangement are candidates for a 'quick look'; therewith, arguing that not only *per se* agreements are covered by the truncated rule of reason, but also arrangements having been on the edge of the rule of reason. Accordingly, the steps of the analysis to be done can be summarized as follows. First, it is to be established 'whether a restraint is of a type traditionally condemned as *per se* unlawful or is so seriously anticompetitive that it becomes a candidate for truncated treatment. (…) If the first test is satisfied, the second issue would be whether defendant has presented competitive justifications that viewed facially, on argument alone, appear legitimate. If not, the conduct would be condemned, just as under modern *per se* analysis. If the second test is satisfied, the third enquiry would be whether the competitive justifications can be sustained as a matter of fact.')

294 7 Phillip Areeda, Antitrust Law ¶ 1507c, at 399-403 (1986).

295 *Matter of Massachusetts Board of Registration in Optometry*, 110 F.T.C. 549, 603-604 (1988). Nevertheless, the FTC, finally, abandoned the notion that the *per se* category was utterly replaced by the 'quick look'. *California Dental Association v FTC*, 526 U.S. 756 (1999). *See* James A. Keyte, *What It Is and How It Is Being Applied: the 'Quick Look' Rule of Reason*, 11-SUM Antitrust 21, 21 (1997).

296 *See* James A. Keyte, *What It Is and How It Is Being Applied: the 'Quick Look' Rule of Reason*, 11-SUM Antitrust 21, 22 (1997); Lawrence A. Sullivan and Warren S. Grimes, The Law of Antitrust: an Integrated Handbook 219 (2000). ('[T]he Court has done nothing to suggest that it would countenance giving up or weakening the *per se* rule in special situations. (…) On the other hand, the fact that challenged conduct bears some surface similarities to a *per se* wrong need not end the inquiry.')

297 493 U.S. 411 (1990).

298 498 U.S. 46 (1990).

299 472 U.S. 284 (1985).

300 466 U.S. 2 (1984).

301 Lawrence A. Sullivan and Warren S. Grimes, The Law of Antitrust: an Integrated Handbook 220 (2000). ('The balanced solution is to continue to recognize the *per se* rules, as the Court is doing, but to concede the possibility that in some limited instances it may be possible to see even on a quick look that the purpose and the likely effect of the challenged conduct is not the cartel-like competition harm at which the *per se* rule is aimed.')

categories, i.e. *per se* illegality and rule of reason. A variant of this approach was the stance that the analysis in cases characterized by the truncated rule of reason completely overruled or replaced the traditional dichotomy and the new test embraced a big rule of reason analysis.[302] The new category replacing *per se* illegality was the pigeonhole of 'inherently suspect' agreements, which, nevertheless, encompassed traditional *per se* agreements and some agreements that were previously part of the rule of reason but close to one of the *per se* categories. Moreover, all agreements had the chance to bring up justifying arguments, though the handling of these arguments was rather truncated in case of 'inherently suspect' agreements.[303] This approach was criticized for its enabling too 'aggressive'

302 *See* Jennifer E. Gladieux, *Towards a Single Standard for Antitrust: the Federal Trade Commission's Evolving Rule of Reason*, 5 George Mason Law Review 471, 471 (1997); Timothy J. Muris, *The New Rule of Reason*, 57 Antitrust Law Journal 859, 859 (1989) (Arguing that 'there is only one form of [antitrust] analysis, the rule of reason'.)

303 *Matter of Massachusetts Board of Registration in Optometry*, 110 F.T.C. 549, 603-604 (1988). ('First (…) there is no bright line that separates *per se* from rule of reason analysis, thus destroying the neat taxonomy that characterized many an antitrust course outline. Second (…) the essential inquiry under both [rules] is the same, *i.e.*, 'whether or not the challenged restraint enhances competition.' (…) One important – perhaps the most important – result of the cases is that the utility of the conventional labeling exercise has been called into question. (…) First, we ask whether the restraint is "inherently suspect". In other words, is the practice the kind that appears likely, absent an efficiency justification, to "restrict competition and restrict output"? If the restraint is not inherently suspect, then the traditional rule of reason, with attendant issues of market definition and power, must be employed. But if it is inherently suspect, we must pose a *second* question: Is there a plausible efficiency justification for the practice? That is, does the practice seem capable of creating or enhancing competition (*e.g.*, by reducing the costs of producing or marketing the product, creating a new product, or improving the operation of the market)? Such an efficiency defense is plausible if it cannot be rejected without extensive factual inquiry. If it is not plausible, then the restraint can be quickly condemned. But if the efficiency justification is plausible, further inquiry – a *third inquiry* – is needed to determine whether the justification is really valid. If it is, it must be assessed under the full balancing test of the rule of reason. But if the justification is, on examination, not valid, then the practice is unreasonable and unlawful under the rule of reason without further inquiry – there are no likely benefits to offset the threat to competition.'). William E. Cohen, *Per Se Illegality and Truncated Rule of Reason: the Search for a Foreshortened Antitrust Analysis* III. 3 (1997), http://www.ftc.gov/opp/jointvent/persepap.shtm. (Arguing that basically all *per se* illegal arrangements are candidates for a 'quick look'; therewith, arguing that not only *per se* agreements are covered by the truncated rule of reason, but also arrangements having been on the edge of the rule of reason. Accordingly, the steps of the analysis to be done are to be summarized as follows. First, it is to be established 'whether a restraint is of a type traditionally condemned as *per se* unlawful or is so seriously anticompetitive that it becomes a candidate for truncated treatment. (…) If the first test is satisfied, the second issue would be whether defendant has presented competitive justifications that viewed facially, on argument alone, appear legitimate. If not, the conduct would be condemned, just as under modern *per se* analysis. If the second test is satisfied, the third inquiry would

antitrust enforcement. Notwithstanding the 'inherently suspect' agreements' chance for raising justifications, it cannot be disregarded that the burden of proof would shift on the defendant, even in case of agreements where traditional rule of reason required the profound analysis of the anti-competitive effects.[304] This approach was also adopted by the FTC; nevertheless, at the end of the day the FTC returned to the traditional characterization and abandoned the above approach, contending that 'although there have been some oblique suggestions in Supreme Court cases that perhaps the categories had merged, the Court later returned to distinguishing between *per se* and rule of reason categories'.[305] Furthermore, the Supreme Court in *California Dental Association* pointed out that 'quick look' cases cannot be interpreted in a way that they extended the category of *per se* illegality, i.e. rule of reason agreements retain their traditional legal status. The Court reversed the FTC's *per se* characterization, holding that restraints on price advertising are to be analysed under the rule of reason. The Court emphasized that in all 'quick look' cases,

> which have formed the basis for what has come to be called abbreviated or 'quick look' analysis under the rule of reason, an observer with even a rudimentary understanding of economics could conclude that the arrangements in question would have had an effect on customers and markets. (…) As in such cases, quick-look analysis carries the day when the great likelihood of anticompetitive effects can easily be ascertained.[306]

Accordingly, 'quick look' does not concern agreements that, beforehand, have been examined under the rule of reason.[307]

---

be whether the competitive justifications can be sustained as a matter of fact.'). *See* Terry Calvani, *Some Thoughts on the Application of the Rule of Reason and the Per Se Rule*, 2003 ALI-ABA Course of Study 27, 34-35 (2003).

304 Joseph Kattan, *The Role of Efficiency Considerations in the Federal Trade Commission's Antitrust Analysis*, 64 Antitrust Law Journal 613, 615 (1996). ('Given the enormous difficulties that can be associated with proving valid efficiencies, the effect of the approach was to condemn conduct that may or may not have been efficient but had not been shown to have anticompetitive effects, solely because the respondent had failed to overcome the complex problems (or costs) of proving that the conduct was positively procompetitive.')

305 *In re California Dental Association*, 121 F.T.C. 190, 199 (1996).

306 *California Dental Association v FTC*, 526 U.S. 756, 770 (1999). *See United States v Brown University*, 5 F.3d 658, 672 (1993), and *Chicago Professional Sports Ltd. Partnership v National Basketball*, 95 F.3d 593, 600 (1996), where the appellate courts refused to apply the 'quick look' and, instead, declared that a full rule of reason was necessary.

307 *See American Ad Management, Inc., v GTE Corp.*, 92 F.3d 781, 789-790 (1996). (Contending that only agreements belonging to one of the *per se* categories may be covered by 'quick look' analysis, while agreements coming traditionally under the rule of reason

Summary

In sum, the analysis under Section 1 is twofold: while only unreasonable restraints of trade are forbidden (rule of reason), in case of certain kinds of agreements this feature is conclusively presumed (*per se* illegality).

Per se agreements are automatically condemned implying that there is no need to consider the market context of the arrangement ('automatic condemnation' rule) and, as a matter of law, no justifying arguments can be heard ('no defence' rule).

This ancient rule of US antitrust was softened by the Supreme Court's introduction of the concept of 'quick look', which provides that a limited 'hearing' of justifying arguments can be granted in order to find out whether these justifications, if proved indeed, are at least theoretically eligible for being accepted; if the arguments meet this burden, they are granted a full scrutiny. Nevertheless, 'quick look' leaves the 'automatic condemnation' rule intact, i.e. the anti-competitive impact of the agreement is presumed and the analysis, in case of a full scrutiny, starts with the proffered justifications. The purview of 'quick look' is ambiguous; one thing remains certain: it applies only in exceptional cases, for the most part to professions and markets where cooperation is necessary 'if the product is to be available at all'.[308]

All agreements that are not presumed to be *per se* illegal deserve a full-blown rule of reason. Under this test, first, the plaintiff has to prove anti-competitive impact, a surrogate of which can be the proof of market power. Once competitive harm is confirmed, the burden shifts to the defendant to proffer justifications. Defendants can argue both that the agreement increases the intensity of competition and that it increases efficiency. If the defendant meets its burden of proof, the plaintiff can try to prove that there are less restrictive ways of achieving the same benefits.

In case of substantiated justifications, the court has to balance the anti-competitive impact and the justifications and decide whether the latter outweigh the former. The relevant question is whether the arrangement in question, at the end of the day, enhances consumer welfare. Since this question cannot be reduced to numerical terms, the court exercises a qualitative balancing. The general perception is that courts tend to show some deference to the sound business decisions of undertakings: in case of plausible and substantiated justifications courts tend to decide for the defendant (see Figure 4.2).

---

remain in this pigeonhole. '[T]his so-called "quick look" analysis is the exception, rather than the rule. "Proving injury to competition in a rule of reason case almost uniformly requires a claimant to prove the relevant market and to show the effects of competition within that market." For many of the same reasons used to apply the rule of reason analysis, the present case does not present the type of naked restraint on price or output that would justify a "quick look". Accordingly, the district court was correct in requiring proof of the relevant geographic and product markets, as well as proof of the effects within these markets.')

308 *National Collegiate Athletic Association v Board of Regents of the University of Oklahoma,* 468 U.S. 85, 100-101 (1984).

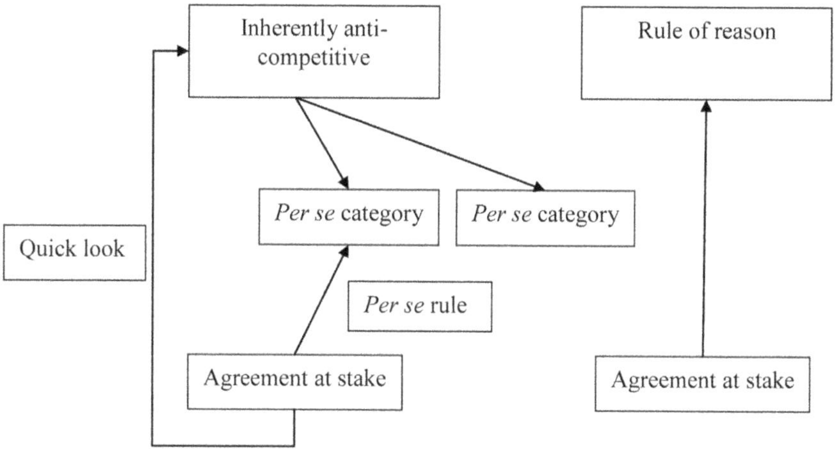

Figure 4.2

Comparative summary

Both US antitrust and EU competition law use a twofold categorization of agreements. In US antitrust law, *per se* illegal agreements are condemned automatically ('automatic condemnation' rule) and without any possibility to consider the defendant's arguments concerning justification ('no defence' rule). This proposition was supplemented with the qualification introduced by the concept of 'quick look', which is a narrow corridor from *per se* agreements to rule of reason: in some cases the court can give a limited chance to the defendant to name its justifications and if these are facially plausible, the court will go on with a full-blown rule of reason, where, nevertheless, the anti-competitive impact of the agreement is presumed. On the other hand, the Supreme Court was not clear about the purview of 'quick look'; however, it seems that this concept applies to professional services and markets that inevitably require some horizontal cooperation.

Per se categories are rather strict, and it is submitted that their inflexible nature was probably the main reason that led to the introduction of 'quick look'.[309]

309 *See* Alan J. Meese, *Farewell to the Quick Look: Redefining the Scope and Content of the Rule of Reason*, 68 Antitrust Law Journal 461, 478-480 (2000). (Criticizing *NCAA* because it 'endorsed *Topco*[, which defined *per se* illegal agreements very broadly,] as the general rule, carving out an exception only for those cases in which some horizontal restraint of competition is necessary to create the product in question', instead of confining the definition of such agreements. 'Moreover, when analyzing the arrangement's "anticompetitive" effects as part of its truncated rule of reason analysis, the Court echoed a concern expressed in *Topco*, by stating that "[i]ndividual competitors lose their freedom to compete." Finally, in an approach more reminiscent of *Von's Grocery* than *Sylvania*,

In *U.S. v Socony-Vacuum Oil Co*, the Supreme Court held that all arrangements tampering with price structures amount to *per se* illegal price-fixing.[310] In *Broadcast Music, Inc. v Columbia Broadcasting System, Inc.*, the Supreme Court encountered an arrangement that did tamper with prices but was apparently not naked.[311] 'Quick look' was introduced to save such agreements from the rigidity of *per se* rules.

Arguably, 'quick look' could be compared to the *prima facie* assessment that occurs in case of interim measures (Article 8 of Regulation 1/2003). Nevertheless, there are numerous fundamental differences between the two concepts. First, interim measures are *per definitionem* provisory, and enable, because of lack of time, an interlocutory decision on the basis of 'balance of probabilities', postponing the final decision on the merits. On the other hand, quick look is a method that governs the final adjudication of the merits. Second, the provisions on interim measures, as noted, are justified by the lack of time: the decision maker, on the basis of Article 8 of Regulation 1/2003, pressed by 'urgency due to the risk of serious and irreparable damage to competition', has to adopt a provisory measure on the basis of the '*prima facie* finding of infringement'. This *prima facie* nature relates to both factual and substantive legal questions. On the other hand, under quick look the quickness of the look at the justifications is not explained by the need of a fast decision but by the fact that the agreements coming under the purview of this concept are, in principle, *per se* illegal. Here, the court is not pressed for time but it gives a limited chance to the defendant to present its justifications concerning an agreement that, otherwise, would be condemned automatically and without a chance for proffering justifying arguments. Under the quick look the agreement gets a full inquiry as regards the anti-competitive projections, taking into account that this concept is applicable only to agreements the anti-competitive nature of which is presumed automatically (anti-competitive by object in the EU; *per se* illegal in the US); i.e. it is fully investigated whether the arrangement fits one of the *per se* categories. The quickness of the quick look is certainly explained by the consideration not to frustrate the advantages of the *per se* rules: i.e. clear-cut provisions, legal certainty, predictability etc.

---

the Court shifted the burden of justification to the defendants, without meaningful proof of anticompetitive effects, let alone proof of market power. (…) But, this simply begs the central question: why subject either restraint to a quick look, instead of the sort of full-blown rule of reason treatment usually accorded ancillary restraints, for instance? The mere fact that a restraint limits the "freedom"' of the parties to it cannot itself constitute cognizable antitrust harm; enforcement of voluntary agreements enhances freedom. Moreover, advances in economic theory of the sort recognized in *Sylvania* have taught that horizontal restraints previously deemed anticompetitive are in many cases procompetitive attempts to minimize the costs associated with market contracting.')

310 *U.S. v Socony-Vacuum Oil Co.*, 310 U.S. 150 (1940). ('Any combination which tampers with price structures is engaged in an unlawful activity.').

311 *Broadcast Music, Inc. v Columbia Broadcasting System, Inc.*, 441 U.S. 1 (1979).

The counterpart of *per se* illegal agreements in Europe is the notion of agreements anti-competitive by object. Nonetheless, the concept of object-type agreements is more flexible than the American notion; or rather, there is some flexibility in the European notion.[312] Moreover, even object type agreements may benefit from an individual exemption under Article 101(3), while *per se* illegal agreements traditionally cannot be justified. However, it is submitted that with the introduction of the 'quick look', the latter has ceased to be a remarkable divergence.

The most important difference between the structure of competition law analysis of US antitrust and EU competition law is admitted to be that the individual exemption of Article 101(3) is, theoretically, available to all agreements and no categories of agreements are as such outright excluded from the chance to meet the requirements of Article 101(3), while in US antitrust law the prohibition of *per se* agreements is watertight.[313] Nevertheless, this proposition was falsified by the Supreme Court's introduction of 'quick look'. Whereas the purview of 'quick look' is ambiguous, it is clear that there is no escape-hatch for all *per se* illegal agreements. It still remains a difference that 'quick look' applies only to some *per se* agreements, e.g. professional services and services that inevitably presuppose some horizontal cooperation, while, theoretically, Article 101(3) is available to all agreements. Nonetheless, it is hardly conceivable that the call of Article 101(3) would be addressed to genuine hardcore agreements; instead, it seems that this proposition is meant to preach the hope of absolution only to those types of agreements that would have a potential for a 'quick look', i.e. professional services that inevitably presuppose some sort of horizontal cooperation.

Agreements not warranting automatic condemnation deserve a full market analysis on both sides of the Atlantic. At the end of the day the two regimes enable the examination of the same issues: the analysis of effect type agreements under Article 101(1) and 101(3) embraces all the aspects that are covered by the rule of reason analysis, and *vice versa*.[314] Nevertheless, the architecture of the analysis and the allocation of the burden of proof are not the same in the two systems; and one should not forget that the devil is in the details.

The European test is determined by the bifurcation of Article 101. First, it is to be analysed whether the agreement has anti-competitive effects under 101(1), a point where the burden of proof is borne by the competition authority or the plaintiff. In this phase some justifications can be brought up by the defendant,

---

312 *See* Richard Whish, Competition Law 120-121 (2009). (Emphasizing that the building of categories of agreements that are anti-competitive by object 'slightly oversimplifies the law'.)

313 Richard Whish, Competition Law 118-119 (2009).

314 Alexander Schaub, *Continued Focus on Reform: Recent Developments in EC Competition Policy*, *in* 2001 Annual proceedings of the Fordham Corporate Law Institute 31, 44 (Hawk ed., 2002). ('Outside the field of hardcore restrictions, Article 81(1) and 81(3), taken together, contain all the constituent parts of a rule of reason.')

because the question to be answered is whether in sum the agreement enhances or sets back competition. It is submitted that in this regard competition means rivalry (competitive process). The second phase of the analysis is Article 101(3), where the defendant bears the burden of proof. Here, the question is not whether the agreement deteriorates the competitive process; if this was not the case, there would be no need to have recourse to Article 101(3). Instead, the question is whether the agreement increases efficiency and whether these efficiency benefits outweigh the harm caused by restricting competition; in other words, the relevant question is whether the ultimate effect on consumer welfare is positive or negative. The European test is structured in a way that the burden of proof regarding arguments that are in accordance with conventional wisdom – i.e. competition in terms of rivalry is the very best mechanism of the market – is placed on the person alleging the infringement of Article 101(1), and the burden of proof regarding arguments that are not in accordance with conventional wisdom – i.e. not competition but cooperation is the best mechanism in the given case – is placed on the defendant.

Under the rule of reason, the plaintiff has to present a *prima facie* case; if anti-competitive impact is proved, the burden of proof shifts to the defendant to proffer justifications, which may relate both to competition (rivalry) and efficiency. If the defendant meets the burden of proof, the court exercises a balancing; the perception is that in case of substantiated justifications courts tend to decide for the defendant.

Accordingly, in US antitrust law it is the defendant that bears the burden of proof regarding justifications, irrespective whether these relate to the enhancement of rivalry or to efficiency benefits. In EU competition law the burden of proof shifts only regarding efficiency benefits, while arguments that the agreement promotes competition in terms of rivalry are to be considered under Article 101(1), where the burden of proof rests on the competition authority or the plaintiff. Nevertheless, it is to be stressed that an undertaking that strives for meeting the conditions of Article 101(3) bears a very heavy burden, as compared to the burden of the defendant in US antitrust law after the plaintiff's having presented a *prima facie* case. Contrary to US antitrust law, where perception suggests that in case of substantiated justifications it is decided for the defendant, in Europe undertakings are advised to act very carefully if the agreement is under the necessity to be examined under Article 101(3).

The foregoing may be traced back to the differences in terms of standard of proof. In the US, 90 per cent of the antitrust cases are private enforcement matters and accordingly tried in civil procedure, where the standard of proof is normally preponderance of evidence (balance of probabilities), i.e. a circumstance is to be regarded as proved if it is more likely than not ('more probable than not'[315]) that it is true. On the other hand, the defendant is subjected to a much heavier burden of proof under Article 101(3).

315 *See* Lord Denning's famous definition in *Miller v. Minister of Pensions* [1947] 2 All ER 372.

In the frame of the effects-analysis (agreements anti-competitive by object in the EU; rule of reason in the US) both systems give ground to public interest arguments to a limited extent. A parallel can be drawn between the *Wouters* jurisprudence of the ECJ and the aftermath of the US judgment in *Goldfarb*. The gist of the *Wouters* doctrine is that restrictive agreements can avoid condemnation under Article 101(1) if they are related to a legitimate public interest objective; in other words: not only commercial but also public interest legitimate ends matter. The *Goldfarb* jurisprudence suggests that in case of professional services the special considerations of self-regulation are to be taken into account. Nevertheless, it is to be stressed that arrangements meriting automatic condemnation (i.e. agreements anti-competitive by object in the EU; *per se* illegality in the US) receive clemency neither under *Wouters*, nor under *Goldfarb*. Furthermore, it is also noteworthy that the perception is that in the US it is hard to find any case where this public interest reasonableness had decisive significance.

It might be tempting to draw a parallel between *Wouters* and the concept of quick look but these two concepts do not square with each other as regards substance. As far as the scope of application is concerned, 'quick look' and *Wouters* could be regarded as parallel concepts. While quick look is, probably, applicable only to professional services and markets where horizontal cooperation is required to make the service available at all, *Wouters* has been applied to liberal arts (professional services) and sport. Nevertheless, the functions of the two concepts differ completely. According to the quick look, otherwise *per se* illegal agreements are granted the chance to raise facially plausible arguments; nevertheless, once such facially plausible justifications are demonstrated, the analysis turns into a full-blown rule, a reason, where the anti-competitive impact of the arrangement is presumed. On the other hand, *Wouters* does not intimate at all that agreements anti-competitive by object could escape Article 101(1) condemnation, but it suggests that the 'reasonableness' standard within the effects-analysis under Article 101(1) contains not only economic aspects but, exceptionally, also public interest arguments. Accordingly, the concept of 'quick look' is exclusively a channel between automatic condemnation and effects-analysis, while *Wouters* suggests that in the frame of the effects-analysis also public interest arguments can be taken into account in case of professional services. As noted above, the counterpart of *Wouters* is rather *Goldfarb* and the judgments built upon it.

Evaluation

Legal certainty, predictability, judicial convenience all justify that there should be agreements that are condemned automatically, without the need to accomplish a costly market analysis and without considering the justifications proffered. The concept of 'quick look' and the notion that even object type agreements can meet the conditions of Article 101(3) are applicable only in highly exceptional cases and, thus, do not endanger the brightness of these rules.

Since both US antitrust and EU competition law analyse the same issues when examining the competitive repercussions of an arrangement and inquire roughly the same ultimate question, i.e. whether consumer welfare is enhanced or decreased at the end of the day, the real question of evaluation is how these tests are structured. In this regard EU competition law's method, if properly construed, could be preferable, as it allocates the burden of proof in accordance with the probable effects. Since common sense suggests that consumer welfare is maximized if there is competition, it is assumed that agreements setting back rivalry are illegal, while rivalry-neutral and rivalry-enhancing ones are lawful. On the other hand, though it is normally not the case, cooperation sometimes, may have a more beneficial impact on consumer welfare: accordingly, EU competition law provides for the analysis of this issue as well; nevertheless, as experience shows that cooperation is the exception and not the rule from the point of view of welfare maximization, in this regard the burden shifts to the defendant.

Nonetheless, the merits of the European system are called in question, because the above structure of analysis is not applied consistently: not all justifications relating to rivalry are considered under Article 101(1), and they are occasionally exiled into Article 101(3).

Chapter V
Fundamentals of the economics of vertical restraints

Economic intuition would suggest that intra-brand restraints may only rarely have anti-competitive consequences; and indeed there are several justifications stressing the economic efficiency of intra-brand restraints, some of which became a commonplace.

First, though vertical intra-brand restraints certainly have the capacity of restricting competition, intuition suggests that this is seldom the case since the producer is not interested in restricting the competition among its distributors. The lower the retail costs are, the smaller the retail price is and hence, the more goods are sold, and the more goods are ordered by the retailers from the supplier. Weak retail competition leads to higher dealer margins, which is detrimental to the producer's interests.[1]

Second, in the absence of producer market power vertical restraints are not capable of influencing the operation of competition appreciably. Again, economic intuition would suggest that intra-brand restraints are the least harmful.

Third, economic intuition would also suggest that if a restraint becomes a settled market practice and there is no market power, it reflects sound business decisions, which are based on and controlled by the market.

Fourth, it cannot be disregarded that distribution is a service 'purchased' by the producer, which can choose between the firm and the market.[2] The choice between

---

1 Cf. *Communication from the Commission on the Application of the Community Competition Rules to Vertical Restraints. Follow-up to the Green Paper on Vertical Restraints.* COM (98) 544 final, 30 September, 1998. OJ [1998] C 365/3. ('The main reason for treating a vertical restraint more leniently than a horizontal restraint lies in the fact that the latter may concern an agreement between competitors producing substitute goods/services while the former concerns an agreement between a supplier and a buyer of a particular product/service. In horizontal situations the exercise of market power by one company (higher price of its product) will benefit its competitors. This may provide an incentive to competitors to induce each other to behave anti-competitively. In vertical situations the product of the one is the input for the other. This means that the exercise of market power by either the upstream or downstream company would normally hurt the demand for the product of the other. The companies involved in the agreement may therefore have an incentive to prevent the exercise of market power by the other (so called self-policing character of vertical restraints).')

2 See R. H. Coase, *The Nature of the Firm*, 4 Economica 386 (1937); Oliver E. Williamson, Markets and Hierarchies: Analysis and Antitrust Implications (1975).

internal distribution and independent dealers depends on different considerations (transaction costs, principal-agent problem etc.) and undertakings, under competitive pressure, are assumed to make the most efficient decisions (otherwise they 'perish'). The law on intra-brand restraints may interfere with the producer's rational choice between the firm and the market since internal instructions and agreements between companies belonging to the same economic entity do not come under the scope of the rule on restrictive agreements; the producer may be induced to integrate (or to grow) vertically in order to avoid the prohibitions: a decision that would not have been made if solely pure efficiency considerations were taken into account. Since internal distribution and independent dealers fulfil the same function, merger control rules on vertical integration are to be taken into account when shaping the provisions on vertical agreements.[3]

Another aspect to be taken into account when analysing intra-brand restraints is that although price and non-price restraints merit separate examination, economically speaking they are the two sides of the same coin. Branded goods, due to product differentiation, have no perfect substitutes and are sold under monopolistic competition: each brand faces a residual demand curve. In this situation the producer has the power to determine the price and the quantity, taking into account the elasticity of the demand curve. Put it at simplest, the profit-maximizing price has a corresponding profit-maximizing quantity, and vice versa. Hence, theoretically, it is irrelevant whether price or quantity is fixed.[4] At least in theory, it makes no difference whether the producer fixes the resale price or assigns exclusive territories (or consumer groups) to different dealers, which will charge the profit-maximizing price in each territory (or for each consumer group). Hence, it would be inconsequent to treat price and non-price restraints completely differently. Nonetheless, it is to be stressed that the foregoing theoretical convergence is less palpable in real life cases. The producer may lack the relevant information, and according to the information at its disposal it may prefer to fix the resale price or to grant exclusive territories.[5]

Below, RPM and territorial restraints will be examined separately, amplifying their risks and efficiency explanations. The negative and positive impacts will be contrasted in order to strike the balance about the competitive consequences.

---

3 Roger J. Van den Berg and Peter D. Camesasca, European Competition Law and Economics 243-245 (2001); Emmanuel P. Mastromanolis, *Insights from U.S. Antitrust Law on Exclusive and Restricted Territorial Distribution: The Creation of a New Legal Standard for European Union Competition Law*, 15 University of Pennsylvania Journal of International Business Law 559, 620-622 (1994).

4 Robert H. Bork, The antitrust paradox. A policy at war with itself 280 (1978); Roger J. Van den Berg and Peter D. Camesasca, European Competition Law and Economics 242 (2001).

5 Cf. Roger J. Van den Berg and Peter D. Camesasca, European Competition Law and Economics 247 (2001). (Asserting that 'great parts of the economic analysis apply, word for word, to both' price and non-price restraints.)

Resale price fixing from an economic perspective

The burning question regarding RPM is the economic impact of resale price fixing and of the fixing of the minimum resale price (RPF). In competition law and policy, the theorem that maximized retail prices may be efficient because they tackle the successive monopoly mark-up problem (double marginalization)[6] is admitted and amounts to a commonplace; hence, below RPF will be analysed in detail.

Risks of RPF

Resale price fixing and minimum resale prices may, under certain circumstances, raise different competition risks. The traditional objections against RPF relate to horizontal concerns; nevertheless, the limited empirical data suggests that such arrangements rarely have horizontal repercussions, and the vertical aspects are the most important issues of examination.

Horizontal concerns of RPF

RPF may conceal a collusion between dealers: the dealer-cartel theory Probably the oldest economic argument against RPF is the dealer-cartel theory, where the supplier is the agent of the distributors and their collusion. At the end of the day, as this theory argues, the effects of these vertical restraints are not divergent from those of horizontal cartels, the only difference being that the cartel is administered and controlled by the producer, which is in a better position to monitor the dealers' compliance since it has a much better overview of the market.[7]

Although RPF might, indeed, conceal a horizontal collusion between dealers, especially, if the latter are powerful enough to force the producer's hand, this is not inevitable. The producer is highly interested in a competitive downstream market and in low dealer margins; it is in its elementary interest to keep distribution costs down: lower resale prices result in higher consumer demand and if the quantity sold increases, dealers will purchase more from the producer. Accordingly, the producer would enter into such an arrangement in two cases: if it is forced to and if it is interested in. Nonetheless, if the distribution segment is not concentrated, there are insubstantial barriers to entry at the retail level or the retail market is not apt for cartelization, the producer could easily find alternative distribution channels and thus preserve its interests. Now then, if the producer is not forced to maintain resale prices, why does it want to?

---

6 See J. J. Spengler, *Vertical Integration and Antitrust Policy*, 58 Journal of Political Economy 347 (1950); D. W. Carlton and J. M. Perloff, Modern Industrial Organization 399 (2000).

7 Richard A. Posner, Antitrust Law. An economic perspective 148 (1976); Robert H. Bork, The antitrust paradox. A policy at war with itself 282 (1978).

RPF may facilitate a manufacturer cartel Parallel systems of similar distribution networks may facilitate the administration of a manufacturer cartel since they enhance price transparency on the market. Individual sales made to wholesalers are normally secret and the price charged by the wholesaler towards the retailers is usually also secret. Cartel members may have only assumptions about the actual prices charged by other cartelist firms, and they may base their estimations on the only publicly available price information, which is the final retail price. If the competitors' retail prices are lower than expected, it is still questionable whether they cheated or the retailers had lower costs.[8]

Although RPF might certainly be used as a device to support a horizontal hardcore cartel, it is obviously not the case that all RPF arrangements are inevitably linked to a producer cartel.

Vertical concerns of RPF

RPF may impede the emergence of more cost-effective distribution methods Another concern related to RPF is that by preventing discounting it may prevent low-cost dealers with innovative distribution methods from entering the market.[9] Some decades ago large hypermarkets reduced resale costs significantly by introducing a new distribution 'service'. Such hypermarkets enjoy significant economies of scale and economies of scope and are more attractive for consumers because they maintain a wider range of products; on the other hand, traditional retail outlets, e.g. grocery stores or supermarkets located in the city centre, still have their merits: they can be approached more conveniently. Internet sales and online marketing are the innovative distribution methods of our age; they enable considerable cost-savings, e.g. no shelves need to be maintained, no stores require heating, fewer salesmen are needed. Nonetheless, traditional resale outlets and virtual shops provide different distribution 'services': while in case of web-shops significant costs can be saved, they normally provide no point-of-sale services as, for instance, display of the goods, the consumer's opportunity to inspect the product, stockpiling and fast delivery (on-line orders are usually executed within days). Nevertheless, the tension between traditional and innovative distributors does not seem to be different from the tension between high-cost and low-cost dealers. These justifications will be considered below in detail.

RPF may prevent price decrease A general fear concerning RPF is that it definitely entails some price increase and impedes price decrease,[10] arguing that if this were not the case there would be no demand for it.

8 Herbert Hovenkamp, Federal Antitrust Policy. The law of competition and its practice 443-445 (1999).

9 *See* Luc Peeperkorn, *Resale Price Maintenance and its Alleged Efficiencies*, 4(1) European Competition Journal 201, 208 (2008).

10 Luc Peeperkorn, *Resale Price Maintenance and its Alleged Efficiencies*, 4(1) European Competition Journal 201, 207 (2008).

This argument seems to be valid only partially: RPF certainly increases the price of some products; nevertheless, the relevant question is whether it increases the market price. The increase in the price of some products is not a problem until consumers have the alternative to purchase competing products at the pre-RPF price. If, for instance, the maintenance of the resale price is justified by the enhancement of the point-of-sale services, the introduction of RPF is not a problem until consumers can choose between high-price high-service, and low-price low-service goods.

Price discrimination RPF can be used as a tool to implement a system of territorial protections. The producer may protect the territorially competent dealer from parallel imports by banning or discouraging exports by other dealers, in addition to attempting to maintain the resale prices in low-price Member States in order to make parallel trade less attractive. This use of RPF is relevant only from the point of view of EU competition law, which fiercely strives against the partitioning of the common market along national borders.

Efficiency explanations (justifications) for RPF

Although, due to the long-standing *per se* condemnation of RPF, there is only limited empirical evidence about the possible merits and drawbacks of RPF, the scholarship is replete with efficiency theories. Albeit these theories do not have general application and provide valid explanation for resale price fixing only under certain circumstances, they suggest that there are cases when RPF is efficient.

Dealer service theory and the free-rider effect

The producer may endeavour to promote non-price competition because it considers that consumers or at least some consumers (marginal consumers)[11] are more sensitive to it. Enhanced quality and the provision of extra-services may increase the demand much more than higher prices may lower it. The producer may restrict or exclude the price competition between the dealers in order to drive the sales efforts of the distributors into the channel of non-price competition.[12] The

11 Marginal consumers are those consumers whose choice is influenced by the change in the features (quality, price) of the product as opposed to infra-marginal consumers who value the goods so much that an insignificant change in the price or other non-price characteristics does not affect their choices. In geometric terms, marginal consumers are those that are situated along the demand curve to the left and in the near of the intersection between the supply and the demand curve.

12 *See* Lester G. Telser, *Why Should Manufacturers Want Fair Trade?*, 3 Journal of Law and Economics 86 (1960). *Cf.* Ward Bowman, *The Prerequisites and Effects of Resale Price Maintenance*, 22 University of Chicago Law Review 825 (1955); Basil S. Yamey, The Economics of Resale Price Maintenance (1954). *Contra* Warren Grimes, *Spiff, Polish, and Consumer Demand Quality: Vertical Price Restraints Revisited*, 80 California Law

restriction of the distributor's power to determine its resale price is justified by the promotion of pre-sale and point-of-sale services. If the producer fixes the resale price, the only field where distributors can compete with each other is the non-price aspects.[13] The prevalence of non-price competition, obviously, does not raise problems until the yield of the dealer's extra services can be harvested by itself.

Nevertheless, extra-service (high-cost) dealers may trigger positive externalities to low-service (low-cost) dealers (e.g. consumers learn about new books in convenient bookstores in the city but order them on-line). Under such circumstances, the producer is interested in having the products on the shelves of the high-cost dealers as this improves the marketability of the product at large. However, if prices are not fixed consumers may take the pre-sale services of high-cost dealers and buy the goods from discounters, which can cut prices since they do not incur the costs of extra services. The chief purpose of RPF in this scenario is to overcome the free-rider problem and to ensure proper dealer services.[14] Under perfect (or less ambitiously: workable) retail competition resellers earn no economic profit since they compete by providing additional services to the customers or by improving the quality of the products or services. Accordingly, higher resale prices do not result in higher margins, as the would-be economic rent is spent on extra services.

A general argument against the above free-rider theory is that high-margins granted to dealers do not ensure that the extra services are indeed provided: retailers may take the higher margin, while not providing the extra services.[15] Obviously, this criticism is very strong if assuming that all dealers are expected to provide the services in question. Nevertheless, in several cases the producer cooperates with both high-cost and low-cost dealers and tries to strike the right balance between the two groups.[16] In several cases the provision of extra-services is not a question

---

Review 815 (1992). (Asserting that RPM may expose consumers to excessively aggressive promotion and makes them enter unwise purchases.)

13 Roger J. Van den Berg and Peter D. Camesasca, European Competition Law and Economics 215 (2001).

14 Richard A. Posner, Antitrust Law. An economic perspective 148-150 (1976).

15 *See* Benjamin Klein and Kevin M. Murphy, *Vertical Restraints as Contract Enforcement Mechanisms*, 31 Journal of Law and Economics 265 (1988); Robert L. Steiner, *Sylvania Economics – a Critique*, 60 Antitrust Law Journal 41, 41-42 (1991); Luc Peeperkorn, *Resale Price Maintenance and its Alleged Efficiencies*, 4(1) European Competition Journal 201, 209 (2008).

16 *See* David A. Butz and Andrew N. Kleit, *Are Vertical Restraints Pro- or Anticompetitive? Lessons from Interstate Circuit*, 44 Journal of Law and Economics 131, 133 and 155 (2001). (Demonstrating the above balancing through *Interstate Circuit v United States*, 306 US 208 (1939), concerning the motion picture theatres, where the term 'first-run movie theatre' (FRT) stands for the high-service high-cost dealer, while the term 'subsequent-run theatre' (SRT) stands for the low-service low-cost dealer. '[T]he model described here shows that when retailers are heterogeneous, a few retailers (FRTs in the case of *Interstate Circuit*) may have a comparative advantage at providing most of the promotional effort for all of the manufacturer's outlets. In this case, RPM serves not to force less efficient outlets

of choice for the dealer. Some outlets – for instance, simply because they are located in the city centre – are more costly and, at the same time, more attractive for consumers than others: the location of the outlet is a service that requires no control and monitoring.

In this context the producer does not insist on the provision of the point-of-sale services by all the dealers; instead, there are certain distributors that provide extra services, while there are certain ones that do not. Under such circumstances, it is not price-cutting but 'excessive' price-cutting that can discourage high-cost dealers from trading with the product.[17] If the difference between the high-cost and price-cutting dealers' prices is not enormous, both dealer groups can get a sufficient share from the turnover of the product: high-cost dealers would sell to the less cost-sensitive, while discounters would sell to the rather cost-sensitive consumers. A very significant difference in the retail prices, however, would make so many less cost-sensitive consumers purchase from discounters that high-cost retailers could not make a living profit from the product concerned and, hence, would drop it.

A variant of the above criticism is that the maintenance of the resale prices is only one of the tools of ensuring the services envisaged by the producer, and contractual stipulations, penalties and monitoring are alternative and more efficient methods of ensuring compliance. While this argument certainly has its merits, it does not explain why the producer may prefer RPF over contractual control. Competition law's confidence in competition would suggest that under competitive circumstances undertakings make the most efficient choices, otherwise they fail. At the same time, there are very strong arguments that while the provision of extra services cannot be controlled easily, resale prices are more transparent and give a proper incentive to provide extra services, thus the combination of the two methods, i.e. RPF and contractual stipulations, yields the best result.

Another criticism of the free rider theory of RPF is that it harms infra-marginal consumers, who are compelled to pay for the services they do not need.[18]

(SRTs) to supply effort that they are not well positioned to provide but rather to prevent them from appropriating the quasi rents of the nondiscount outlets that do provide that effort. The result is that nondiscount outlets provide more promotional effort. Thus, higher prices at SRTs encouraged Interstate Circuit to promote films more aggressively, for the simple reason that it was better able to generate and appropriate the returns from such promotions.') (Here, the purpose of the RPM is not to induce discounters to make the promotional efforts; quite the contrary, '[t]he manufacturer's objective is to provide incentives for full-service outlets (rather than discounters) to put forth additional effort. (…) Its effect is to increase the difference in point-of-sale services offered by the two retailer types.')

17 The very limited empirical record shows that in the late 1930s in the US, in the period when states were empowered to legalize RPF, the minimum prices imposed by producers on drugstores were low and chain stores often still charged considerably less than independent drugstores. H. J. Ostlund and C. R. Vickland, Fair Trade and the Retail Drug Store (1940).

18 Frederic M. Scherer, *The Economics of Vertical Restraints*, 52 Antitrust Law Journal 687, 700 (1983); William S. Comanor, *Vertical Price-Fixing, Vertical Market*

While the product's utility for marginal consumers is roughly equal to its price, infra-marginal consumers value the product significantly more than the price. In other words, marginal consumers are located along the demand curve near the intersection between the price and the demand curve, while infra-marginal consumers represent the upper left segment of the demand curve. Since infra-marginal consumers are less price sensitive, that is their price-flexibility is lower, the producer has to take only marginal consumers into account, when deciding whether to provide the extra-services or not.[19]

The problem with the infra-marginal consumers theory is that it pre-supposes some market power on the part of the producer; nevertheless, under workable competition in the absence of market power, it seems hardly convincing that infra-marginal consumers would be really captured and could not find any other brand that is cheaper but is mingled with a lower level of pre-sale or point-of-sale services.[20] If the cross-elasticity of the residual demand curve is high enough, which is, by the way, based on the availability and price of alternative sources of substitutable products, the producer cannot arrange its marketing policy in favour of its marginal consumers without the risk of losing some of its infra-marginal ones. Consequently, this criticism of the free rider theory of RPM works only in case of perceptible market power.

Protecting different channels of distribution

There is benign explanation for RPF even in cases where the services provided by some dealers do not cause positive externalities to those who do not provide them and there is no free-riding.[21] For instance, traditional retail outlets are threatened by innovative distribution methods as demand for the former decreases; nevertheless, they do not expire, and may try to find some protection from this competitive pressure: they may stop trading with products that can be found on the 'shelves' of web-shops or large hypermarkets; alternatively, they may complain to the producer that if they do not get some protection, e.g. RPM, they would drop the merchandise in question. In this case, one may ask again: why is the producer interested in protecting high-cost dealers? One reason could be the free-rider rationale: high-cost dealers may trigger positive externalities to low-cost dealers. Another explanation could be that

---

Restrictions, and the New Antitrust Policy, 98 Harvard Law Review 983, 990-998 (1985); William S. Comanor and John B. Kirkwood, *Resale Price Maintenance and Antitrust Policy*, 3(3) Contemporary Policy Issues 9 (1985); Frederic M. Scherer and David Ross, Industrial Market Structure and Economic Performance 541-548 (3d ed. 1990).

19 A. Michael Spence, *Monopoly, quality, and regulation*, 6 Bell Journal of Economics 417, 417-419 (1975); William S. Comanor, *Vertical Price-Fixing – Vertical Market Restrictions, and the New Antitrust Policy*, 98 Harvard Law Review 983 (1985).

20 Roger J. Van den Berg and Peter D. Camesasca, European Competition Law and Economics, 220 (2001).

21 *See* Greg Shaffer, *Rendering Alternative Offerings Less Profitable with Resale Price Maintenance*, 3(4) Journal of Economics and Management Strategy 639 (1995). (Giving an explanation for RPM in cases where free-riding is not a problem.)

some consumers would prefer the point-of-sale services high-cost dealers provide (note that the location of the outlet or the physical presence of the goods on the shelves of the shop are also point-of-sale services), and the producer does not want to lose these channels of distribution. Assume that there is no free-riding here as the extra-services of the high-cost dealers do not trigger positive externalities to low-cost dealers. The producer may stick to high-cost dealers because they are the exclusive or primary channel for reaching certain consumer groups (those, who are not cost-sensitive and do not want to travel to distant hypermarkets). Of course, it could be argued that since there is no free-riding involved in the foregoing scenario, why should the producer protect high-cost dealers? In the absence of RPM, consumers would have the chance to choose between products with and without point-of-sale services. The answer could be that the appreciation of point-of-sale services is a matter of degree; some consumers are extremely keen on point-of-sale services, while others' choice would depend on how low the prices of the discounters are. With a moderate RPM the producer may preserve both channels of distribution and embrace the widest spectrum of consumers.

Obviously, the question is whether RPF is efficient under the above circumstances; notwithstanding the fact that it obviously increases the resale price, producers striving to achieve the widest possible product coverage seem to be efficient, as far as there is strong inter-brand competition. Consumers retain the chance to purchase cheap brands that are normally sold in discount shops, and, if inefficient, the RPF arrangement would fail in case there is workable inter-brand competition.

Quality certification

Reputable dealers may provide non-tangible services, which enhance the general marketability of the brand: producers may find it reasonable to pay with RPF for the style or quality certification provided by these prestigious dealers. If prestigious dealers have the reputation of selling only high quality merchandise, the fact that they carry the products is an information service, and non-reputable dealers can free-ride on the reputable dealers' investment. This strategy may be rational even when the producer can select the dealers who can carry the goods (selective distribution): the producer may not tie down which dealers can carry the goods but attach accentuated importance to the fact that quality 'certifying' dealers have it on stock.[22]

Tackling distribution risks attached to uncertain demand

RPM may also be used to tackle problems caused by uncertain demand.[23] Dealers have limited shelf and stock space and may be reluctant to carry products which

22 Howard P. Marvel and Stephen McCafferty, *Resale Price Maintenance and Quality Certification*, 15(3) Rand Journal of Economics 346 (1984).

23 Patrick Rey and Jean Tirole, *The Logic of Vertical Restraints*, 76 American Economic Review 921 (1986); Richard J. Gilbert and Paul Klemperer, *An Equilibrium Theory of Rationing*, 31(1) Rand Journal of Economics 1 (2000); Howard P. Marvel, *The*

have an uncertain demand. The producer can encourage dealers by taking the commercial risk of the distribution, i.e. the producer can retain title over the goods, thus, if unsold they can be returned at no loss. Nevertheless, the foregoing generosity does not make up for the overhead expenditures and the opportunity costs: these risks stay with the dealer. RPM could be a device to share the risk between the producer and the dealers in case the latter are more risk-averse.[24]

Under such circumstances, the producer can encourage dealers in two ways: it may guarantee a minimal resale price level or pay slotting allowance. The problem with the latter could be that it shifts all risk onto the producer, contrary to RPM which splits the risk, and makes the dealer less interested in the promotion of the merchandise: if the extra remuneration paid by the producer is not dependent on the quantity sold, the dealer might not be interested in promoting the brand.[25]

Non-price restraints: a clear-cut case for the free-rider theory

Non-price restraints, i.e. territorial and customer group restrictions, present a clear-cut case for the free-riding rationale. While they may raise the same risks as price restraints, their virtue of tackling the problem of free-riding is evident.

Formally, a system of territorial protections imposed by the producer may resemble a market-sharing cartel concluded by the dealers (dealer cartel theory); moreover, parallel systems of territorial exclusivities of different producers may, likewise, facilitate the operation and administration of a producer cartel. Nevertheless, these theories cannot be squared with the fact that the producer is not interested in the restriction of dealer competition. A distributor-compelled restraint is hardly realistic given the fact that it would require the 'trans-territorial' cooperation of some of the dealers with the exclusion of others. Assistance to a producer cartel could be a problem; nevertheless, such facilitating effects do not have automatic anti-competitive consequences and cannot be condemned in general, in the absence of a real danger of cartelization.

Resale Price Maintenance Controversy: Beyond the Conventional Wisdom, 63 Antitrust Law Journal 59, 73-77 (1994) ('RPM will thus be most desirable when without it retailers would be reluctant to hold adequate inventories for fear of dramatically lower prices in the event of low demand. This explanation for RPM is most compelling when demand is highly variable and when inventories are either perishable or costly to hold over to future demand periods.'); Raymond Deneckere, Howard P. Marvel and James Peck, *Demand Uncertainty, Inventories, and Resale Price Maintenance*, 87 American Economic Review 619 (1997).

24 J. R. Gould and L E. Preston, *Resale Price Maintenance and Resale Outlets*, 32 Economica 302 (1965).

25 *Contra* Roger J. Van den Berg and Peter D. Camesasca, European Competition Law and Economics 222 (2001). (Arguing that although RPM 'may provide benefits to retailers by reducing the extent to which their profits vary with sales, this use of the practice may not be socially desirable due to the adverse effects on consumers'.)

The efficiency theories of territorial restraints are mainly based on the free-rider rationale,[26] a phenomenon more visible than in case of price restraints. Penetrating a market involves considerable risks, while it requires substantial investment in terms of marketing efforts and promotion. No distributor would invest in promoting a certain brand in an area if it cannot be sure that it will get exclusive rights for recovering its investment. All this is prevalent to a greater extent with regard to new markets. The free rider theory justifies that producers grant 'property-like' rights to distributors in order to make them interested in promoting the brand. These 'property-like' rights are more tangible when the distributor is allotted a land where it can 'crop and harvest'.

Conclusions on intra-brand restraints

In sum, RPF cannot be adjudicated universally: it certainly may have advantages and drawbacks; nevertheless, it depends on the circumstances which effects prevail. It is also certain that the maintenance of the resale price is sensible only in the case of branded goods.

Accordingly, the question is whether RPF can be condemned generally or a more detailed analysis of the case would be warranted. Thus much is certain that RPF leads to higher resale prices for the brand concerned and it may harm infra-marginal consumers. Nevertheless, it is not obvious whether RPF entails higher market prices in general, since other brands – if economically efficient – can still decide not to follow an RPF policy. It is also expected that RPF leads to higher sales volumes; otherwise, why would the producer be interested in it.

Interestingly, the limited empirical data concerning RPF strongly suggests that horizontal collusion is seldom an issue: a survey on cases litigated between 1976 and 1982 shows that only 7.2 per cent of 153 reported RPF cases involved allegations of horizontal (either producer or dealer) collusion, or put it more demonstratively: 82.8 per cent of the cases did not involve even allegations of horizontal collusion.[27] Another survey based on 47 litigated FTC RPF cases between 1965 and 1982 for which retail market structure information was available showed that 43 cases involved at least 100 rival dealers. Due to the high number of dealers widespread dealer collusion was unlikely. The conclusion of the survey was that 'for the majority of these (47) cases the use of RPM was not likely motivated by collusive dealers who had successfully coerced their suppliers into using RPM to facilitate a widespread dealers' cartel'.[28]

26 Roger J. Van den Berg and Peter D. Camesasca, European Competition Law and Economics 226-228 (2001).

27 Pauline M. Ippolito, *Resale Price Maintenance: Empirical Evidence from Litigation*, 34 Journal of Law and Economics 263 (1991).

28 Thomas Overstreet, Resale Price Maintenance: Economic Theories and Empirical Evidence 80 (Bureau of Econ., Fed. Trade Comm'n 1983). *See also* Stanley

Resale price maintenance has several alternatives, e.g. dealer services can be contracted for directly, distributors' risk aversion can be handled through slotting allowances. Nevertheless, the question is not whether substitutes exist: the problems RPF aims at do exist and producers certainly try to find second-best solutions for tackling them, if the first-best is not lawful. The question is whether these substitutes are more welcome from the point of view of competition and economic efficiency. If the producer does not have market power, RPF is not inherently anti-competitive and it is preferred by competitive producers, economic intuition would suggest that it has significant efficiency advantages over its substitutes.[29]

Naturally, the final question is whether RPF is harmful to consumers at large? Economic theory suggests that in concrete cases detailed economic analysis could ensure that it does not cause consumer harm, provided there is sufficient inter-brand competition, ensuring the optimal balance between point-of-sale services and price reductions, and consumers' choice is preserved (different producers use different methods of distribution).

As far as territorial restraints are concerned, the vast majority of economists share the common ground that though they definitely restrict intra-brand rivalry, or possibly even completely exclude it, they have very strong pro-competitive effects and, hence, merit a full-blown analysis.

Finally, the perspectives of vertical integration are to be taken into account too. Market operators could feel forced to resort to other patterns of organization, i.e. integration, in order to achieve results condemned by the law on vertical restraints; this may happen if vertical restraints are more stringently controlled than vertical mergers. The aftermath of the most famous EU vertical restraint case is very telling: some time after the ECJ's judgment in Consten and Grundig, Grundig acquired many of its exclusive distributors, including Consten,[30] thus abolishing all competition law concerns. This argument is a fortiori applicable to licensing agreements, where there would be no competition in the absence of the vertical (technology transfer) agreements; the licensor could opt for exploiting the IP rights itself and preserve the monopoly granted by IP law.[31]

I. Ornstein, *Resale Price Maintenance and Cartels*, 30 Antitrust Bulletin 401 (1985). (Concluding that hints of a cartel were present in less than one third of the RPF cases.); Andrew N. Kleit, *Efficiencies without Economists: the Early Years of Resale Price Maintenance*, 59 Southern Economic Journal, 597 (1993). (Reaching a similar conclusion regarding RPF's use as a cartelization tool.)

29 Howard P. Marvel, *The Resale Price Maintenance Controversy: Beyond the Conventional Wisdom*, 63 Antitrust Law Journal 59, 78 (1994).

30 Valentine Korah and Denis O'Sullivan, Distribution Agreements under the EC Competition Rules 62 (2002).

31 Robert C. Lind and Paul Muysert, *The European Commission's Draft Technology Transfer Block Exemption Regulation and Guidelines: a Significant Departure from Accepted Competition Policy Principles*, 25(4) European Competition Law Review 181, 184 (2004).

Chapter VI

Resale price fixing: the schism?

There is a fundamental divergence between US antitrust and EU competition law as far as RPF is concerned, due to the Supreme Court's *Leegin* judgment in 2007. For decades, the two sides of the Atlantic had the common ground that the fixing of concrete or minimum resale prices is a pernicious restraint of trade and should be condemned without ado, even if, after *Monsanto*, there was a very significant divergence concerning the meaning of the term 'agreement to fix the price'; as noted above, in *Monsanto* the Supreme Court held that only agreements determining a particular price or price level are covered by *per se* illegality, while terminating a discounter is not an 'agreement to fix the price' – even if this is the corollary of the complaint of one of the non-price-cutting dealers. At the same time, in US antitrust law RPF covenants were *per se* illegal, while in EU competition law they have been characterized as anti-competitive by object with no real chance for an individual exemption. This common understanding changed in 2007. Although, in this respect, the 2010 *Guidelines on Vertical Restraints* slightly depart from the *Old Guidelines* of 2000, as a matter of practice, they seem to fail to produce fundamental changes.

RPF in EU competition law: all quiet on the European front?

Notwithstanding US antitrust law's departure from the traditional stance on RPF in *Leegin*, EU competition law's approach has been very hostile towards RPF. Under EU law, while maximum resale price fixing and recommended prices are not hardcore restrictions and are to be condemned only if they have anticompetitive effects,[1] the fixing of concrete or minimum resale prices is anti-competitive by object under Article 101(1) and has only an improbable chance for meeting the

1 The ECJ granted leave to a price recommendation system in *Pronuptia* holding that 'although provisions which impair the franchisee's freedom to determine his own prices are restrictive of competition, that is not the case where the franchisor simply provides franchisees with price guidelines, so long as there is no concerted practice between the franchisor and the franchisees or between the franchisees themselves for the actual application of such prices'. Case 161/84 *Pronuptia de Paris GmbH v Pronuptia de Paris Irmgard Schillgallis* ECR [1986] 353, para 25. The ECJ has not ruled on maximum resale price yet. Likewise, the Commission also takes a more relaxed view with regard to recommended prices and maximum price fixing. *See Guidelines on Vertical Restraints*, paras 226-229; Case COMP/B-1/38348 *Repsol CPP SA* OJ [2004] C 258/03, paras 18-20.

requirements of individual exemption under Article 101(3).[2] The perspective for the latter is theoretically always, practically almost never realistic:[3] theoretically, all agreements, including vertical covenants fixing the resale price, are fit for individual exemption, while practically they are scarcely able to deserve it. Furthermore, the stance that RPF agreements automatically violate Article 101(1) with a theoretical and moderate chance for individual exemption under Article 101(3) is conceptually flawed: while Article 101(3) covers (productive) efficiency arguments, all theories advocating RPF argue that it enhances rivalry, which is a value to be examined under Article 101(1).

Although less palpable than in case of territorial protection, EU law's approach towards RPF is influenced not only by antitrust traditionalism, but also by the purpose of market integration (single market imperative).[4] RPF could be used to maintain more or less uniform prices in different Member States, thus impeding the inter-state flow of goods; or it could also be used to back a system of territorial protection.[5]

The position that fixed and minimum resale prices are anti-competitive by object (and thus fall foul of Article 101(1) automatically) is firm in EU competition law. In *SA Binon & Cie v SA Agence et messageries de la pressem*,[6] in an Article 234 reference, the ECJ ruled that RPF covenants 'constitute, of themselves, a restriction of competition'[7], i.e. they are anti-competitive by object, as one example of agreements mentioned in Article 101(1)(a) ('directly or indirectly fix purchase or selling prices or any other trading conditions').[8] The foregoing position was

---

2 Mart Kneepkens, *Resale Price Maintenance: Economics Call for a More Balanced Approach*, 28(12) European Competition Law Review 656, 656 (2007). (Stating that in practice RPF is 'subject to a *per se* prohibition'.)

3 *See* Alison Jones, *Resale Price Maintenance: a Debate about Competition Policy in Europe*, 5(2) European Competition Journal 479, 501-502 (2009).

4 *See* Valentine Korah and Denis O'Sullivan, Distribution Agreements under the EC Competition Rules 105 (2002); Lennart Ritter and W. David Braun, European Competition Law: a Practitioner's Guide 269-270 (3d ed., 2005); Femi Alese, *Unmasking the Masquerade of Vertical Price Fixing*, 28(9) European Competition Law Review 514, 525 (2007).

5 As shown by several Commission decisions. *See* 77/66/EEC *GERO-fabriek* OJ [1977] L 16/8, para II(3)(c); 2002/190/EC *JCB* OJ [2002] L 69/1, paras 168-172.

6 Case 243/83 *SA Binon and Cie v SA Agence et messageries de la pressem* [1985] ECR 2015.

7 Or as the authentic French version of the judgment says: '*sont en elles-memes restrictives de concurrence*'.

8 Para 44. ('[P]rovisions which fix the prices to be observed in contracts with third parties constitute, of themselves, a restriction on competition within the meaning of Article 85(1) which refers to agreements which fix selling prices as an example of an agreement prohibited by the Treaty.')

re-affirmed in *SPRL Louis Erauw-Jacquery v La Hesbignonne SC*;[9] in *Pronuptia de Paris GmbH v Pronuptia de Paris Irmgard Schillgallis*[10] the ECJ showed tolerance towards recommended prices, nonetheless, the judgment's language makes clear that mandatory fixed resale prices are automatically restrictive.[11] In accordance with the jurisprudence on RPF, the Commission's decisional practice is replete with cases where the anti-competitive nature of RPF was established,[12] and the 'soft law' documents issued by the Commission also adopt this approach.[13] Though formally relating to Article 101(3), it is telling that all block exemption regulations on distribution agreements – i.e. distribution agreements in general and specifically automotive distribution – unequivocally characterize RPF as hardcore and as falling outside of the safe harbour of the block exemption. It is important to emphasize that the notion of RPF covers not only express covenants but also arrangements that trigger the same or similar consequences indirectly.[14]

---

9 Case 27/87 *SPRL Louis Erauw-Jacquery v La Hesbignonne SC* [1988] ECR 1919, paras 12-15. (Condemning the fixing of the minimum "resale" price in a technology transfer agreement concerning plant breeders' rights.)

10 Case 161/84 *Pronuptia de Paris GmbH v Pronuptia de Paris Irmgard Schillgallis* [1986] ECR 353.

11 Para 25.

12 73/322/EEC *Deutsche Philips GmbH* OJ [1973] L 293/40, para 2(b); 77/66/EEC *GERO-fabriek* OJ [1977] L 16/8, para II(3)(c). (Here RPF was also used as a device to partition the common market.); 80/1333/EEC *Hennessy-Henkell* OJ [1980] L 383/11, para 20 (Asserting that RPF 'has the object of limiting (…) [the distributor's] freedom to fix resale prices, prevents the exclusive dealer from fixing them freely on the basis of the conditions obtaining on the market.'); 97/123/EC *Novalliance/Systemform* OJ [1996] L 47/11, para 81; 2001/135/EC *Nathan-Bricolux* OJ [2001] L 54/1, para 72. (Expressly characterizing RPF as anti-competitive by object.); 2002/190/EC *JCB* OJ [2002] L 69/1, paras 168-172 (Here RPF was also used as a device to partition the market.); Case COMP/37.975 *PO/Yamaha* Commission decision of 16.07.2003 (unpublished but available at http://ec.europa.eu/competition/antitrust/-cases/decisions/37975/en.pdf), paras 88, 127. 137, 144 and 155-156. (Designating RPF as restrictive by object and 'obvious restriction of competition'.); 2001/711/EC *Volkswagen* OJ [2001] L 262/14, paras 71 and 74. (Stating that there was no need to show effects as RPF is anti-competitive by object.); 2001/135/EC *Nathan-Bricolux* OJ [2001] L 54/1, paras 86 and 88. (Designating RPF as restrictive by object.) This approach was taken by the Commission from the beginning of EU competition law. *See* VALENTINE KORAH AND DENIS O'SULLIVAN, DISTRIBUTION AGREEMENTS UNDER THE EC COMPETITION RULES 105-106 (2002).

13 *Guidelines on Vertical Restraints*, paras 48 and 223; *Guidelines on Article 101(3)*, para 23; *Notice on Agreements of Minor Importance*, para 11(2).

14 It is essential to stress that in EU competition law RPM also covers resale price maintenance 'achieved through indirect means', *Guidelines on Vertical Restrains*, para 48. ('However, RPM can also be achieved through indirect means. Examples of the latter are an agreement fixing the distribution margin, fixing the maximum level of discount the distributor can grant from a prescribed price level, making the grant of rebates or reimbursement of promotional costs by the supplier subject to the observance of a given price level, linking the prescribed resale price to the resale prices of competitors, threats,

Article 4 of the BER characterizes RPF as hardcore and deprives it of the benefit of the block exemption.

> The exemption provided for in Article 2 shall not apply to vertical agreements which, directly or indirectly, in isolation or in combination with other factors under the control of the parties, have as their object:
>
> (a) the restriction of the buyer's ability to determine its sale price, without prejudice to the possibility of the supplier to impose a maximum sale price or recommend a sale price, provided that they do not amount to a fixed or minimum sale price as a result of pressure from, or incentives offered by, any of the parties.

Article 4 of the MVBER repeats the above provision regarding the motor vehicle sector.

> Hardcore restrictions
>
> 1. The exemption shall not apply to vertical agreements which, directly or indirectly, in isolation or in combination with other factors under the control of the parties, have as their object:
>
> (a) the restriction of the distributor's or repairer's ability to determine its sale price, without prejudice to the supplier's ability to impose a maximum sale price or to recommend a sale price, provided that this does not amount to a fixed or minimum sale price as a result of pressure from, or incentives offered by, any of the parties.

The same language is used by Article 4(2)(a) of the TTBER.

> 2. Where the undertakings party to the agreement are not competing undertakings, the exemption provided for in Article 2 shall not apply to

---

intimidation, warnings, penalties, delay or suspension of deliveries or contract terminations in relation to observance of a given price level. Direct or indirect means of achieving price fixing can be made more effective when combined with measures to identify price-cutting distributors, such as the implementation of a price monitoring system, or the obligation on retailers to report other members of the distribution network that deviate from the standard price level. Similarly, direct or indirect price fixing can be made more effective when combined with measures which may reduce the buyer's incentive to lower the resale price, such as the supplier printing a recommended resale price on the product or the supplier obliging the buyer to apply a most-favoured-customer clause. The same indirect means and the same "supportive" measures can be used to make maximum or recommended prices work as RPM. However, the use of a particular supportive measure or the provision of a list of recommended prices or maximum prices by the supplier to the buyer is not considered in itself as leading to RPM.') *See* Case 86/82 *Hasselblad (GB) Limited* v *Commission* [1984] ECR 883, para 49. (In this case a clause enabled the producer to control dealers' advertisements as regards selling prices and empowered it to prohibit such advertisements.)

> agreements which, directly or indirectly, in isolation or in combination with other factors under the control of the parties, have as their object:
> (a) the restriction of a party's ability to determine its prices when selling products to third parties, without prejudice to the possibility of imposing a maximum sale price or recommending a sale price, provided that it does not amount to a fixed or minimum sale price as a result of pressure from, or incentives offered by, any of the parties.

As no block exemption regulation covers agreements containing RPF, the subsequent question is whether such arrangements are capable of benefiting from an individual exemption under Article 101(3). Although, as noted above, the GC declared in *Matra Hachette* 'that, in principle, no anti-competitive practice can exist which, whatever the extent of its effects on a given market, cannot be exempted, provided that all the conditions laid down in Article 85(3) of the Treaty are satisfied',[15] both judicial and decisional practice,[16] as well as the Commission's

15 Case T-17/93 *Matra Hachette SA v Commission* [1994] ECR II-595, para 85. *See also Guidelines on Article 101(3)*, para 46. ('Article 81(3) does not exclude a priori certain types of agreements from its scope. As a matter of principle all restrictive agreements that fulfil the four conditions of Article 81(3) are covered by the exception rule.'). *See also* Case C-209/07 *Competition Authority v Beef Industry Development Society Ltd and Barry Brothers (Carrigmore) Meats Ltd* [2008] ECR I-8637, paras 21 and 39.

16 In *Hennessy-Henkell*, the Commission considered that although the exclusivity would encourage the distributor to invest thus ensuring a wider distribution of the products, it asserted that the fixing of the resale price by the German distributor deprived the exclusivity of the chance to be exempted under Article 101(3), as the fixed prices forestalled that the benefits resulting from the improvements in distribution introduced by the exclusivity would be passed on to the consumers. 80/1333/EEC *Hennessy-Henkell* OJ [1980] L 383/11, paras 28, 30 and 32. ('For such improvement to be effective, however, the exclusive dealer would have to be able to fix resale prices freely on the basis of the cost price of the products purchased from the manufacturer and by adapting his profit margin to the sales policy determined by him on the basis of the conditions obtaining on the market. This requirement is essential if Hennessy products are to penetrate the German market better, and to combat competition from other brands.') ('Nor can it be concluded that a fair share of the benefits which could result from exclusive distribution is being set aside for consumers. An improvement in distribution should be accompanied, particularly, by a reduction in sales prices to consumers, whereas (...) [the distributor] is not free to take a decision on this, and it is clear from the manner in which the agreement has been applied that Hennessy has prevailed upon Henkell to fix higher prices than those which ought to have ensued from the agreement.') ('By contrast, the restriction of the concessionaire's freedom to fix his resale prices, contained in Article 6, cannot be regarded as indispensable to the attainment of the objectives of the agreement, even if the products in question are considered, as Hennessy considers them, to be luxury products.') The Commission also refused the argument that RPF was necessary for preserving the luxurious image of the brand. The Commission apparently proceeded from the proposition that the chief benefit of the improvement of distribution could be the decrease of the price of the product in question and RPF is by its very nature incapable of producing such effects. In

'soft law' instruments[17] suggest that Article 101(3) is a theoretically always, practically almost never open haven for RPF;[18] albeit the 2010 *Guidelines on Vertical Restraints* contain the siren song of a substantial analysis; this will be examined below.

In *SA Binon & Cie v SA Agence et messageries de la pressem*,[19] interestingly, the ECJ did not say that it would be highly unlikely for RPF to fulfil the conditions of Article 101(3) but ruled that the Commission was to take account of the factors mentioned by the undertaking concerned.[20] Nevertheless, it is fairly doubtful whether any relevant conclusion could be extracted from the neutral language of

---

Yamaha the Commission used a very unconditional language characterizing both RPF and absolute territorial protection as arrangements that cannot meet the requirements of Article 101(3) by their very nature; a language going far beyond the fact pattern of the case. Case COMP/37.975 *PO/Yamaha* Commission decision of 16.07.2003 (unpublished but available at http://ec.europa.eu/competition/antitrust/cases/decisions/37975/en.pdf), para 175. ('The Agreements in question were not notified. If such agreements had been notified, they could not have been exempted individually from the application of Article 81(1) of the Treaty and Article 53(1) of the EEA Agreement, since the conditions necessary for granting an exemption are not met due to the nature of the restrictions of competition. Territorial protection and resale price maintenance are hardcore restrictions that do not meet the cumulative conditions of Article 81(3) of the Treaty and Article 53(3) of the EEA Agreement. They do not contribute to improving the production or, in this case, the distribution of goods, nor are consumers allowed a share of the resulting benefit.')

17 *Guidelines on Article 101(3)*, paras 46 and 79. ('However, severe restrictions of competition are unlikely to fulfil the conditions of Article 81(3). Such restrictions are usually blacklisted in block exemption regulations or identified as hardcore restrictions in Commission guidelines and notices. Agreements of this nature generally fail (at least) the two first conditions of Article 81(3). They neither create objective economic benefits nor do they benefit consumers. (...) Moreover, these types of agreements generally also fail the indispensability test under the third condition.') ('Restrictions that are black listed in block exemption regulations or identified as hardcore restrictions in Commission guidelines and notices are unlikely to be considered indispensable.')

18 *See* Valentine Korah and Denis O'Sullivan, Distribution Agreements under the EC Competition Rules 233 (2002). (Noting that '[i]n brief, although *Matra Hachette* suggests that no restriction of competition is beyond exemption, there appears to be no real possibility of redeeming the so-called "hardcore" restraints, and their inclusion in any distribution arrangement – even one which would otherwise satisfy the conditions for exemption under Regulation 2790/99 – exposes the parties to serious risk of fines and nullity. Businesses would be well advised simply to avoid such restraints entirely.')

19 Case 243/83 *SA Binon and Cie v SA Agence et messageries de la pressem* [1985] ECR 2015.

20 Para 46. ('If, in so far as the distribution of newspapers and periodicals is concerned, the fixing of the retail price by publishers constitutes the sole means of supporting the financial burden resulting from the taking back of unsold copies and if the latter practice constitutes the sole method by which a wide selection of newspapers and periodicals can be made available to readers, the Commission must take account of those factors when examining an agreement for the purposes of Article 85(3).')

the judgment. At all events, until the entry into force of Regulation 1/2003/EC on 1 May 2004, the Commission had monopoly over the application of Article 101(3),[21] and it had never ever granted individual exemption to an RPF covenant.[22] Since then, the application of EU competition law, including Article 101(3), has been decentralized; nevertheless, it is scarcely conceivable that this provision would be interpreted, otherwise, in practice, especially as the formation of competition policy, contrary to enforcement, has remained essentially centralized.

Nevertheless, it is noteworthy that in *Newspaper distribution contracts in Belgium – AMP* the Commission did send a comfort letter (but not a formal decision!) for an RPF arrangement and expressly came to the conclusion that it met the conditions of Article 101(3).[23] In the case it was the essential characteristic of the market that the products (newspapers and magazines) had an extremely short life span and the scheme was based on a sale or return system. Nevertheless, it is submitted that the dealers in this case were possibly acting as agents, as they did not acquire title over the periodicals and all the risk of non-sale was borne by the producer. The Commission noted that '[i]t is therefore economically acceptable in the distribution system concerned that the operator *who incurs the main economic risk* should control the selling price'. This circumstance may have influenced the Commission's analysis considerably.

As far as the perspectives of RPF in EU competition law are concerned, the 2010 *Guidelines on Vertical Restraints* expressly highlight that albeit the hardcore restrictions enumerated in Article 4 of the BER, including resale price fixing and minimum resale price fixing, are presumed to violate Article 101(1) and not to meet the conditions of Article 101(3), this presumption is rebuttable, and the parties may have an improbable but not unrealistic chance to survive on the basis

21 Regulation 17, Article 9(1).

22 *See* Richard Whish, Competition Law 637 (2009). Nonetheless, the Commission in *Volkswagen*, while finding that the conditions of Article 101(3) were not met, refrained from condemning RPF in general (stressing that the requirements of an individual exemption were not met *in this case*) and seriously examined the justifications submitted by Volkswagen. 2001/711/EC *Volkswagen* OJ [2001] L 262/14, para 95. ('Resale price maintenance does not contribute to improving the production or (in this case) the distribution of goods. Although, according to Volkswagen AG, it is intended to improve the profitability of German Volkswagen dealers and help them attain or maintain the standards of service prescribed by Volkswagen AG, and hence could, according to this argument, contribute to safeguarding as many dealerships as possible, there is no evidence to suggest that safeguarding individual dealerships which under normal competitive conditions would not be viable would appreciably improve the distribution of goods or that this alleged improvement might offset the disadvantages of the restriction of competition. Furthermore, there is not the slightest guarantee that the larger profits earned by Volkswagen dealers as a result of their refusing to grant discounts on the purchase of new VW Passat cars will be used to safeguard dealerships.')

23 Cases IV/C-2/31.609 and 37.306, XXIXth *Report on Competition Policy* 161 (1999).

of individual exemption.[24] Although the inclusion of RPF into the agreement 'gives rise to the presumption that the agreement is unlikely to fulfil the conditions of Article 101(3)', the 'undertakings have the possibility to plead an efficiency defence under Article 101(3) in an individual case'.[25] Until this point the 2010 *Guidelines* depart from the *Old Guidelines* of 2000 only slightly: it has always been possible to plead an efficiency defence under Article 101(3). This possibility remains also under the 2010 *Guidelines* highly exceptional, but is, notwithstanding the above conceptual arguments, to be regarded as practically prohibited. This proposition is underpinned by the conceptual placement of the treatment of RPF, i.e. Article 101(3), which entails considerable uncertainty. The BER boosts this when it does not simply blacklist RPF but pronounces it to be hardcore. Namely, if an agreement contains a blacklisted clause (as enumerated in Article 5 of the BER), the agreement itself does not lose the block exemption but this exclusion is limited to the incriminated contractual provision. On the other hand, if an agreement contains a hardcore restraint (as enumerated in Article 4), the entire agreement loses the block exemption's safe harbour. Accordingly, testing an RPF clause under Article 101(3) risks not simply this clause but the entire distribution agreement, thus raising the stakes.

The novelty of the 2010 *Guidelines on Vertical Restraints* is that they provide examples of when RPF could meet the requirements of Article 101(3); they list three cases where efficiency benefits may be present. First, RPF may be an efficient means of introducing and promoting a new product:

> Most notably, where a manufacturer introduces a new product, RPM may be helpful during the introductory period of expanding demand to induce distributors to better take into account the manufacturer's interest to promote the product. RPM may provide the distributors with the means to increase sales efforts and if the distributors on this market are under competitive pressure this may induce them to expand overall demand for the product and make the launch of the product a success, also for the benefit of consumers.[26]

---

24 *Guidelines on Vertical Restraints*, para 47. ('The Block Exemption Regulation contains in Article 4 a list of hardcore restrictions which lead to the exclusion of the whole vertical agreement from the scope of application of the Block Exemption Regulation. Including such a hardcore restriction in an agreement gives rise to the presumption that the agreement falls within Article 101(1). It also gives rise to the presumption that the agreement is unlikely to fulfil the conditions of Article 101(3), for which reason the block exemption does not apply. However, undertakings have the possibility to demonstrate pro-competitive effects under Article 101(3) in an individual case. In case the undertakings substantiate that likely efficiencies result from including the hardcore restriction in the agreement and that in general all the conditions of Article 101(3) are fulfilled, this will require the Commission to effectively assess the likely negative impact on competition before making the ultimate assessment of whether the conditions of Article 101(3) are fulfilled.')

25 Para 223.

26 Para 225.

It is to be stressed that the footnote attached to the above provides that the supplier may resort to RPF if it is not practical to impose on all dealers by contract effective promotion requirements.

Second, a coordinated short term low price campaign in a franchise system or similar distribution system applying a uniform distribution format may also justify the application of 'fixed resale prices, and not just maximum resale prices'.[27]

Third, pre-sales services, especially in case of experience or complex products, may also justify RPF, if necessary for tackling the free-rider problem.

> In some situations, the extra margin provided by RPM may allow retailers to provide (additional) pre-sales services, in particular in case of experience or complex products. If enough customers take advantage from such services to make their choice but then purchase at a lower price with retailers that do not provide such services (and hence do not incur these costs), high-service retailers may reduce or eliminate these services that enhance the demand for the supplier's product. RPM may help to prevent such free-riding at the distribution level. The parties will have to convincingly demonstrate that the RPM agreement can be expected to not only provide the means but also the incentive to overcome possible free riding between retailers on these services and that the pre-sales services overall benefit consumers as part of the demonstration that all the conditions of Article 101(3) are fulfilled.[28]

Notwithstanding the 2010 *Guidelines*' above siren song, it is expected that the fixing of the resale prices and minimum resale prices will remain rather risky from a competition law point of view, without having any secure leaning as to when it may be practised. Namely, the burden on undertakings pleading an efficiency defence under Article 101(3) is extremely high and, besides the above three examples, the 2010 *Guidelines* seem to offer only a little more than what was offered by the *Old Guidelines* of 2000: RPF is unlikely to fulfil the requirements of an individual exemption but theoretically this is possible. Accordingly, EU competition law saw only a minor refinement and not a comprehensive reform.

The *de facto* outright prohibition of RPF has been frequently criticized[29] and seems to be at variance with the state of the law in other fields. First, for long, both EU courts and the Commission recognized the validity of the free-rider argument, though as relation to territorial protection, without giving any indication why this theory should not be applied to RPF.[30] Now, as noted above, the 2010 *Guidelines*

27 Para 225.

28 Para 225.

29 Femi Alese, *Unmasking the Masquerade of Vertical Price Fixing*, 28(9) European Competition Law Review 514, 525 (2007).

30 *Guidelines on Article 101(3)*, para 82; Joined Cases 56/64 and 58/64 *Consten and Grundig v Commission* [1964] ECR 299, p. 342.; Case T-168/01 *GlaxoSmithKline Services Unlimited v Commission* [2006] ECR II-2969, para 273.

on Vertical Restraints indicate the Commission's intention to apply the free-riding theory also to RPF.[31] Second, the ECJ expressly recognized in *Metro/Saba* that although price competition must never be eliminated, it does not have absolute precedence in all cases and restraints on resale prices could be pro-competitive.

> [A]lthough price competition is so important that it can never be eliminated it does not constitute the only effective form of competition or that to which absolute priority must in all circumstances be accorded. The powers conferred upon the Commission (…) show that the requirements for the maintenance of workable competition may be reconciled with the safeguarding of objectives of a different nature and that to this end certain restrictions on competition are permissible, provided that they are essential to the attainment of these objectives and that they do not result in the elimination of competition for a substantial part of the common market. For specialist wholesalers and retailer the desire to maintain a certain price level, which corresponds to the desire to preserve, in the interests of consumers, the possibility of the continued existence of the channel of distribution in conjunction with new methods of distribution based on a different type of competition policy, forms one of the objectives which may be pursued without necessarily falling under the prohibition contained in article 85 (1), and, if it does fall thereunder, either wholly or in part, coming within the framework of article 85 (3). That argument is strengthened if, in addition, such conditions promote improved competition inasmuch as it relates to factors other than prices.[32]

Nevertheless, as far as the authoritative nature of the above passage is concerned, the fly in the ointment is that the Commission decision under review dealt with different stipulations in a selective distribution agreement, which did not relate directly to prices but the whole distribution system had such an aggregate effect.

The judicial and decisional practice has been at fault for a comprehensive explanation why RPF is treated as anti-competitive by object, albeit some hints were given. One reason could be the elimination of intra-brand price competition; in *SPRL Louis Erauw-Jacquery v La Hesbignonne SC* the ECJ referred to the dealer-cartel theory.[33]

The Commission's 2010 *Guidelines on Vertical Restraints* contain a detailed enumeration of the competition risks of RPF:[34] first, it may facilitate collusion

31 *Guidelines on Vertical Restraints*, para 225.

32 Case 26/76 *Metro SB-Großmärkte GmbH and Co. KG v Commission* ECR [1977] 1875.

33 Case 27/87 *SPRL Louis Erauw-Jacquery v La Hesbignonne SC* [1988] ECR 1919, para 15. (Asserting that the parallel employment of RPF clauses in different agreements entails that 'those agreements have the same effects as a price system fixed by a horizontal agreement'.)

34 Contrary to the *Old Guidelines* of 2000 that failed to demonstrate with compelling arguments that RPF is 'always or almost always' anti-competitive and, in para 112, pointed

between suppliers, second, it may facilitate collusion between dealers, third, 'it may more generally soften competition between manufacturers and/or between retailers', fourth, 'the immediate effect of RPM will be that all or certain distributors are prevented from lowering their sales price for that particular brand', fifth, 'it may lower the pressure on the margin of the manufacturer, in particular where the manufacturer has a commitment problem', sixth, it 'may be implemented by a manufacturer with market power to foreclose smaller rivals', seventh, RPF 'may reduce dynamism and innovation at the distribution level'.[35]

It is welcome that the Commission in the 2010 *Guidelines* got rid of the argument that one of the main risks of RPF is that it reduces intra-brand competition;[36] intra-brand competition has no independent significance if inter-brand competition is effective.

While RPF agreements may entail all the above impacts, these effects are not necessarily attached to these arrangements. By way of example, price-transparency-induced horizontal concerns emerge only if RPF is widely practised in the industry and the market is susceptible of tacit coordination; as far as the risk of price increase is concerned, RPF relates to the price of *a particular brand* and *not to the market price*; hence, the increase of the market price is not necessary. All in all, these examples suggest that RPF is *not always* risky but it may raise concerns *under certain circumstances*. Accordingly, the circumstances of the case at stake must be taken into account in order to ascertain whether these potential negative effects are indeed present.

RPF in US antitrust law: hundred years' war and the triumph of the free-rider rationale

In US antitrust law maximum and recommended resale prices have been considered under the rule of reason for long. On the other hand, the fixing of concrete and minimum resale prices had been *per se* illegal for almost a century. The stance taken by the Supreme Court in *Dr. Miles* (1911) was overruled in a long-awaited judgment in *Leegin* (2007). Therewith, it is worthy of note that the hostile approach against RPF was considerably diluted in *Monsanto*,[37] where the Supreme Court, whilst preserving *per se* illegality, held that the agreement between the producer

only to two main negative effects: '(1) a reduction in intra-brand price competition, and (2) increased transparency on prices. (…) Increased transparency on price and responsibility for price changes makes horizontal collusion between manufacturers or distributors easier, at least in concentrated markets. The reduction in intra-brand competition may, as it leads to less downward pressure on the price for the particular goods, have as an indirect effect a reduction of inter-brand competition.'

35 Para 224.

36 See *Old Guidelines on Vertical Restraints*, para 112.

37 *Monsanto Co. v Spray-Rite Service Corp.*, 465 U.S. 752 (1984).

and a complaining distributor to expel a price-cutting dealer from the distribution network does not qualify as an agreement on the resale price. It is also interesting that this odd grasp of agreement was heavily and admittedly influenced by the arguments that actually justify the complete withdrawal of RPF from the *per se* illegality pigeonhole (free-riding, dealer services etc.).

The outright prohibition of resale price fixing was based on several arguments that were not backed or verified by sound economic theory. First, courts placed excessive emphasis on the role of intra-brand competition, disregarding the fact that the real ring of rivalry is among the brands. Second, the protection of small and medium-size companies and the respect for the enterprises' right to compete also played a central role in condemning a business policy that envisaged eliminating the most important playing field of the dealers, which were typically small businesses. Finally, the foregoing stance was induced also by a goodly amount of formalism: it seemed to be contradictory to countenance uniform and consented prices between competing dealers imposed centrally by the producer, while chasing with fire and sword any agreement between these dealers if concluded in a decentralized manner.

In the first RPM case, *Dr. Miles Medical Co. v John D. Park & Sons Co.*,[38] the manufacturer of patented pharmaceuticals fixed the minimum resale price in its distribution contracts. The Supreme Court held that the anti-competitive effects of such agreements are evident; nevertheless, it did not back its wide-ranging and unconditional prohibition with any valid economic argument. The Court's reasoning was based on two points, besides the bare declaration that it is obvious 'that these agreements restrain trade'. First, the Court was concerned about competition between dealers, i.e. intra-brand competition, which was, as the Court stated, excluded completely in case of resale price-fixing.

> [A]ll competition between retailers is destroyed, for each such retailer can obtain his supply only by signing one of the uniform contracts prepared for retailers, whereby he covenants not to sell to anyone who proposes to sell again unless the buyer is authorized in writing by the complainant, and not to sell at less than a standard price named in the agreement. Thus all room for competition between retailers, who supply the public, is made impossible.[39]

The second ground of the outright prohibition of the minimum resale price was the theory that it is not allowed to impose on distributors restrictions that they cannot stipulate between themselves. This argument is clearly based on the dealer-cartel theory described above.

> [T]he [producer] can fare no better with its plan of identical contracts than could the dealers themselves if they formed a combination and endeavored to establish

38 220 U.S. 373.

39 *Id.* at 400.

> the same restrictions, and thus to achieve the same result, by agreement with each other. *If the immediate advantage they would thus obtain would not be sufficient to sustain such a direct agreement, the asserted ulterior benefit to the [producer] cannot be regarded as sufficient to support its system.*[40]

The Court, presumably as a corollary of the notion that centrally imposed resale prices are *like* horizontally agreed prices, came to the conclusion that RPM favours resellers; nevertheless, it did not explain why it was the manufacturer who introduced, administered and defended this arrangement.[41] Anyhow, the legal test to be applied with regard to vertical price fixing was established: *per se* illegality, the same fate as for horizontal price fixing.

At the same moment, it is remarkable what Justice Holmes said in his dissent. It sowed the seeds of what would nowadays be called the prevalence of inter-brand competition over intra-brand rivalry, stating that the Court 'greatly exaggerate[d] the value and importance to the public of competition in the production or distribution of an article (here it is only distribution) as fixing a fair price'.[42] If there is sufficient inter-brand competition, intra-brand restrictions simply lose their relevance from a competition law point of view, provided that the brand concerned has no market power. In the absence of market power, the producer has no chance to raise prices over the competitive level. Hence, if there is no market power, the business policy of the undertakings should be adjudicated by the market and not by the judiciary. As Justice Holmes concluded in his dissent: the producer 'knows better than we do what will enable it to do the best business'.[43]

The Court later on confined the above hostile approach towards RPM. First, it exempted recommended prices,[44] and afterwards, it gave the green light to maximum price fixing, thus keeping only the fixing of concrete and minimum prices in the *per se* illegality pigeonhole. Although the Supreme Court initially condemned maximum price fixing in *Albrecht v Herald Co.*,[45] 29 years later, in 1997, it overruled that precedent in *State Oil Co. v Khan.*[46]

The *per se* condemnation of vertical resale price fixing was, nevertheless, not uninterrupted, though the short intermezzo was not due to the Supreme

40 *Id.* at 407.

41 *Id.* at 407.

42 *Id.* at 412.

43 *Id.* at 412.

44 See *United State v Colgate and Co.*, 250 U.S. 300 (1919).

45 390 U.S. 145 (1968). In *Albrecht v Herald Co.* the publisher of a daily newspaper terminated its business relationship with one of its distributors because the latter applied higher resale prices than the ones determined by the publisher. This conduct was condemned by the Court. *Id.* at 149.

46 118 S.Ct. 275. In *State Oil Co. v Khan* the defendant, a retail gasoline station, purchased gas from the plaintiff at a given price and it was required to put, at most, a margin of 3.25 cents per gallon. All surpluses over the allowed margin were to be transferred to State Oil.

Court's overruling of *Dr. Miles*. In 1937 the Miller-Tydings Act[47] was adopted, and strengthened in 1952 by the McGuire Act,[48] which granted states the right to opt out from the *per se* rule, and several used the opportunity to enact such statutes.[49] Nevertheless, in 1975 the Consumer Goods Pricing Act[50] repealed the Miller-Tydings Act and the McGuire Act, thus reinstating the omnipotence of *Dr. Miles*. There was a 'general dissatisfaction with the effects of legal vertical price fixing [which] led to the repeal of those statutes'.[51] Nevertheless, it should be pointed out that while the Miller-Tydings Act of 1937 enabled only the exemption of voluntary vertical agreements on the resale price, it did not empower states to compel retailers' adherence to the producer's resale pricing policy if there was no prior covenant.[52] On the other hand, the McGuire Act of 1952 permitted states to enact laws according to which the producer's RPF agreement with one of the retailers had the effect of binding all dealers, not only the ones that consented to it.[53] Unfortunately, there is no comprehensive empirical evidence concerning this era's retail prices. A survey focusing on drugs shows that in this segment the producers normally increased the then prevailing discounter prices only slightly in order to preserve the dual distribution system, i.e. independent dealers providing services and discounting chain stores providing no services.[54]

Although the *per se* illegality of RPF reigned for almost a century (from 1911 to 2007), its purview was widely confined in 1984 by the Supreme Court's judgment in *Monsanto*. As mentioned above, the hostile attitude towards RPM yielded up its soul in 2007 (*Leegin*); nevertheless, it received a mortal hurt already in 1984 (*Monsanto*). In the latter case, the Supreme Court held that the producer is entitled to announce in advance the pricing policy it favours and terminate the distributorship of a discounter following complaints from non-price-cutting dealers, stressing that an agreement with a dealer to terminate a discounter for price-cutting is not an agreement to fix the resale price. Thus, building on *Monsanto*, producers could virtually maintain resale prices without inserting express stipulations into the distribution agreements.

---

47 Pub. L. No. 314, 50 Stat. 693 (1937).

48 Pub. L. No. 542, 66 Stat. 631 (1952).

49 Naturally, even during the above period the *per se* rule remained applicable to arrangements not covered by state law. *See Simpson v Union Oil Co.,* 377 U.S. 13 (1964).

50 Pub. L. No. 94-145, 89 Stat. 801 (1975).

51 *See* Donald L. Beschle, *What, Never? Well, Hardly Ever: Strict Antitrust Scrutiny as an Alternative to Per Se Antitrust Illegality*, 38 Hastings Law Journal 471, 479 (1987).

52 See *Schwegman Bros. v Calvert Distillers Corp*., 341 U.S. 384 (1951).

53 *See* Donald L. Beschle, *What, Never? Well, Hardly Ever: Strict Antitrust Scrutiny as an Alternative to Per Se Antitrust Illegality*, 38 Hastings Law Journal 471, 479 fn 33 (1987). *Cf. Parke, Davis and Co. v Health Cross Stores, Inc.*, 364 F.2d 214 (1966). (Inquiring whether the McGuire Act meets respective constitutional standards.)

54 *See* H. J. Ostlund and C. R. Vickland, Fair Trade and the Retail Drug Store (1940).

In *Leegin Creative Leather Products, Inc. v PSKS, Inc.*, a highly divided Supreme Court, in a five-to-four judgment, finally overruled *Dr. Miles*, expressly disapproving the formalist analysis of RPF and the dealer-cartel theory, especially because in several (or rather all) other respects 'the Court rejected the approach of reliance on rules governing horizontal restraints when defining rules applicable to vertical ones'.[55] After recognizing that 'the reasons upon which Dr. Miles relied do not justify a *per se* rule', the Court started examining the economic effects of vertical minimum price fixing in order to decide 'whether the *per se* rule is nonetheless appropriate'.[56]

The logic applied by the Court thereafter was the following: there is neither chance, nor need to determine whether the fixing of the resale price is simply good or bad. As far as antitrust characterization is concerned, the proper question is whether the arrangement at stake always or almost always tends to restrict competition without a potential for redeeming virtue; the question is not whether the arrangement at stake is normally or usually detrimental to competition but whether it is always of such a nature. The role of economic pros and cons at this level of antitrust analysis is restricted to answering the query whether the fixing of the resale price can have potentially plausible justifications. The task of characterization is not a matter of balancing but it is about searching for potentially plausible theories supporting the arrangement concerned. Therewith, the fact may have incited sympathy in the Court that 'a manufacturer has no incentive to overcompensate retailers with unjustified margins. The retailers, not the manufacturer, gain from higher retail prices.'[57] And in case the producer imposes RPF, it is reasonable to assume that it has good reasons to do that.

Accordingly, the Court enumerated the potential advantages and risks attached to resale price fixing and came to the conclusion that 'notwithstanding the risks of unlawful conduct, it cannot be stated with any degree of confidence that resale price maintenance "always or almost always tend[s] to restrict competition and decrease output"'.[58] The Court perceived such justifications for vertical price restraints that are similar to vertical non-price restraints. First, the fixing of the minimum resale price can stimulate inter-brand competition by reducing intra-brand rivalry. Second, it can 'give consumers more options so that they can choose among low-price, low-service brands; high-price, high-service brands; and brands that fall in between'.[59] Third, it can enhance retail services. 'Absent vertical price restraints, the retail services that enhance interbrand competition might be underprovided' and 'discounting retailers can free ride on retailers who furnish services'.[60] Therewith, the fixing of the minimum resale price, as a contract

55 127 S.Ct. 2705, 2714 (2007).
56 *Id.* at 2714.
57 *Id.* at 2714 and 2719.
58 *Id.* at 2717.
59 *Id.* at 2715.
60 *Id.* at 2708.

enforcement device, can enhance retail services also in cases where free-riding is not a real hazard: it may be difficult for the producer to enforce a contract specifying the whole spectrum of the required retail services. On the other hand, it may be more efficient for the producer to guarantee a particular margin to the retailer and to threaten termination once the distributor does not comply with the retail service requirements. Fourth, the fixing of the minimum resale price can ease the market entry of new enterprises and brands and this increases inter-brand competition.

The Court also drew an inventory of the potential risks of the fixing of the minimum retail price. First, it could assist a producer cartel by identifying price-cutting cartelists. Second, it can also be used for the sake of a retailer cartel: distributors might conclude a cartel and request the producer to administer it. Finally, both producers and distributors could abuse RPF. For instance, a dominant retailer could compel the producer to impose minimum resale prices in order to get protection from the competitive pressure induced by more efficient discounters, thus hindering innovation. At the same time, a producer with market power could use the fixing of the minimum resale price in order to cut smaller rivals' or new entrants' access to distribution channels by 'giv[ing] retailers an incentive not to sell [their] products'; such a practice would be tantamount to a constructive non-compete.

On the basis of the above enumerated advantages and risks, the Court was ready to take the position that '[t]hough each side of the debate can find sources to support its position, it suffices to say here that economics literature is replete with procompetitive justifications for a manufacturer's use of resale price maintenance'.[61]

The Court mentioned three factors that should be taken into account when adjudicating RPF in a given case. First, the number and market power of the producers committed to RPF can provide important instruction. When only few producers with no market power employ RPF, there is little likelihood of any producer or retailer cartel, as inter-brand competition would easily dampen any endeavour for higher prices. Nevertheless, if numerous manufacturers apply RPF, the case would merit a closer scrutiny.[62] Second, it could also be of relevance

---

61 *Id.* at 2714.

62 *Id.* at 2719. ('When only a few manufacturers lacking market power adopt the practice, there is little likelihood it is facilitating a manufacturer cartel, for a cartel then can be undercut by rival manufacturers. Likewise, a retailer cartel is unlikely when only a single manufacturer in a competitive market uses resale price maintenance. Interbrand competition would divert consumers to lower priced substitutes and eliminate any gains to retailers from their price-fixing agreement over a single brand. Resale price maintenance should be subject to more careful scrutiny, by contrast, if many competing manufacturers adopt the practice.')

where the initiative of RPF originates from: the retailer or the producer.[63] Finally, the Court also emphasized the relevance of market power when inquiring whether a producer or retailer can abuse RPF for anti-competitive purposes.[64] Of course, the foregoing enumeration of the relevant factors is certainly not exhaustive since courts have not had the chance to subject minimum resale price fixing cases to a full-blown inquiry, due to the century-long *per se* illegality rule, and, hence, they could not gain considerable experience in this regard. Nevertheless, as courts gain experience concerning the fixing of the resale price by 'applying the rule of reason over the course of decisions, they can establish the litigation structure to ensure the rule operates to eliminate anticompetitive restraints from the market and to provide more guidance to businesses'.[65]

Comparative summary

As demonstrated above, there is a fundamental divergence between US antitrust and EU competition law, both in law and in fact, concerning the treatment of the fixing of concrete or minimum resale prices, while the approaches of the two regimes regarding maximum resale price fixing and recommended resale prices roughly coincide. The latter two kinds of arrangements are to be examined under the rule of reason in US antitrust law, while in EU competition law they are declared lawful if neither the supplier's, nor the buyer's market share exceeds 30 per cent and even above this threshold they can be condemned only if they have anti-competitive effects.[66]

In US antitrust law, the *per se* illegality of RPF was utterly abolished in *Leegin* (2007), nevertheless, in *Monsanto* (1984) the Supreme Court sympathized with the producer imposing RPF and with the free-riding rationale, and confined the application of *per se* illegality to agreements that relate positively to the resale price, i.e. prior announcements to terminate in case of discounting, communication between the producer and non-discounting dealers and agreements to terminate the price-cutter were not covered by *per se* illegality. Accordingly, it is to be

63 *Id.* at 2719. ('If there is evidence retailers were the impetus for a vertical price restraint, there is a greater likelihood that the restraint facilitates a retailer cartel or supports a dominant, inefficient retailer. See Brief for William S. Comanor et al. as *Amici Curiae* 7-8. If, by contrast, a manufacturer adopted the policy independent of retailer pressure, the restraint is less likely to promote anticompetitive conduct.')

64 *Id.* at 2720. ('As a final matter, that a dominant manufacturer or retailer can abuse resale price maintenance for anticompetitive purposes may not be a serious concern unless the relevant entity has market power. If a retailer lacks market power, manufacturers likely can sell their goods through rival retailers. And if a manufacturer lacks market power, there is less likelihood it can use the practice to keep competitors away from distribution outlets.')

65 *Id.* at 2720.

66 Article 3 of the BER.

emphasized that the virtual divergence between US antitrust and EU competition law, in this regard, started 23 years before *Leegin*.

For a long time, US antitrust and EU competition law had been in line: in the US RPF was *per se* illegal, while in the EU it was automatically condemned under Article 101(1) and had practically no chance to survive under Article 101(3); at least, with one doubtful exception, there had been no agreement that could have done it in the Commission's decisional practice,[67] although before Regulation 1/2003/EC all agreements caught by Article 101(1) were to be notified to the Commission if they wanted to gain an individual exemption under Article 101(3). As noted above, this accordance, contrary to the majority view, collapsed long before *Leegin*. This was already a accomplished fact after *Monsanto*, where the Supreme Court inflected the notion of agreement in the context of RPF insomuch that it confined the applicability of the *per se* prohibition to the utmost extent: it was held that terminating a discounter for price-cutting after non-discounting distributors' complaining does not imply RPF, provided there is no agreement directly relating to prices. This divergence became complete in *Leegin*, which abolished the *per se* condemnation of RPF.

In EU competition law, RPF covenants are anti-competitive by object under Article 101(1) and might, at least in theory, benefit from an individual exemption under Article 101(3). Nevertheless, there has been no formal decision allowing RPF under Article 101(3). The jurisprudence of the EU courts, the Commission's 'soft law' instruments and its decisional practice all suggest that the chances of RPF surviving are theoretically always, practically almost never realistic.

As far as the perspectives of RPF are concerned, there is an ever-growing school of thought in Europe on RPF and on the need for reform concerning its treatment. There is, nevertheless, a danger that the issues of RPF will be forced into Article 101(3)'s bed of Procrustes,[68] which is, however, not the proper place for examining them. As noted above, Article 101(3) focuses, or rather

67 Nevertheless, the Commission, as noted above, in *Newspaper distribution contracts in Belgium – AMP* sent a comfort letter (but not a formal decision!) concerning an RPF arrangement, and came to the conclusion that it met the conditions of Article 101(3). Cases IV/C-2/31.609 and 37.306, XXIXth *Report on Competition Policy* 161 (1999).

68 *See* Luc Peeperkorn, *Resale Price Maintenance and its Alleged Efficiencies*, 4(1) European Competition Journal 201, 204 and 212 (2008). (Asserting that it can be argued that the hardcore approach of EU competition law is 'in a way an application of what is described (…) [in *Leegin*] by the Supreme Court'.) ('One could conclude that the *Leegin* judgment provides the US authorities and courts with the possibility of applying the same policy towards RPM as is currently applied in the EU, though it remains to be seen how US policy will develop.'); Alison Jones, *Resale Price Maintenance: a Debate about Competition Policy in Europe*, 5(2) European Competition Journal 479, 513 (2009). (Arguing that the Commission could be encouraged to consider the pro-competitive merits of RPM under Article 101(3).); Frederik Van Doorn, *Resale Price Maintenance in EC Competition Law: The Need for a Standardised Approach* (6 November 2009) (available at SSRN: http://ssrn.com/abstract=1501070), 1 and 23-24.

should focus, on questions of (productive) efficiency, while the vast majority of economic justifications for RPF assert that it increases rivalry, i.e. the intensity of competition. The currently effective BER and *Guidelines on Vertical Restraints* (both adopted in 2010) foreshadow this approach and seem to turn this danger into reality: while the new BER and the new *Guidelines*, similarly to old ones, consider RPF as hardcore and anticompetitive by object, the 2010 *Guidelines* expressly encourage undertakings to test RPF agreements under Article 101(3) and declare that the exemptibility of such arrangements is an exceptional but not a completely unrealistic perspective.

It is submitted that after *Leegin* the two regimes are not in line with each other, notwithstanding the fact that the European approach towards RPF is said to have changed and a 'full-blown' enquiry is promised under Article 101(3). First, under the rule of reason the plaintiff has to show a *prima facie* case (competitive harm or market power); on the other hand, in EU competition law RPF is a *per se* violation of Article 101(1). Second, the enquiry of the justifications and the balancing of the pros and cons of RPF – taking into account the present conceptual location of RPF, which exiles it to Article 101(3) – would be far more burdensome for defendants than the treatment they can expect on the other side of the Atlantic. The reason is not only the one mentioned above, i.e. Article 101(3) focuses on (productive) efficiency benefits, but it is also to be taken into account that the status of justifications under the rule of reason and Article 101(3) is different. The application of the latter is almost, though not completely, exceptional, where a heavy burden of proof rests on the shoulders of the undertaking concerned, which assumes all uncertainties and risks of evaluation. What is more, a rather detailed set of substantiated and empirically verifiable evidence is to be submitted in order to succeed. On the other hand, concerning the rule of reason the general perception is that plausible and reasonably substantiated allegations of justification can save the defendant. This may be due to the circumstance that in the US more than 90 per cent of the antitrust matters are litigated in civil procedure where the usual standard of burden of proof is preponderance of evidence (balance of probabilities) and this applies also to the proof of justifications.

Evaluation

Both US antitrust and EU competition law share the general proposition that the application of automatic condemnation should be restricted to practices that, due to their nature, are always or almost always anti-competitive without the perspective of a redeeming virtue. Economic theory shows that RPF is in several cases reasonably justifiable. Economic scholarship provides several examples where the producer's endeavour to maintain prices is socially beneficial because it enhances competition. Accordingly, the *per se* condemnation of RPF is not justified, and those instances are to be singled out where there is no competitive harm, either because there are no anti-competitive repercussions (e.g. the market position of the parties is trivial) or because they are outweighed by pro-competitive effects (e.g. the RPF handles a market failure).

There is an internal inconsistency in automatically condemning RPF, while affording the chance of full-blown analysis for vertical non-price restraints: at the end of the day they have the same effects, at least in theory. It is an economic commonplace that price and quantity are in inverse relation with each other. Assume that, due to the fact that the goods are branded, and hereupon differentiated, the proper economic model to be applied is that of monopolistic competition. Here, the manufacturer faces a residual demand curve, which is sufficiently elastic in order to bar the producer from acting like a monopolist; however, it still has some playing field owing to the loyal customers of the brand. Since the price and the quantity of the goods are determined by the profit-maximizing point of the residual demand curve, from an economic point of view, it is indifferent whether it is the price or the quantity that is fixed in advance. When the producer assigns an exclusive territory or consumer group(s) to the distributor it has some ideas, at least theoretically, about the profit-maximizing price of the territory or customer group in question. Accordingly, assigning a restricted number of consumers, i.e. quantity, to the distributor implies that the producer determines the dealer's profit-maximizing price indirectly.[69] The real difference between the two methods – that is fixing the resale price directly or indirectly through non-price restrictions – lies in the details: normally, this convergence works only in theory since due to imperfect information it is almost impossible for the producer to determine the quantity that triggers exactly the price the producer endeavours.

It is submitted that in EU competition law the main problem is that conceptually the question of RPF has been pushed in the pigeonhole of Article 101(3). While the latter is certainly the proper place for measuring productive efficiency arguments, several of the supporting theories of RPF stress that in some cases RPF may actually increase the intensity of competition in terms of rivalry. For instance, the enhanced services provided by the retailers may increase the demand for the product and thus trigger competitive pressure on competing products; producers may have access to distribution channels not available for them in the absence of RPF etc. These theories, in fact, argue that RPF increases rivalry but, by way of example, normally reveal no cost-savings. Another rule of thumb regarding RPF is that it cannot interfere with the proper functioning of the competitive process if there is no market power, an issue also belonging to the analysis under Article 101(1). As the economic criticism of the present state of law and the impact of *Leegin* is growing, EU competition law is being compelled to react to the points raised. There is a danger (and this danger became a reality in the 2010 *Guidelines on Vertical Restraints*) that the analysis of RPF will be forced into Article 101(3); the reaction will probably be that RPF as such is not *per se* illegal (a notion unknown for EU competition law anyway) and it can be regarded as lawful if it

69 Robert H. Bork, The antitrust paradox. A policy at war with itself 282 (1978).

fulfils the requirements of individual exemption.[70] Nevertheless, this escape hatch seems to drive RPF onto a field where it cannot win the battle, as Article 101(3) deals with productive efficiency, a benefit normally not attributed to RPF.

Although the 2010 *Guidelines on Vertical Restraints* suggest that undertakings should test their RPF agreements under Article 101(3), the 2010 BER, inconsistently, discourages them from this: it maintains the 1999 BER's approach and it does not simply exclude RPF from the block exemption but regards it as hardcore. As noted above, if an agreement contains a blacklisted clause (as enumerated in Article 5 of the BER), the agreement itself does not lose the block exemption but this exclusion is limited to the incriminated contractual provision. On the other hand, if an agreement contains a hardcore restraint (as enumerated in Article 4), the entire agreement loses the block exemption's safe harbour. Accordingly, testing an RPF clause under Article 101(3) risks not simply this clause but the entire distribution agreement, thus unnecessarily raising the stakes.

As noted above, one of the strongest arguments for RPF is that if implemented by a small supplier and it is not widespread in the industry (no cumulative effects), it is simply not capable of being harmful; an argument that does not fit Article 101(3); on the other hand, this argument suggests that instead the *Notice on Agreements of Minor Importance* should be amended so as to cover agreements containing RPF if market share is low.[71]

The 2010 regulatory package of vertical restraints ignores the transaction costs and realities of competition assessment and balancing. The Article 101(3) assessment is very expensive and time-consuming, and definitely needs specialized expertise. If individual exemption under the notification system amounted to a torture, this is the truer in respect of self-assessment under Article 101(3). Such resources normally pertain to big enterprises; nevertheless, they are the ones where a stringent RPF policy would be justified. On the other hand, normally, the Article 101(3) assessment requires, subjectively, much higher efforts and induces, proportionally, higher transaction costs in case of undertakings of which the market power is smaller. Although it is normally the small enterprises that, due to the low market share, should be allowed to fix the resale price, they are also the ones that shrink from the Article 101(3) assessment due to the high legal and analysis expenses. It is to be noted that legal costs emerge not only in the phase of the preliminary self-assessment but also during the subsequent potential competition procedure.

70 Para 47 of the Commission's *Guidelines on Vertical Restraints* encourages hardcore restrictions to try to meet the conditions of Article 101(3). This siren song is repeated specifically regarding RPF in para 223 of the *Guidelines on Vertical Restraints*.

71 The approach that RPFs of minor importance cannot raise competition concerns and are, hence, in accord with competition law appears, for instance, in Section 13 of the Hungarian Competition Act (Law No LVII of 1996), which regards RPF below 10 per cent market share as *de minimis* and thus lawful.

The status of (relative) territorial protection demonstrates the mistreatment of RPF. The most important argument for territorial protection is the free-rider theory. The story of the parasite dealer intruding in the field cultivated by the local distributor and free-riding on its investments is so picturesque that competition law waives the claim to inquire in detail whether free-riding is a real problem in the particular case, whether the territorially competent trader would assume distributorship, whether it would take on the efforts and expenses of promotion on the optimal level or whether there would be under-investment. Here, competition law is satisfied in that it regards these restraints as lawful in the absence of market power (according to the BER under 30 per cent market share) and presumes that they are justified and follow a legitimate end. In other words, competition law accepts that *in abstracto* these restraints aim at tackling the free-rider problem and does not analyse whether this consideration is present *in concreto*. Several agreements involving territorial protection would fail if it were required to be proved under Article 101(3) that the restraint's purpose and actual effect is the tackling of the free-rider problem, the supplier would find no trader to deal with the merchandise, dealers would not be incited to promote the merchandise and hence, there would be under-investment in the promotion efforts and finally, there is no alternative and less restrictive method to handle free-riding.

The fact that there is a conceptual escape hatch for RPF in the form of Article 101(3) appears to be rather a disadvantage: in US antitrust law the compelling economic criticism concerning the status of RPF resulted in the comprehensive revision of the law; in EU competition law the perspective of such a fundamental re-thinking of the features and consequences of RPF seems to be delayed or even impeded by the opportunism enabled by Article 101(3). This is what the 2010 *Guidelines on Vertical Restraints* seem to have done: only a minor refinement, not a comprehensive reform.

Chapter VII

Non-price restraints: territorial exclusivity – from foe to friend

It may seem odd but concerning territorial exclusivity, for a decade (between 1967 and 1977), EU competition law followed a much more economic approach than US antitrust law. Notwithstanding the Supreme Court's classification of territorial exclusivity as a rule of reason restraint in 1963 (*White Motor*), four years later it held that such arrangements are *per se* illegal (*Schwinn*); and this rule reigned for ten years, until 1977 (*Sylvania*). On the other hand, primarily due to the influence of the free-riding rationale, in the EU territorial exclusivity has always been judged according to its effects (*Technique Minière*), provided, it did not ban passive sales (absolute territorial protection); a circumstance that turns the entire arrangement into an agreement anti-competitive by object (*Consten and Grundig*). Nevertheless, this advantage of EU competition law evaporated once US courts started scrutinizing territorial restraints under the rule of reason, while the ban on passive sales remained sacrosanct in the EU.

Vertical territorial restraints in EU competition law: the taboo of market integration

As opposed to price-related vertical restrictions, non-price restrictions are treated more laxly in EU competition law, which has a fairly unique feature: one of the central purposes of EU competition law is market integration, a target not present in any other competition law on the globe. The end of market integration has palpable effects on several rules, the most idiosyncratic being the treatment of vertical territorial restrictions.[1] It implies that market operators are not allowed to re-build the barriers to free movement (of goods, services, capital and persons), which were abolished by the rules of the internal market.[2] Whereas EU

1 *See* 2003/675/EC *PO Video Games, PO Nintendo Distribution and Omega – Nintendo* OJ [2003] L 255/33. para 374. ('[T]he infringement had the object of enhancing the territorial protection awarded to exclusive distributors to a state of absolute territorial protection and eliminating in each territory all competition with the distributor of the products in that territory. It also had the object of artificially partitioning the single market, thereby jeopardising a fundamental principle of the Treaty. Restrictions of this kind are by their nature very serious violations of Article 81(1) of the Treaty and 53(1) of the EEA Agreement.').

2 See Luc Gyselen, *Vertical Restraints in the Distribution Process: Strength and Weakness of the Free Rider Rationale under EEC Competition Law*, 21 Common Market

competition law, similarly to US antitrust, recognizes and follows the free-rider theory, beyond a certain point the purpose of market integration overshadows this justification and turns the otherwise benign treatment of territorial protection into *quasi per se* illegality. The purpose of market integration in the sense of free movement contrasts with the free-rider rationale: virtually all territorial restraints devoted to tackle the free-rider problem, to some extent, impede the intra-Union free movement. Once this tension reaches an appreciable level, the single market imperative prevails,[3] a conclusion frequently criticized in the scholarship.[4]

In 1966 the ECJ rendered two judgments within two weeks, which laid down the foundation stones of EU law on territorial exclusivity. While the law on vertical restraints has undergone several changes in the last four decades, the approach fixed in 1966 remained essentially intact: EU competition law does not tolerate absolute territorial exclusivity, whereas relative territorial exclusivity can be acceptable.

In the first case, *Société Techniquliedekere Minière (L.T.M.) v Maschinenbau Ulm GmbH (M.B.U.)*,[5] the ECJ held that 'it may be doubted whether there is an interference with competition if the said agreement [containing relative territorial protection] seems really necessary for the penetration of a new area by an undertaking'.[6] The distribution arrangement at stake, while encompassing territorial exclusivity, did not contain export bans and was mainly based on areas of primary responsibility.

The Court also gave a list of factors to be taken into account when evaluating vertical territorial restraints:

Law Review 647, 650-651 (1984); Jean-Yves Art and Dirk van Liedekerke, *Developments in EC Competition Law in 1994 – an Overview*, 32(4) Common Market Law Review 921, 930 (1995); Lennart Ritter and W. David Braun, European Competition Law: a Practitioner's Guide 269 (3d ed., 2005).

3 See Emmanuel P. Mastromanolis, *Insights from U.S. Antitrust Law on Exclusive and Restricted Territorial Distribution: The Creation of a New Legal Standard for European Union Competition Law,* 15 University of Pennsylvania Journal of International Business Law 559, 565 (1994).

4 Baden Fuller, *Economic Issues Relating to Property Rights in Trade Marks, Important Bans, Differential Pricing, Restrictions on Resale and Repackaging*, 6 European Law Review 162 (1981); Valentine Korah, *Goodbye, Red Label; Condemnation of Dual Pricing by Distillers*, 3 European Law Review 62 (1978); Ivo Van Bael, *Heretical Reflections on the Basic Dogma of EEC Antitrust: Single Market Integration*, 10(1) Revue Suisse du Droit International de la Concurrence 39 (1980). For cases where export bans, irrespective of whether imposed in law or in fact, were condemned automatically, *see e.g.* Case T-43/92 *Dunlop Slazenger International Ltd v Commission* [1994] ECR II-441, para 52; Case T-77/92 *Parker Pen Ltd v Commission* [1994] ECR II-549, para 37; Case T-66/92 *Herlitz AG v Commission* [1994] ECR II-531, para 29.

5 Case 56/65 *Société Technique Minière (L.T.M.) v Maschinenbau Ulm GmbH (M.B.U.)* [1966] ECR 235.

6 *Id.* at 250.

> it is appropriate to take into account in particular the nature and quantity, limited or otherwise, of the products covered by the agreement, the position and importance of the grantor and the concessionaire on the market for the products concerned, the isolated nature of the disputed agreement or, alternatively, its position in a series of agreements, the severity of the clauses intended to protect the exclusive dealership or, alternatively, the opportunities allowed for other commercial competitors in the same products by way of parallel re-exportation and importation.[7]

Two weeks later, in *Consten and Grundig v Commission*,[8] the ECJ categorically condemned an arrangement granting absolute territorial protection for a distributor.[9] The Court was heavily concerned about the export ban embedded in the distribution scheme of Grundig. The producer 'undertook not to deliver even indirectly to third parties products intended for the area covered by the contract', imposed export-bans on Consten, as well as on other distributors, and assigned the 'gint' trademark to Consten in order to afford protection against parallel import.[10] The ECJ held that absolute territorial protection, as the one granted in the fact pattern, was anti-competitive by object. Although the Court did not declare that such arrangements cannot ever fulfil the requirements of Article 101(3), it was rather hostile towards such schemes when affirming the decision of the Commission that refused to grant an individual exemption. Obviously, the most important concern was that absolute territorial protection 'results in the isolation of the French market and makes it possible to charge for the products in question prices which are sheltered from all effective competition'.[11]

It is worth noting that whereas the Court seemingly recognized the general validity of the free-rider argument submitted by Grundig and Consten, its

---

7 *Id.* at 250.

8 Joined Cases 56/64 and 58/64 *Consten and Grundig v Commission* [1964] ECR 299.

9 The approach employed in *Consten and Grundig v Commission* was not unprecedented. Leon J. de Keyser, *Territorial Restrictions and Export Prohibitions under the United States and the Common Market Antitrust Laws*, 2 Common Market Law Review 271, 287-289 (1965). (Citing AG Lagrange's opinion in Case 13/61 *Kledingverkoopbedrijf de Geus en Uitdenbogerd v Robert Bosch GmbH and Maatschappij tot voortzetting van de zaken der Firma Willem van Rijn* [1962] ECR 45, national judgments and a Commission decision; concluding that in the light of these cases 'it cannot be said that the Grundig-Consten decision came as a surprise'.) *See* Valentine Korah and Denis O'Sullivan, Distribution Agreements under the EC Competition Rules 59 (2002). ('The law and practice relating to exclusive distribution was developed in the 1960s before any other aspect of competition law. The Commission's earliest decisions in 1964 related to exclusive distribution systems, most of which included export restraints to prevent poaching in other dealers' territories.')

10 Joined Cases 56/64 and 58/64 *Consten and Grundig v Commission* [1964] ECR 299, 343.

11 *Id.* at 343.

enthusiasm for these economic arguments was relatively modest. First, although the Court recognized that inter-brand competition is more important than intra-brand rivalry, it added immediately that this proposition does not entail that an agreement restricting intra-brand competition could escape the prohibition of Article 101(1) merely because it might increase inter-brand competition.[12] Second, the Court was rather hostile against product differentiation, strong trademarks and brand image, viewing trademarks as one kind of wicked restrictions of competition: it asserted that as product differentiation decreases substitutability, it diminishes rivalry.[13]

Société Technique Minière (L.T.M.) v Maschinenbau Ulm GmbH (M.B.U.) and *Consten and Grundig v Commission* established two fundamental propositions: absolute territorial protection (export bans) is anti-competitive by object, *per se* infringing Article 101(1),[14] while relative territorial protection is an 'effect-type' agreement. *Consten and Grundig v Commission* appears also to strongly suggest that absolute territorial protection can hardly meet the requirements of Article 101(3). These propositions have ossified in the last four decades.[15] In order to distinguish the contemptible territorial exclusivities from the welcome ones, the concept of active/passive sales was developed. Accordingly, a passive transaction is a sale for which the dealer made no efforts: these are the unsolicited orders addressed to it; on the other hand, active transactions are sales that are entailed by the distributor's endeavours.[16] Location clauses, areas of primary responsibility

12 *Id.* at 342.

13 *Id.* at 343. ('[T]he more producers succeed in their effort to render their own makes of product individually distinct in the eyes of the consumer, the more the effectiveness of competition between producers tend to diminish.')

14 In *Miller* the ECJ held that an export-ban violates Article 101(1) irrespective of whether the measure was actually enforced by the parties; a statement suggesting that export bans amount to a *per se* infringement of Article 101(1). Case 19/77 *Miller International Schallplatten GmbH v Commission* [1978] ECR 131, para 7. (Holding that 'the fact that the supplier is not strict in enforcing such prohibitions cannot established that they had no effect since their very existence may create a "visual and psychological" background which satisfies consumers and contributes to a more or less rigorous division of the markets.'); Case T-66/92 *Herlitz AG v Commission* [1994] ECR II-00531, para 40. (Extending the holding of *Miller* in order to refuse an allegation that export-prohibitions were not implemented.); Case T-77/92 *Parker Pen Ltd v Commission* [1994] ECR II-549, para 55. (Extending *Miller* in order to refuse an allegation that export-prohibitions were not implemented.)

15 Richard Whish, Competition Law 629 (2009). ('[B]ecause of the single market imperative in Community competition law, absolute territorial protection almost always infringes Article 81(1) and only rarely would benefit from Article 81(3).'); Kassie Smith, *Vertical Agreements Affecting Distribution or Supply*, *in* Bellamy and Child's European Community Law of Competition 6.084 (Peter Roth and Vivien Rose ed., 2008).

16 *See* Regulation 1983/83 OJ [1983] L 173/1, Article 2(2)(c). (The regulation defined active sales as follows: 'the obligation to refrain, outside the contract territory and in relation to the contract goods, from seeking customers, from establishing any branch, and from maintaining any distribution depot'.). *See also Guidelines on Vertical Restrains*, para 51. ('[T]he Commission interprets "active" and "passive" sales as follows: "Active"

and restrictions on advertisements are considered as restraints on active sales. An outright prohibition on export, i.e. forbidding both active and passive sales, amounts to an absolute territorial protection, while the mere exclusion of active sales qualifies as relative territorial protection.

The Internet presents novel and complicated questions. The Commission considers the use of the Internet, i.e. having a website, not to be a form of active sales, though acknowledging the 'extraterritorial' effects of such websites: a website is equally accessible by any consumer on the globe, disregarding certain countries where access to the net is restricted or controlled. Interestingly, according to the Commission, the language of the website, in itself, does not make a difference in this regard.[17] While acknowledging that language restrictions cannot be squared with the fundamental values of EU law, the language options used on a website, taking into account the circumstances, may give clear indication as to who the targeted consumers are. For instance, a Hungarian language option used on the website of a Slovak distributor can certainly be considered to be passive selling as 10 per cent of the population in Slovakia speaks Hungarian as their mother tongue. On the other hand, it is not easy to argue that a Portuguese distributor's Hungarian language webpage does not aim at customers located in Hungary.

Indeed, the ECJ has never regarded an absolute territorial protection in a distribution arrangement as not anti-competitive by object. The *Guidelines on Vertical Restraints* contain a very tight exception in this regard, providing that even an absolute territorial protection clause may be lawful for two years if it is necessary for penetrating a new market.

> A distributor which will be the first to sell a new brand or the first to sell an existing brand on a new market, thereby ensuring a genuine entry on the relevant market, may have to commit substantial investments where there was previously

---

sales mean actively approaching individual customers by for instance direct mail, including the sending of unsolicited e-mails, or visits; or actively approaching a specific customer group or customers in a specific territory through advertisement in media, on the internet or other promotions specifically targeted at that customer group or targeted at customers in that territory. Advertisement or promotion that is only attractive for the buyer if it (also) reaches a specific group of customers or customers in a specific territory, is considered active selling to that customer group or customers in that territory. "Passive" sales mean responding to unsolicited requests from individual customers including delivery of goods or services to such customers. General advertising or promotion that reaches customers in other distributors' (exclusive) territories or customer groups but which is a reasonable way to reach customers outside those territories or customer groups, for instance to reach customers in one's own territory, are considered passive selling. General advertising or promotion is considered a reasonable way to reach such customers if it would be attractive for the buyer to undertake these investments also if they would not reach customers in other distributors' (exclusive) territories or customer groups.')

17 *Guidelines on Vertical Restrains*, para 52-53. See *Old Guidelines on Vertical Restraints*, para 51.

> no demand for that type of product in general or for that type of product from that producer. Such expenses may often be sunk and in such circumstances the distributor may not enter into the distribution agreement without protection for a certain period of time against (active and) passive sales into its territory or to its customer group by other distributors. For example such a situation may occur where a manufacturer established in a particular national market enters another national market and introduces its products with the help of an exclusive distributor and where this distributor needs to invest in launching and establishing the brand on this new market. Where substantial investments by the distributor to start up and/or develop the new market are necessary, restrictions of passive sales by other distributors into such a territory or to such a customer group which are necessary for the distributor to recoup those investments generally fall outside the scope of Article 101(1) during the first two years that the distributor is selling the contract goods or services in that territory or to that customer group, even though such hardcore restrictions are in general presumed to fall within the scope of Article 101(1).[18]

The ECJ, though very exceptionally, was less categorical in an IP context and in two unique cases gave the green light to arrangements built upon absolute territorial protection.[19] The dawn of the case-law on licensing began in a similar fashion to that on distribution agreements. In *Nungesser v Commission*,[20] the first ECJ case on technology transfer, the Court followed the pattern established in *Consten and Grundig*: exclusive licenses warranting absolute territorial protection were considered to be anti-competitive by object, while open exclusive licenses (equivalents of relative territorial protection) were considered to necessitate effects-analysis.

> [There are] two legal situations which are not necessarily identical. The first case concerns a so-called open exclusive licence or assignment and the exclusivity of the licence relates solely to the contractual relationship between the owner of the right and the licencee, whereby the owner merely undertakes not to grant

---

18 Para 61.

19 It is to be stressed that the purview of these cases is rather narrow, *see* Valentine Korah and Denis O'Sullivan, Distribution Agreements under the EC Competition Rules 82-83 (2002) ('It is arguable that the rationale of encouraging investment is of general application, but the judgments in *Coditel* and *Louis Erauw-Jacquery* were carefully qualified, and it is doubtful whether they will be greatly extended beyond their special sectors.'), *see also* Richard Whish, Competition Law 761 (2009). ('[W]here a licensor grants a licensee absolute territorial protection against any form of intra-technology competition there will almost certainly be an infringement of Article 81(1) and it is unlikely that the terms of Article 81(3) will be satisfied'); and the Commission opines that the *Erauw-Jacquery* judgment applies only to basic seeds, 1999/6/EC *SICASOV* OJ [1999] L4/27, paras 50 and 53.

20 Case 258/78 [1982] ECR 2015.

> other licences in respect of the same territory and not to compete himself with the licensee on that territory. On the other hand, the second case involves an exclusive licence or assignment with absolute territorial protection, under which the parties to the contract propose, as regards the products and the territory in question, to eliminate all competition from third parties, such as parallel importers or licensees for other territories.[21]

Nevertheless, later cases established limited exceptions to the foregoing proposition.

In *Coditel II*, the dealer that acquired exclusive distribution rights in Belgium over the film entitled 'Le Boucher' (The Butcher) sued three cable television companies because the latter retransmitted the film broadcasted in Germany. The ECJ held that the very special features of performing rights and the film producers' need to achieve an adequate rate of return might warrant absolute territorial protection from re-transmissions and, hence, an effect-based analysis is to be carried out. According to the Court, the relevant question is

> whether or not the exercise of the exclusive right to exhibit a cinematographic film creates barriers which are artificial and unjustifiable in terms of the needs of the cinematographic industry, or the possibility of charging fees which exceed a fair return on investment, or an exclusivity the duration of which is disproportionate to those requirements, and whether or not, from a general point of view, such exercise within a given geographic area is such as to prevent, restrict or distort competition within the common market.[22]

In *Louis Erauw-Jacquery v La Hesbignonne SC*, the ECJ held that a provision of an agreement that 'prohibits the licensee from selling and exporting the basic seed is compatible with Article 85(1) of the Treaty in so far as it is necessary in order to enable the breeder to select the growers who are to be licensees'.[23] Basic seeds are a very special commodity: they are covered by plant breeders' rights and used for producing certified seeds, which are sold to farmers. Basic seeds are multiplied by propagators. The Court explained the above exceptional rule with the circumstance that

> the development of the basic lines may involve considerable financial commitment. Consequently, a person who has made considerable efforts to develop varieties of basic seed which may be the subject-matter of plant breeders' rights must be allowed to protect himself against improper handling of those varieties of

21 Para 53.

22 Case 262/81 *Coditel SA, Compagnie générale pour la diffusion de la télévision, and others v Ciné-Vog Films SA and others* [1982] ECR 3381, para 19.

23 Case 27/87 *SPRL Louis Erauw-Jacquery v La Hesbignonne SC* [1988] ECR 1919, para 11.

> seeds. To that end the breeder must have the right to reserve propagation for the propagating establishments chosen by him as licensees. To that extent the clause prohibiting the licensee from selling and exporting basic seeds does not come within the prohibition laid down by Article 81(1) of the Treaty.[24]

It is noteworthy that the free-rider rationale appears in none of the above judgments, even though this theory is *a fortiori* valid in case of technology transfer: normally, licensees invest more capital and need more protection than distributors;[25] instead, the ECJ was persuaded by different arguments. In *Coditel II* the fundamental theory of IP was used: the legal exclusivity afforded to the owner of the IP is meant to enable the latter to recover its investment and to serve as an incentive for future creations. The ECJ was concerned about whether the owner of the IP could properly exploit the term of exclusivity, or get an adequate return, if territorial protection was not permitted. There was a fear that competition law unduly interferes with IP law's mechanism of operation. On the other hand, in *Louis Erauw-Jacquery v La Hesbignonne SC* the main concern related to the peril of the 'improper handling of those varieties of seeds'. Although in both cases the ECJ worried whether investments get an adequate return, obviously due to the fact that it was the internal logic of IP law that changed the picture, it was always the producer's (or rather the IP owner's) and not the distributor's investment that mattered.

It is also interesting that in the above cases the ECJ granted leave already under Article 101(1), without getting to Article 101(3); nevertheless, it is to be added that these matters reached the Court on the basis of Article 234 references and at the relevant time individual exemption under Article 101(3) came under the Commission's exclusive competence; hence, the position that these restraints are to be examined under Article 101(3) would have, in fact, meant that they are illegal, since only the Commission was entitled to apply Article 101(3).

Some years ago, in *GlaxoSmithKline AEVE*[26] the GC was close to diluting the imperative nature of the prohibition on absolute territorial protection and to create a narrow exception; however, the judgment was annulled on appeal: the ECJ[27] reiterated the categorical nature of the traditional principle.

---

24 *Id.* at para 10.

25 *See* VALENTINE KORAH, INTELLECTUAL PROPERTY RIGHTS AND THE EC COMPETITION RULES 28 (2006) ('In principle a licensee may need more protection from dealers and other licensees than does a dealer. Not only does it have to establish a market, usually it also has to set up a production line and may still have to develop the technology. A licensee often has to invest more capital than a dealer and accept greater risk.')

26 Case T-168/01 *GlaxoSmithKline Services Unlimited v Commission* [2006] ECR II-2969. The judgment of the GC was delivered on 27 September 2006. The incriminated arrangement in this case was that the producer charged different prices for its products depending on whether they were sold within or outside Spain.

27 Joined Cases C-468/06 to C-478/06 Sot. *Lélos kai Sia EE and Others v GlaxoSmithKline AEVE Farmakeftikon Proionton, formerly Glaxowellcome AEVE* [2008] ECR I-07139.

The GC seems to have been heavily influenced by the peculiar features of the pharmaceutical industry.

> While it has been accepted since then that parallel trade must be given a certain protection, it is therefore not as such but, as the Court of Justice held, in so far as it favours the development of trade, on the one hand, and the strengthening of competition, on the other hand (Case C-373/90 *X* [1992] ECR I-131, paragraph 12), that is to say, in this second respect, in so far as it gives final consumers the advantages of effective competition in terms of supply or price (*Tepea* v *Commission*, paragraph 118 above, paragraphs 43 and 56). Consequently, while it is accepted that an agreement intended to limit parallel trade must in principle be considered to have as its object the restriction of competition, that applies in so far as the agreement may be presumed to deprive final consumers of those advantages.[28]

Thereafter, the GC embarked on examining the special features of the pharmaceutical industry and concluded that, mainly due to the fact that prices are heavily regulated in the different Member States, it cannot be assumed that the restriction of parallel trade works effectively for the detriment of consumers.

> That circumstance means that it cannot be presumed that parallel trade has an impact on the prices charged to the final consumers of medicines reimbursed by the national sickness insurance scheme and thus confers on them an appreciable advantage analogous to that which it would confer if those prices were determined by the play of supply and demand.[29]

Nevertheless, on appeal the ECJ overturned the above interpretation rather quickly and reiterated the ancient rule that absolute territorial protection is anti-competitive by object.

> In relation to the application of Article 85 of the EEC Treaty (Article 85 of the EC Treaty (...)), the Court has held that an agreement between producer and distributor which might tend to restore the national divisions in trade between Member States might be such as to frustrate the objective of the Treaty to achieve the integration of national markets through the establishment of a single market. Thus on a number of occasions the Court has held agreements aimed at partitioning national markets according to national borders or making the interpenetration of national markets more difficult, in particular those aimed

28 Case T-168/01 *GlaxoSmithKline Services Unlimited v Commission* [2006] ECR II-2969, para 121.

29 *Id.* at para 134.

> at preventing or restricting parallel exports, to be agreements whose object is to restrict competition within the meaning of that Treaty article.[30]

The Commission's decisional practice is replete with cases where absolute territorial protection was automatically condemned under Article 101(1).[31] The Commission's soft law instruments are also in accordance with this approach.[32] It is noticeable that the *Notice on Agreements of Minor Importance*, which regards vertical agreements under 15 per cent market share[33] as not capable of appreciably affecting competition, classifies absolute territorial protection as hardcore and withdraws it from the benign presumption of no appreciable effect on competition. In other words, the Commission's stance is that absolute territorial protection cannot be regarded as not restricting competition even if the parties' market share is trivial. The notion of absolute territorial restriction also embraces measures that do not involve an express export ban but apply means that entail similar consequences indirectly.[34]

---

30 Joined Cases C-468/06 to C-478/06 Sot. *Lélos kai Sia EE and Others v GlaxoSmithKline AEVE Farmakeftikon Proionton, formerly Glaxowellcome AEVE* [2008] ECR I-7139, para 65.

31 97/123/EC *Novalliance/Systemform* OJ [1997] L 047/11, 60; 2001/135/EC *Nathan-Bricolux* OJ [2001] L 054/1, para 72; 2002/190/EC *JCB* OJ [2002] L 069/1, para 75; 2001/146/EC *Opel* OJ [2001] L 59/1, para 118; 2002/758/EC *Mercedes-Benz* OJ [2002] L 257/1, paras 175-177.

32 *Guidelines on Article 101(3)*, paras 23 and 55. ('Restrictions that are blacklisted in block exemptions or identified as hardcore restrictions in guidelines and notices are generally considered by the Commission to constitute restrictions by object.' And absolute territorial protection is consistently classified as a hard-core restriction.) (Asserting that 'in the case of hardcore restrictions (…) [anti-competitive] effects are presumed'.); *Guidelines on Vertical Restraints*, para 47 ('Where such a hardcore restriction is included in an agreement, that agreement is presumed to fall within Article 101(1).')

33 It is the market share 'held by each of the parties to the agreement (…) on any of the relevant markets affected by the agreement' that is to be taken into account. *Notice on Agreements of Minor Importance*, para 7(b).

34 *See Guidelines on Vertical Restraints*, para 50. ('That may be the result of direct obligations, such as the obligation not to sell to certain customers or to customers in certain territories or the obligation to refer orders from these customers to other distributors. It may also result from indirect measures aimed at inducing the distributor not to sell to such customers, such as refusal or reduction of bonuses or discounts, termination of supply, reduction of supplied volumes or limitation of supplied volumes to the demand within the allocated territory or customer group, threat of contract termination, requiring a higher price for products to be exported, limiting the proportion of sales that can be exported or profit pass-over obligations. It may further result from the supplier not providing a Union-wide guarantee service under which normally all distributors are obliged to provide the guarantee service and are reimbursed for this service by the supplier, even in relation to products sold by other distributors into their territory. Such practices are even more likely to be viewed as a restriction of the buyer's sales when used in conjunction with the implementation by the supplier of a

The following have been considered to have similar consequences to absolute territorial protection: withdrawal and exclusion of bonuses when the dealer exported the goods,[35] imposition of penalties on export,[36] obligation imposed on the exclusive distributor to pass on to the producer orders from customers from outside the assigned territory.[37] In *Volkswagen*, EU courts sanctioned the Commission's condemnation of the '15 per cent' rule according to which, when calculating bonus, a dealer's sales outside the contract territory were taken into account only up to the limit of 15 per cent of the total sales.[38] In *Mercedes-Benz*, the producer instructed the dealers to 'require a 15 per cent deposit in cases of parallel exports'.[39] In other cases, undertakings were condemned for operating a detecting, monitoring and alerting mechanism in order to identify parallel trade.[40] In *Tipp-Ex* the Commission condemned a covenant according to which the dealer undertook 'not to sell the contract goods to customers who to his knowledge intend to resell them in areas outside the contract territory'.[41]

Interestingly, however, the GC in *JCB Service* held that a fee paid by the selling dealer to the dealer in the territory of which the customer is located could

---

monitoring system aimed at verifying the effective destination of the supplied goods, such as the use of differentiated labels or serial numbers. However, obligations on the reseller relating to the display of the supplier's brand name are not classified as hardcore.') *See also* IV/36.957/F3 *Glaxo Wellcome*, IV/36.997/F3 *Aseprofar and Fedifar*, IV/37.121/F3 *Spain Pharma*, IV/37.138/F3 *BAI*, IV/37.380/F3 *EAEPC* OJ [2001] L 302/1, paras 116, 118, 119 and 124-125. For a long list of examples of other measures that prevent parallel imports indirectly, *see* Kassie Smith, *Vertical Agreements Affecting Distribution or Supply*, *in* BELLAMY AND CHILD'S EUROPEAN COMMUNITY LAW OF COMPETITION 6.058 (Peter Roth and Vivien Rose ed., 2008); 93/554/EEC *Zera/Montedison, Hinkens/Stähler* OJ [1993] L 272/28, paras 96-126. (Treating product differentiation aimed at thwarting parallel trade as absolute territorial protection.)

35 For cases where bonuses were withdrawn or not applicable when the dealer exported the goods, *see* 85/617/EEC *Sperry New Holland* OJ [1985] L 376/21, para 55. ('Dealers must have the right to supply farmers from other territories without being penalized by the withdrawal of bonuses. Therefore agreements or practices concerning bonuses which are conditional on the machine not subsequently being exported by the customer are prohibited. The same rationale might apply to the condition that the machine is registered for use within the territory of the dealer or that the warranty service be completed within that territory.'). 2001/146/EC *Opel* OJ [2001] L 59/1, para 131.

36 93/46/EEC *Ford Agricultural* OJ [1993] L 20/1, paras 13-14. (Discounts depended on non-export and penalties were imposed for exporting); *Organon*, XXVth *Report on Competition Policy 1995* 37-38 (1996). (Making discounts dependent on whether the goods were sold domestically or exported.)

37 95/477/EC BASF Lacke+Farben AG, and Accinauto SA OJ [1995] L 272/16.

38 Case T-62/98 *Volkswagen* v *Commission* [2000] ECR II-2707, para 49; on appeal Case C-338/00 *Volkswagen AG v Commission* [2003] ECR I-09189, para 44.

39 2002/758/EC *Mercedes-Benz* OJ [2002] L 257/1, paras 102-103.

40 See 2003/675/EC *PO Video Games, PO Nintendo Distribution and Omega – Nintendo* OJ [2003] L 255/33.

41 87/406/EEC *Tipp-Ex* OJ [1987] L 222/1, para 13. (See Article 14 of the agreement.)

be in conformity with EU competition rules, provided the amount of the fee is a realistic assessment of the expenditures related to the latter's after-sale services.[42]

It is highly unlikely that an absolute territorial protection arrangement could benefit from Article 101(3),[43] a proposition accepted in the scholarship with one accord.[44] First of all, it is to be emphasized that absolute territorial protection schemes are regarded as hardcore and as such not covered by the BER.

> Article 4
> Restrictions that remove the benefit of the block exemption – hardcore restrictions
> The [block] exemption provided for in Article 2 [of the BER] shall not apply to vertical agreements which, directly or indirectly, in isolation or in combination with other factors under the control of the parties, have as their object:
> (...)
> (b) the restriction of the territory into which, or of the customers to whom, a buyer party to the agreement, without prejudice to a restriction on its place of establishment, may sell the contract goods or services, except:
> (i) the restriction of active sales into the exclusive territory or to an exclusive customer group reserved to the supplier or allocated by the supplier to another buyer, where such a restriction does not limit sales by the customers of the buyer.[45]

---

42 Case T-67/01 *JCB Service v Commission* [2004] ECR II-49, para 149.

43 A proposition not made completely clear in *Consten and Grundig*, see Leon J. de Keyser, *Territorial Restrictions and Export Prohibitions under the United States and the Common Market Antitrust Laws*, 2 Common Market Law Review 271, 290-293 (1965). (Asserting that exemption under Article 101(3) is possible for absolute territorial protection), but became clear subsequently. *See* Valentine Korah and Denis O'Sullivan, Distribution Agreements under the EC Competition Rules 233 (2002). (Noting that '[i] n brief, although Matra Hachette suggests that no restriction of competition is beyond exemption, there appears to be no real possibility of redeeming the so-called "hardcore" restraints, and their inclusion in any distribution arrangement – even one which would otherwise satisfy the conditions for exemption under Regulation 2790/99 – exposes the parties to serious risk of fines and nullity. Businesses would be well advised simply to avoid such restraints entirely.')

44 Luc Gyselen, *Vertical Restraints in the Distribution Process: Strength and Weakness of the Free Rider Rationale under EEC Competition Law*, 21 Common Market Law Review 647, 660 (1984). ('Territorial restraints upon intra-brand competition which ossify parallel trade and thus stifle price competition have virtually no chance of being exempted. Outright export bans will virtually never meet the Article 85 para. 3 indispensability test.'); Paul M. Taylor, *The Vertical Agreements Regulation*, 3 The Cambridge Yearbook of European Legal Studies 525, 538 (2000).

45 The BER practically repeats Article 4(b) of the Old BER but adds that restrictions on the buyer's place of establishment are not regarded as hardcore; a rule probably implied also in the old text. *See* Article 4(b) of the Old BER. In the Old BER, the phrase 'without prejudice to a restriction on its place of establishment' was missing.

It is noticeable that the above provision of the BER, which is in accordance with Article 4 of the Old BER, departs from the block exemption regulations before 1999. The Old BER was a paradigm shift in comparison to earlier block exemption regulations, introducing a new-style vertical regime. The paradigm shift did not affect the treatment of territorial protection fundamentally, nonetheless, the approach, to some extent, changed also in this regard. In old-style vertical block exemption regulations (i.e. regulations before 1999) restrictions on active sales were block-exempted unconditionally.[46] The Old BER introduced the requirement of 'reservation', i.e. restrictions on active sales are acceptable only if they relate to a territory reserved for the supplier itself or assigned by the supplier to another dealer. This principle was maintained by the new BER.

Another interesting point regarding Article 4(b) of the BER is that it speaks only about restrictions on the buyer's freedom to sell; consequently, restrictions on the supplier are covered by the block exemption, irrespective of whether they cover both active and passive sales.[47] On the other hand, this wording (that is, active sales are not hardcore if they relate to a territory or consumer group reserved for a *supplier* or another *buyer*) also implies that this requirement is not met if the territory or customer group is reserved to a *licensee*.[48] The language of Article 4(b) fails to take into account the perspective of vertical arrangements

---

46 Regulation 67/67/EEC OJ [1967] L 57/849, Article 2(1)(b). ('[N]o restriction on competition shall be imposed on the exclusive dealer other than (…) the obligation to refrain, outside the territory covered by the contract, from seeking customers for the goods to which the contract relates, from establishing any branch, or from maintaining any distribution depot.'). This formulation was practically repeated by subsequent block exemption regulations. Regulation 1983/83 OJ [1983] L 173/1, Article 2(2)(c) (The regulation provided that 'no restriction on competition shall be imposed on the exclusive distributor other than: (…) (c) the obligation to refrain, outside the contract territory and in relation to the contract goods, from seeking customers, from establishing any branch, and from maintaining any distribution depot.'); Regulation 4087/88 OJ [1988] L 359/46, Article 2(d). (Using the same unconditional language concerning territorial protection in franchise agreements, and white-listing 'an obligation on the franchisee to refrain, outside the contract territory, from seeking customers for the goods or the services which are the subject-matter of the franchise'.) The same legislative practice featured the regulations on motor vehicle distribution. Regulation 123/85 OJ [1985] L 15/16, Article 3(8)-(9); Regulation 1475/95 OJ [1995] L 145/25, Article 3(8)-(9).

47 *See* Luc Peeperkorn, *E.C. Vertical Restraints Guidelines: Effects Based or Per Se Policy? – a Reply*, 23(1) European Competition Law Review 38 (2002); Mario Filipponi, Luc Peeperkorn and Donncadh Woods, *Chapter 9: Vertical Agreements*, *in* The EC Law of Competition § 9.216 (Jonathan Faull and Ali Nikpay ed., 2007).

48 For a categorical opinion, which can be hardly opposed, *see* Valentine Korah and Denis O'Sullivan, Distribution Agreements under the EC Competition Rules 62 (2002). ('The lack of protection possible under Regulation 2790/99 for technology licensees makes no sense.'). *See also* Valentine Korah, *Draft Block Exemption for Technology Transfer*, 25(5) European Competition Law Review 247, 258 (2004). ('I regret that the Commission assumes that all Member States are served by distributors, or all by licensees, when often some areas are exploited one way and some another.')

where technology-transfer and distribution are combined. This failure deprives also vertical structures of the benefit of block exemption that otherwise would be perfectly in conformity with the principles of the BER.

For instance, the owner of a particular technology may decide to license the technology regarding certain Member States, and to produce the goods in other Member States and employ exclusive distributors. Nevertheless, a restriction on the distributors' active sales outside the contract territory would not be covered by the BER, since the applicability of the block exemption fails at the point of 'reservation': the territories of the licensees are not reserved for the supplier or a buyer. In the above fact pattern the condition that the territory is reserved for the supplier or another buyer would not be met, because the territory is in fact reserved for a licensee.

Likewise, the language of Article 4(b) of the BER seems to deprive semi-exclusivity arrangements (i.e. when there are more than one 'exclusive' distributor) from the benefit of the block exemption, despite being justified by the same reasons as those warranting the block exemption of one-distributor territorial protection. For instance, if a territory is allotted to two exclusive distributors, the conditions of Article 4(b) of the BER are not met, which seems to have in mind the typical scenario of a single exclusive distributor ('allocated by the supplier to *another buyer*'). Accordingly, if a supplier appoints one exclusive distributor for Member State 'A', and two distributors for Member State 'B', the restriction of the former's active sales to Member State 'B' are not block-exempted as the latter is not reserved to 'another buyer'.[49]

49 *See* FRANK WIJCKMANS, FILIP TUYTSCHAEVER AND ALAIN VANDERELST, VERTICAL AGREEMENTS IN EC COMPETITION LAW §§ 188-189 (2006). This interpretation is reinforced by para 51 of the *Guidelines on Vertical Restraints*. ('A territory or customer group is exclusively allocated when the supplier agrees to sell its product *only to one distributor* for distribution in a particular territory or to a particular customer group and the exclusive distributor is protected against active selling into its territory or to its customer group by all the other buyers of the supplier within the Union, irrespective of sales by the supplier.'). Emphasis added. *See* Romano Subiotto and Filippo Amato, *The Reform of the European Competition Policy Concerning Vertical Restraints*, 69 Antitrust Law Journal 147, 175 (2001). ('[T]he requirements contained in Article 4(b), first indent, of Regulation 2790/99, are designed to permit restrictions on active sales on a distributor or franchisee only when they are genuinely justified by the need to protect the promotional efforts of another distributor/franchisee or of the supplier within another territory or customer group. It is not clear, why, unlike under the previous block exemption regime, the Commission considers restrictions on active sales aimed at compelling the distributor or franchisee to concentrate its sale efforts within the contract territory no longer worth automatic exemption.' This statement seems to be applicable also to the 2010 BER.) *See also* Frank Wijckmans and Filip Tuytschaever, *Active Sales Restrictions Revisited*, 25(2) European Competition Law Review 107, 109 (2004). If the supplier distributes the goods in some Member States, while using exclusive distributors in others, the supplier and the buyer can be regarded as competitors. Nevertheless, this circumstance does not preclude the application of the BER, as far as the conditions of Article

On the other hand, the *Guidelines on Vertical Restraints* suggest that the requirement of 'reservation' is met also in case of sole distributorship, i.e. when a single distributor is appointed in a given area but the supplier reserves the right to effect sales towards this territory.

> A territory or customer group is exclusively allocated when the supplier agrees to sell its product only to one distributor for distribution in a particular territory or to a particular customer group and the exclusive distributor is protected against active selling into its territory or to its customer group by all the other buyers of the supplier within the Union, *irrespective of sales by the supplier*.[50]

When discussing the BER's approach towards vertical intra-brand territorial restrictions, it is worthwhile looking at the Commission's attitude as regards territorial restraints within selective distribution schemes. Namely, in case of selective distribution even restrictions on active sales are considered to be hardcore under the BER, hence the combination of territorial protection and selective distribution is problematic. Article 4(c) of the BER characterizes as hardcore 'the restriction of active or passive sales to end users by members of a selective distribution system operating at the retail level of trade, without prejudice to the possibility of prohibiting a member of the system from operating out of an unauthorised place of establishment'. Accordingly, practically no territorial restriction – neither absolute, nor relative – can be imposed on retailers if the producer opts for selective distribution.[51] Therewith, Article 4(d) of the BER characterizes as hardcore 'the restriction of cross-supplies between distributors within a selective distribution system, including between distributors operating at different level of trade'.[52] Accordingly, no territorial restrictions can be applied as to the supplies between the members of the selective distribution system. *Ergo*, the only acceptable territorial restriction is the restriction on the wholesaler to

---

2(4)(a) of the BER are fulfilled. ('The exemption provided for in paragraph 1 shall not apply to vertical agreements entered into between competing undertakings. However, it shall apply where competing undertakings enter into a non-reciprocal vertical agreement and: (a) the supplier is a manufacturer and a distributor of goods, while the buyer is a distributor and not a competing undertaking at the manufacturing level.')

50 Para 51. Emphasis added.

51 *See Guidelines on Vertical Restraints*, para 152, 169 and 185. ('A combination of exclusive distribution and selective distribution is only exempted by the Block Exemption Regulation if active selling in other territories is not restricted.') ('A combination of exclusive customer allocation and selective distribution is normally a hardcore restriction, as active selling to end-users by the appointed distributors is usually not left free.') ('The combination of selective distribution with a location clause, protecting an appointed dealer against other appointed dealers opening up a shop in its vicinity, may in particular fulfil the conditions of Article 101(3) if the combination is indispensable to protect substantial and relationship-specific investments made by the authorised dealer.')

52 Article 4(c) and 4(d) of the BER repeat Article 4(c) and 4(d) of the Old BER.

serve end users outside the territory; hardly a new freedom as wholesalers can be enjoined from selling to end users anyhow: Article 4(b)(ii) exempts 'the restriction of sales to end users by a buyer operating at the wholesale level of trade'. All in all, it seems that territorial protection and selective distribution cannot be effectively combined, since apart from restrictions on the place of establishment no substantial territorial restrictions can be maintained.

The 'reservation' requirement may cause problems of interpretation in case the supplier combines territorial exclusivity with selective distribution in a way that it appoints exclusive distributors in some Member States, while using selective distribution in others: it is questionable whether the Member States covered by selective distribution qualify as being 'reserved' for another buyer. The literal interpretation of the BER suggests a negative answer, while logic would dictate the contrary. The situation is the same if the supplier uses semi-exclusivity (shared exclusivity), i.e. it appoints two exclusive distributors for the same Member State.[53]

The MVBER in fact repeats the above provisions of the BER.

> Article 4
> Hardcore restrictions
> 1. The exemption shall not apply to vertical agreements which, directly or indirectly, in isolation or in combination with other factors under the control of the parties, have as their object:
>
> (…)
>
> (b) the restriction of the territory into which, or of the customers to whom, the distributor or repairer may sell the contract goods or services; however, the exemption shall apply to:
>
> (i) the restriction of active sales into the exclusive territory or to an exclusive customer group reserved to the supplier or allocated by the supplier to another distributor or repairer, where such a restriction does not limit sales by the customers of the distributor or repairer …

Although it cannot be excluded that a measure treated as hardcore in the block exemption regulations can meet the requirements of Article 101(3), the regulations' enumerations of hardcore restrictions are very telling about the Commission's stance. Therewith, the Commission's soft law instruments and its decisional practice are replete with indications of the proposition that absolute territorial protection is simply not capable of fulfilling the conditions of Article 101(3), as it fails at least at the point of indispensability.[54] In *Nathan-Bricolux*, in the context

53 *See* Frank Wijckmans, Filip Tuytschaever and Alain Vanderelst, Vertical Agreements in EC Competition Law §§ 5.122-5.123 and § 7.07 (2006).

54 The same applies in this regard as to RPF. *Guidelines on Article 81(3)*, paras 46 and 79. ('However, severe restrictions of competition are unlikely to fulfil the conditions of Article *101*(3). Such restrictions are usually blacklisted in block exemption regulations or identified as hardcore restrictions in Commission guidelines and notices. Agreements of this nature

of an express export ban, the Commission declared categorically that '[a]n export prohibition of this nature falls under Article 85(1) and cannot be exempted under Article 85(3).'[55] In some cases the Commission decision regarded as a virtue under Article 101(3) that passive sales were not excluded.[56] In *Yamaha*, the Commission used a very unconditional language characterizing both RPF and absolute territorial protection as arrangements that cannot meet the requirements of Article 101(3) by their very nature; a language going far beyond the fact pattern of the case.[57] A similarly categorical language was used in *Peugeot*, suggesting that even though theoretically all types of agreements may benefit from an individual exemption, absolute territorial protection tends not to meet the requirements of Article 101(3) by nature.[58] For the time being no formal Commission decision can be found that

---

generally fail (at least) the two first conditions of Article 81(3). They neither create objective economic benefits nor do they benefit consumers. (…) Moreover, these types of agreements generally also fail the indispensability test under the third condition.) ('Restrictions that are blacklisted in block exemption regulations or identified as hardcore restrictions in Commission guidelines and notices are unlikely to be considered indispensable.'); *Guidelines on Vertical Restrains*, para 47. ('It is also presumed that the agreement [containing a hardcore restraint] is unlikely to fulfil the conditions of Article 101(3)'.)

55 2001/135/EC *Nathan-Bricolux* OJ [2001] L 054/1, para 107; 2002/190/EC *JCB* OJ [2002] L 069/1, para 45.

56 97/780/EC *Unisource* OJ [1997] L 318/1, para 89; 97/781/EC *Uniworld* OJ [1997] L 318/24, para 75. *See* Kassie Smith, *Vertical Agreements Affecting Distribution or Supply*, *in* BELLAMY AND CHILD'S EUROPEAN COMMUNITY LAW OF COMPETITION 6.106 (Peter Roth and Vivien Rose ed., 2008). ('A restriction, whether direct or indirect, on cross-supplies between authorized distributors leads to the partitioning of the market and will almost certainly not benefit from Article 101(3).')

57 Case COMP/37.975 *PO/Yamaha* Commission decision of 16.07.2003 (unpublished but available at http://ec.europa.eu/competition/antitrust/cases/decisions/37975/en.pdf), para 175. ('The Agreements in question were not notified. If such agreements had been notified, they could not have been exempted individually from the application of Article 81(1) of the Treaty and Article 53(1) of the EEA Agreement, since the conditions necessary for granting an exemption are not met due to the nature of the restrictions of competition. Territorial protection and resale price maintenance are hardcore restrictions that do not meet the cumulative conditions of Article 81(3) of the Treaty and Article 53(3) of the EEA Agreement. They do not contribute to improving the production or, in this case, the distribution of goods, nor are consumers allowed a share of the resulting benefit.').

58 86/506/EEC *Peugeot* OJ 1986 L295/19, [1989] 4 CMLR 371, para 38. ('Admittedly, a system of agreements containing restrictive conditions such as those included in the Peugeot distribution agreements can, in theory, have beneficial effects, as are essential if the agreements are to qualify for exemption within the meaning of Article 85 (3). This possibility is ruled out, however, where dealers are unable to order new cars of the make in question in order to satisfy demand on the part of customers who are nationals of another Member State (always provided such cars are marketed in that other State.') *See* Luc Gyselen, *Vertical Restraints in the Distribution Process: Strength and Weakness of the Free Rider Rationale under EEC Competition Law*, 21 Common Market Law Review 647, 660 (1984).

would have granted individual exemption to absolute territorial exclusivity in a distribution scheme. This fact is all the more important because until the entry into force of Regulation 1/2003/EC the Commission had legal monopoly over granting individual exemptions under Article 101(3).

In the light of the ECJ's more tolerant jurisprudence regarding licensing agreements it is not surprising that the TTBER adopts a slightly more permissive approach, the most important practical difference being that the licensee's passive sales to the territory or customer group reserved for the licensor can be restricted, while in case of distribution agreements restraints on the dealers' passive sales to the territory reserved for the producer qualify as hardcore.

The TTBER block-exempts all restraints on active and certain prohibitions on passive sales. Restrictions on active sales are not regarded as hard-core at all and contrary to the BER there is no requirement of 'reservation', i.e. it is not required that the territory or customer group in question be reserved for the producer or another dealer. Therewith, Article 4(2)(b) of the TTBER provides that although 'the restriction of the territory into which, or of the customers to whom, the licensee may passively sell the contract products' is hardcore and thus excluded from the benefit of the block exemption regulation, this categorical condemnation does not apply to certain cases, from which the following are relevant for the present analysis:

> (i) the restriction of passive sales into an exclusive territory or to an exclusive customer group reserved for the licensor,
> (ii) the restriction of passive sales into an exclusive territory or to an exclusive customer group allocated by the licensor to another licensee during the first two years that this other licensee is selling the contract products in that territory or to that customer group.[59]

---

59 *See Guidelines on the Assessment of Technology Transfer Agreements*, paras 99-101. (Giving explanations.) For a criticism of these provisions *see* Valentine Korah, Intellectual Property Rights and the EC Competition Rules 66 (2006). ('[The producer] can probably protect the territory of an exclusive distributor: if no licence has been granted for the territory protected, it may be reserved for the licensor. It is anomalous that a licensee can be kept out of the territory of a distributor indefinitely, but that a licensee can be protected from passive sales for only two years after it starts to market the protected products. Moreover, under the vertical restraints regulation, a dealer cannot be kept from selling even actively into the exclusive territory allocated to a licensee.') Article 4(2)(b) of the TTBER also excepts from hardcore categorization some non-price restraints that relate to special cases like production of spare parts, producing the contract products only for a particular customer, protecting retailers from the direct sales of the wholesaler, selective distribution systems: '(iii) the obligation to produce the contract products only for its own use provided that the licensee is not restricted in selling the contract products actively and passively as spare parts for its own products, (iv) the obligation to produce the contract products only for a particular customer, where the licence was granted in order to create an alternative source of supply for that customer, (v) the restriction of sales to

Accordingly, sales restrictions on the licensor are not hardcore and thus they are block-exempted; restrictions on the licensee's passive sales are tolerated if they aim at providing territorial protection for the licensor or they are used during the first two years when entering a new market. The latter is the technology transfer counterpart of the rule included in the *Guidelines on Vertical Restraints* that provides that even an absolute territorial protection clause may be lawful for two years if it is necessary for opening up a new market.[60]

The reason that territorial exclusivity is so sensitive for EU competition law is the single market imperative, which has basically two projections. On the one hand, the purpose of market integration is an institutional target: no hindrances against intra-Union trade should be tolerated, i.e. undertakings are not allowed to covertly reproduce those state measures that were broken down vehemently on the basis of the four freedoms.[61] In this regard the parallel trader is not a 'parasite' dealer free-riding on the efforts of the exclusive distributors but a 'hero because his sales foster the free movement of the brand within the common market and thus contribute to market integration'.[62] The intra-Union flow of goods is considered to be a value in itself. Furthermore, parallel trade has the inherent tendency of equalizing the prices in the different Member States through the mechanism of arbitrage.[63] On the other hand, the single market imperative is considered to imply the fundamental and inalienable right of consumers to purchase wherever they want. This right is symbolic, categorical and cannot be subjected to economic scrutiny, that is, it is not a matter of economics.[64]

---

end-users by a licensee operating at the wholesale level of trade, (vi) the restriction of sales to unauthorised distributors by the members of a selective distribution system'.

60 Para 61.

61 I.e. the rules of the internal market, especially the ones on free movement of goods, but also including the free movement of persons, services and capital.

62 Luc Gyselen, *Vertical Restraints in the Distribution Process: Strength and Weakness of the Free Rider Rationale under EEC Competition Law*, 21 Common Market Law Review 647, 648-649 (1984). See also Leon J. de Keyser, *Territorial Restrictions and Export Prohibitions under the United States and the Common Market Antitrust Laws*, 2 Common Market Law Review 271, 294 (1965); Vivien Rose and Peter Roth, *Article 81(1)*, *in* Bellamy and Child's European Community Law of Competition 2.068 (Peter Roth and Vivien Rose ed., 2008); Doris Hildebrand, The role of economic analysis in the EC competition rules 279 (1998); Joanna Goyder, EU Distribution Law 73 (4th ed., 2005); Valentine Korah and Denis O'Sullivan, Distribution Agreements under the EC Competition Rules 62 (2002).

63 *See* Mario Filipponi, Luc Peeperkorn and Donncadh Woods, *Chapter 9: Vertical Agreements*, *in* The EC Law of Competition § 9.09 (Jonathan Faull and Ali Nikpay ed., 2007); Thomas Hays, Parallel Importation under European Union law 130 (2003); Doris Hildebrand, The role of economic analysis in the EC competition rules 278 (1998); Valentine Korah and Denis O'Sullivan, Distribution Agreements under the EC Competition Rules 263 (2002).

64 *See* 2001/146/EC *Opel* OJ [2001] L 59/1, 129-130 paras. ('[T]he basic rights of the European consumer include the right to be able to purchase a motor vehicle within the

EU competition law's dilemma lies in the fact that while acknowledging the validity of the free-rider theory, it is also bound by the single market imperative. The conundrum in EU competition law is how to reconcile these two values that are mutually exclusive.[65] The answer given by the judicial and decisional practice seems to be the following: a solution is to be found that eliminates neither value but combines them in a way that it gives something to both of them. Accordingly, the watertight isolation of national markets, in terms of intra-brand competition, cannot be accepted, and likewise, some form of territorial protection is to be countenanced. This approach, hallmarked by the targets of reconciling and preserving the two values, leads to a system where absolute territorial protection is in fact *per se* illegal, while relative territorial protection is condemned only if it has anti-competitive effects. Nonetheless, this is a perverse compromise because relative territorial exclusivity often fails to ensure adequate protection and to be a means that tackles the free-rider problem.

Vertical non-price restraints in US antitrust law: all's well that ends well

The treatment of vertical non-price restraints has been fluctuant and controversial throughout the life of US antitrust law. The Supreme Court changed sides four years after its reluctance in *White Motor Co. v United States* to condemn territorial and customer exclusivity automatically and furnishing them a full trial, and in *United*

---

common market in the Member State where it is offered at the most favourable price. This right includes, but is not limited to, new motor vehicles which are offered by the authorised dealers in the volumes and specifications which are required to satisfy the demand of end consumers in the respective contract territory of the dealer. This right is protected, in practice, by the Community competition rules on parallel trade. In the light of these rules, market partitioning through arrangements concerning restricted supply of motor vehicles to dealers in the distribution network cannot be accepted. Such arrangements have as their object a restriction of competition within the meaning of Article 81.') *See also* Mario Filipponi, Luc Peeperkorn and Donncadh Woods, *Chapter 9: Vertical Agreements*, *in* The EC Law of Competition § 9.09 (Jonathan Faull and Ali Nikpay ed., 2007). ('The possibility of passive sales was also seen as necessary to protect what was seen as the fundamental right of consumers or their agents to purchase wherever they want. This right is the symbol of the internal market. Such was the strength of feeling with respect to the right to make parallel trade and passive sales, that any attempt in a distribution system to frustrate these rights was almost treated as a *per se* infringement of Article 81.')

65 Vivien Rose and Peter Roth, *Article 81(1)*, *in* BELLAMY AND CHILD'S EUROPEAN COMMUNITY LAW OF COMPETITION § 2.068 (Peter Roth and Vivien Rose ed., 2008); Claus-Dieter Ehlermann, *The Contribution of EC Competition Policy to the Single Market*, 29 Common Market Law Review 257, 262 (1992); Derek Ridyard and Simon Bishop, *E.C. Vertical Restraints Guidelines: Effects Based or Per Se Policy*, 23(1) European Competition Law Review 35, 35-36 (2002). (Designating the case of market-partitioning as the Commission's schizophrenia.)

States v Arnold Schwinn Co., on the basis of rather formalist arguments, it considered that such arrangements were *per se* illegal. Nevertheless, *Schwinn* was good law only for 10 years and was overruled in *Continental T.V. Inc. v GTE Sylvania Inc.*

In *White Motor Co. v United States*,[66] the Supreme Court came to the conclusion that the features of territorial and customer exclusivity raise several questions that can be answered only after a full trial and the District Court rendered a summary judgment too quickly holding that territorial and customer exclusivity clauses are *per se* illegal. The Court was probably influenced by the appellant's free-riding arguments, who asserted that 'a distributor or dealer must make vigorous and intensive efforts in a restricted territory, and if he is to be held responsible for energetic performance, it is fair, reasonable, and necessary that appellant protect him against invasions of his territory by other distributors or dealers of appellant'.[67] Whereas asked to extend the *per se* illegality of horizontal market sharing to vertical arrangements (certainly by way of analogy and on the basis of the dealer-cartel theory), the Court refused the quick condemnation; nevertheless, it is worthy of note that although *White Motor* is normally read as a precedent where it was held that vertical territorial and customer exclusivities were to be evaluated under the rule of reason, the Court simply hesitated whether an outright prohibition would be adequate for such agreements.

> We are asked to extend the [*per se* illegality of] (…) horizontal arrangements among competitors to divide territory (…) to a vertical arrangement by one manufacturer restricting the territory of his distributors or dealers. *We intimate no view one way or the other on the legality of such an arrangement, for we believe that the applicable rule of law should be designed after a trial.*[68]

> A vertical territorial limitation may or may not have that purpose or effect. We do not know enough of the economic and business stuff out of which these arrangements emerge to be certain.[69]

In the last paragraph of the judgment the Court stressed as far as possible that it does 'not intimate any view on the merits'[70] of vertical exclusivity.

However, the opinion of the majority turned out to be less important than the dissent of Justice Clark, since the latter was actually endorsed four years later by the Supreme Court. Justice Clark's dissent was based on radically formalist arguments, some of which may seem to be fairly perverse for contemporary competition policy. As a response to the manufacturer's, at least on the face of it, plausible economic justifications – as, for instance, the free-rider rationale, the

---

66 372 U.S. 253, 256 (1963).
67 *Id.* at 256.
68 *Id.* at 261.
69 *Id.* at 263.
70 *Id.* at 264.

precedence of inter-brand competition over intra-brand rivalry – Justice Clark simply stated that all these 'are economic arguments or business necessities none of which have any bearing on the legal issue'.[71] The dissent rested on two pillars. The first was the notion of 'atomistic competition', implying that intra-brand and inter-brand rivalry should have equal rank. The dissent argued that the exclusion of free-riding 'may be good for [the manufacturer] (…) but [it is] (…) disastrous for free competitive enterprise and, if permitted, will destroy the effectiveness of the Sherman Act'.[72] The dissent also stated that 'the existence of interbrand competition has never been a justification for an explicit agreement to eliminate competition'.[73] The dissent's notion of competition is also revealed by its language: vertical exclusivity 'is made solely for the purpose of eliminating competition' and it amounts to a 'suppression of competition', which 'is in and of itself a public injury'.[74] The second proposition was that the *per se* condemnation of horizontal market sharing agreements compels similar treatment for vertical territorial division.

> [The manufacturer] seems to place some halo around its agreements because they are vertical. But the intended and actual effect is the same as, if not even more destructive than, a price-fixing agreement or any of its *per se* counterparts. (…) It is hard for me to draw a distinction on the basis of who initiates such a plan.[75]

Finally and interestingly, Justice Clark, in conformity with the indication of the majority, asserted that '[c]ertainly the decision has no precedential value in substantive antitrust law'.[76]

Four years after *White Motor*, the Court turned the whole story upside-down and the dissent, in fact, became the law. In *United States v Arnold Schwinn Co.* the Court, using a far poorer argumentation than Justice Clark in his dissent, held that vertical territorial exclusivity should be considered under the *per se* illegality rule.

> Once the manufacturer has parted with title and risk, he has parted with dominion over the product, and his effort thereafter to restrict territory or persons to whom the product may be transferred – whether by explicit agreement or by silent combination or understanding with his vendee – is a *per se* violation of Section 1 of the Sherman Act.[77]

71 *Id.* at 279.
72 *Id.* at 278.
73 *Id.* at 278.
74 *Id.* at 281.
75 *Id.* at 279-280.
76 *Id.* at 283.
77 388 U.S. 365, 382 (1967).

Unfortunately, it is very hard to understand the Court's motives of characterizing vertical territorial exclusivity as *per se* illegal, apart from the reference to 'the ancient rule against restraints on alienation' where one 'has parted with dominion over the goods'.[78] Whereas the Court noted that 'such restraints are so obviously destructive of competition that their mere existence is enough', it failed to give any detailed explanation, nay, it expressly acknowledged that such territorial restraints do have a pro-competitive potential.[79] Nevertheless, that circumstance did not warrant a rule of reason treatment for such arrangements. Instead, the Court established that in case of consignment sales territorial exclusivity may be condemned only if it is '"unreasonably" restrictive of competition',[80] while characterizing such restraints in resale contracts as *per se* illegal.

The only thing that saved Schwinn's franchise scheme was that it rested, for the most part, on a system of consignment sales; that is title and risk remained with the producer.[81] As established by the Court, in genuine resale agreements territorial exclusivity clauses 'are so obviously destructive of competition that their mere existence is enough. If the manufacturer parts with dominion over his product or transfers risk of loss to another, he may not reserve control over its destiny or the conditions of its resale'.[82]

The *Schwinn* rule reigned for 10 years and it was overruled in *Continental T.V. Inc. v GTE Sylvania Inc.*,[83] where the Court held that vertical territorial restrictions may have pro-competitive effects fairly outweighing the alleged anti-competitive repercussions and, accordingly, there is no reason to treat them as *per se* illegal. The fact pattern was a clear example for a case where the system of territorial restrictions generated salient market results: after Sylvania's having suffered a considerable decrease in market share (to 1 per cent or 2 per cent), introduced a system of location restrictions, which entailed a successful expansion (to approximately 5 per cent market share).[84] Since there was intensive competition in the market (the market share of 5 per cent made Sylvania the eighth television producer in the country), it could hardly be argued that vertical territorial exclusivity, notwithstanding the very good appreciation of the competitive market itself, was anti-competitive. The considerable success in competition strongly suggested that this practice was competitive and efficient.

78 *Id.* at 380. This was expressly admitted by the Supreme Court in *Continental T.V., Inc. v GTE Sylvania Inc.*, 433 U.S. 36, 51 (1977), which overruled in *Schwinn.* ('Only four years later the Court in *Schwinn* announced its sweeping *per se* rule (…) with no explanation of its sudden change in position.')

79 388 U.S. 365, 379-380 (1967).

80 *Id.* at 380.

81 *Id.* at 381.

82 *Id.* at 379.

83 433 U.S. 36 (1977).

84 *Id.* at 38-39.

The Supreme Court's perception was that in *Schwinn* the Court tried to reconcile the perceived pro-competitive values of territorial exclusivity with the formalist arguments justifying *per se* illegality, and this endeavour lead to a perverted compromise: the 'distinction between sale [i.e. resale distribution] and nonsale [i.e. consignment] transactions resulted from the Court's effort to accommodate the perceived intrabrand harm and interbrand benefit of vertical restrictions'.[85] Nonetheless, this border line was considered to be too formalistic. The Supreme Court made it clear that 'departure from the rule-of-reason standard must be based upon demonstrable economic effect rather than as in *Schwinn* upon formalistic line drawing'.[86] So the question to be answered was whether territorial exclusivity, irrespective of whether inserted into agency or distribution contracts, should, in general, be examined under the *per se* rule or under the rule of reason.[87] Heavily influenced by the free-rider theory,[88] and the notion that 'when interbrand competition exists (…) [intrabrand restrictions simply cannot cause harm, as interbrand competition] provides a significant check on the exploitation of intrabrand market power because of the ability of consumers to substitute a different brand of the same product',[89] the Court acknowledged that vertical territorial exclusivity has economic utility,[90] and concluded 'that the appropriate decision is to return to the rule of reason that governed vertical restrictions prior to *Schwinn*'.[91]

It is noteworthy, especially in the context of EU competition law's distinction between active and passive sales, that in *Sylvania* the Supreme Court expressly refused to attach significance to the intensity of territorial protection. In *Sylvania*, the producer imposed location clauses, i.e. distributors could operate only at particular locations or location but they were not forbidden to sell outside the assigned territory. The Court refused to distinguish this case from *Schwinn* on the basis that in the latter the distributors were forbidden to sell outside the territory assigned to them, holding that '[i]n intent and competitive impact, the retail-customer restriction in *Schwinn* is indistinguishable from the location restriction in the present case'.[92]

The rule of reason implies that in the first step the plaintiff has to show adverse effects on inter-brand competition or, as a surrogate, supplier market power, a proxy of which is market share. Market share around and below 20 per cent has

85 *Id.* at 53.

86 *Id.* at 58-59.

87 *Id.* at 57. ('We conclude that the distinction drawn in *Schwinn* between sale and non-sale transactions is not sufficient to justify the application of a *per se* rule in one situation and a rule of reason in the other. The question remains whether the *per se* rule stated in *Schwinn* should be expanded to include non-sale transactions or abandoned in favor of a return to the rule of reason.')

88 *Id.* at 54-55.

89 *Id.* at 52.

90 *Id.* at 58.

91 *Id.* at 59.

92 *Id.* at 46.

generally been considered to be too small;[93] nonetheless, for instance, in *Winter Hill Frozen Foods and Services, Inc. v Haagen-Dazs Co., Inc.* the District Court of Massachusetts found that 43 per cent market share, which declined from 61 per cent, did not establish market power.[94]

So far so good. The Court rejected the traditional concern for the autonomy of independent businessmen and the method of formalism when evaluating vertical restraints. Among others, these were the principles that supported the *per se* condemnation of vertical price restraints; hence, the judgment in *Sylvania* introduced inconsistency into the treatment of vertical restraints. Justice White pointed out in his concurring opinion rather clearly that 'the effect, if not the intention, of the Court's opinion is necessarily to call into question the firmly established *per se* rule against price restraints'.[95] Nevertheless, this contradiction was maintained in the case law for additional three decades.[96]

Comparative summary

Nowadays, with the exception of absolute territorial protection, there is convergence between US antitrust and EU competition law as regards territorial exclusivity. While it is impossible to make a numerical comparison in terms of market share, the existence of a relatively high, market power indicating market share is a necessary prerequisite in both systems. Interestingly, the distinction between absolute and relative territorial protection (active and passive sales) has not emerged in the judicial practice of the Supreme Court: absolute territorial protection and areas of primary responsibility have been treated alike; the Supreme

93 *See Assam Drug Co., Inc. v Miller Brewing Co., Inc.*, 798 F.2d 311, 318 (1986) (19.1 per cent market share.); *JBL Enterprises, Inc. v Jhirmack Enterprises, Inc.*, 698 F.2d 1011, 1017 (1983); *Carlson Mach. Tools. Inc. v American Tool, Inc.*, 678 F.2d 1253, 1259 (1982) (less than 10 per cent market share); *Blanton Enterprises, Inc. v Burger King Corp.*, 680 F.Supp. 753, 767 (1988) (7.5 to 10 per cent market share); *Donald B. Rice Tire Co., Inc. v Michelin Tire Corp.*, 483 F.Supp. 750, 761 (1980) (7.9 per cent market share); *Matter of Beltone Electronics Corp.*, 100 F.T.C. 68, 209-210 (1982) (market share declining from 21 per cent to 16 per cent).

94 *Winter Hill Frozen Foods and Services, Inc. v Haagen-Dazs Co., Inc.*, 691 F.Supp. 539, 547-548 (1988) (43 per cent market share, which declined from 61 per cent two years earlier). For cases where market share was high enough to make the territorial restraint invalid *see Graphic Products Distributors, Inc. v ITEK Corp.*, 717 F.2d 1560, 1570 (1983) (market share over 70 per cent); *Kohler Co. v Briggs and Stratton Corp.*, not reported in F.Supp., 1986 WL 946 (1986) (supplier had 62 per cent market share).

95 *Id.* at 70.

96 See *Leegin Creative Leather Products, Inc. v PSKS, Inc.*, 127 S.Ct. 2705, 2718 (2007).

Court in *Sylvania* expressly refused to make such a distinction.[97] And indeed, the foregoing distinction seems to be rather constrained.

The exception of absolute territorial protection is a very serious shortcoming in the system of EU competition law. The outright prohibition of absolute territorial exclusivity is a missing brick in the wall of territorial protection that in some markets can make the whole building crumble. It depends on the circumstances of the industry whether relative territorial protection is indeed a form of protection against free-riding or it is rather useless: search costs, transportation costs, price of the goods, consumer preferences etc.

Evaluation

The effect-analysis of territorial exclusivity is certainly in conformity with sound economic theory and a very welcome approach. However, the treatment of absolute territorial protection in Europe warrants a much longer evaluation.

In EU law the notion that absolute territorial protection is an evil that EU competition law should always chase is the result of a compromise. Nevertheless, this compromise is only a formal reconciliation of the free-rider rationale and the purpose of market integration, since customers and parallel traders can exploit the perspectives of passive sales and circumvent the territorially competent dealer.[98] Of course, this perspective of circumvention is a question of degree and it depends on the value of the goods and the costs of information. Consumers, when purchasing a particular merchandise, pay two types of costs: the price, which is an out-of-pocket cost, and search costs, which may encompass out-of-pocket costs, the time spent for finding the merchandise etc. If the search costs are low as compared to the price, consumers will be ready to invest extra effort in finding the cheapest source of the goods. The possibility that active sales can be prohibited ensures only that dealers in other Member States cannot mitigate the customers' search costs; nevertheless, this is an obviously imperfect defence for the local distributor: although the exclusive dealer of another Member State cannot help the customers to cross the river, they can cross the bridge on their own. What is more, parallel dealers are free to do

97 *Continental T.V., Inc. v GTE Sylvania Inc.*, 433 U.S. 36, 46 (1977).

98 *See* Paul M. Taylor, *The Vertical Agreements Regulation*, 3 The Cambridge Yearbook of European Legal Studies 525, 539 (2000). (Stressing 'the ease with which a ban on passive sales can be eclipsed merely by the customer requesting the supply, as it is quite likely to do in response to web-site advertising'.) *Contra* Giorgio Monti, *Article 81 EC and Public Policy*, 39 Common Market Law Review 1057, 1067 (2002). (Submitting that 'the distinction between active and passive sales makes economic sense', for the following reasons. First, the most effective way for the free rider to use the marketing efforts of another is through active sales, which are forbidden. (…) Conversely, if a distributor exploits the territorial protection he has received by behaving anticompetitively, buyers will have an incentive to invest resources in finding alternative suppliers outside the territory.')

what appointed distributors cannot do: they may mitigate the consumers' search costs; parallel dealers may appear and, free from the obligations of the appointed distributors, may deliver customers across the river. The shielding effects of the search costs are particularly diminishing in the age of the Internet,[99] especially as the Commission, in general, does not consider the World Wide Web to be a form of active selling, though acknowledging the 'extraterritorial' effects of websites.[100]

Clearly, a ban on active sales is normally not completely ineffective: some customers could be discouraged by the inconvenience of searching new sources of goods; these are the ones who have high search costs. The question is whether this is sufficient for tackling the problem of free-riding.

At the same moment, the right-based rationale does not explain the rigid interdiction of passive sales in general. The argument that European citizens have the right to purchase goods and services in the common market wherever they want is valid only on the retail level and only regarding consumers; nevertheless, territorial exclusivity is normally, though certainly not always, imposed in wholesale markets.

Likewise, it is not defined what the purpose of market integration is: does it mean that artificial borders should not thwart the free flow of goods and services, or does it also encompass 'forced' integration? It could be fairly doubted that the latter would be the case. It seems to be highly questionable whether EU competition law is meant to extort the flow of goods where market realities and sound business mechanisms would not ensure it.[101] The logic of competition law

99 Valentine Korah and Denis O'Sullivan, Distribution Agreements under the EC Competition Rules 62 (2002). ('Now that it is so easy for customers to click on to advertisements on the internet and order products with their credit cards, protection from active sales is of little value for products which can conveniently be mailed and which few customers want to inspect.')

100 *Guidelines on Vertical Restraints*, paras 52-53.

101 *See* Valentine Korah and Denis O'Sullivan, Distribution Agreements under the EC Competition Rules 62 (2002). ('The drawback of looking to the symptom of price differentials between Member States rather than to the disease of different conditions in different Member States, especially when imposed by legislative or administrative measures of the States themselves, may have been to worsen the isolation of national markets.'); Emmanuel P. Mastromanolis, *Insights from U.S. Antitrust Law on Exclusive and Restricted Territorial Distribution: The Creation of a New Legal Standard for European Union Competition Law,* 15 University of Pennsylvania Journal of International Business Law 559, 615 (1994). ('Unless the different conditions causing the price variations are assimilated and other differences in economic conditions in the various Member States cease to exist, the equalization of prices in the abstract may have no rational basis. This is especially true with regard to external conditions, which manufacturers and their distributors are unable to control.'); *Cf.* Sandra Marco Colino, Vertical agreements and competition law: a comparative study of the EU and US regimes 194 (2010). ('The European institutions need to accept that, in the "EU-ropean" context, historical and cultural barriers to trade exist within the Member States which are virtually impossible to overcome.')

is, or rather should be, not be the same as that of the rules on the free movement of goods: while in case of common market rules the targets are Member State measures, competition law is addressed to business decisions based on market considerations. The problem with borrowing methods from the regulation of the common market is that in the field of competition law this approach can easily trigger the opposite result: it may discourage undertakings from entering new markets.[102] Finally, competition rules on territorial exclusivity may be especially harmful for poor Member States: as the profit-maximizing price is lower in poor countries, if parallel trade cannot be restricted, producers may find it reasonable not to supply cheap markets or to set a much higher price for them than the price charged if re-exportation was limited.

---

102 Doris Hildebrand, The role of economic analysis in the EC competition rules 279 (1998). (Warning that 'competition law, if applied in a way to make entry possible without any limitations, will, in the long run, abolish competition itself, because nobody would take the risk of opening and developing new markets by investing money in new distribution systems'.); Emmanuel P. Mastromanolis, *Insights from U.S. Antitrust Law on Exclusive and Restricted Territorial Distribution: The Creation of a New Legal Standard for European Union Competition Law,* 15 University of Pennsylvania Journal of International Business Law 559, 614-615 (1994). ('European officials may wish that integration is achieved due to the existence of parallel imports, which equalize the resale prices of national distributors of manufacturers, i.e., at an intrabrand level. Nonetheless, integration may eventually be prevented at the interbrand level as more entrepreneurs think carefully before expanding operations into different Member States or selectively operating in only a few other states in order to avoid opportunistic activities within their distribution networks.')

Chapter VIII
Final conclusions

The purpose of the present book was to demonstrate, through the example of vertical intra-brand restraints, how the treatment of restrictive agreements in the two leading competition laws of the globe differs and to evaluate, comprehensively, the two regulatory patterns from this comparative perspective. Accordingly, the constituent elements of the prohibition were examined: the concept of agreement, as well as the substance and the architecture of the rule on restrictive agreements. Thereafter, the economics of vertical intra-brand restraints was explored, presenting the economic risks and advantages of these restrictions and drawing a balance on the economic impact. Finally, US and EU law on RPF and territorial exclusivity arrangements were analysed from a critical perspective.

The concept of agreement

Both EU competition and US antitrust law subject express agreements to antitrust scrutiny. Business strategies implemented unilaterally are not caught in the net of the law on restrictive agreements. Nonetheless, the two legal systems follow a completely different approach concerning tacit agreements (agreements implied in fact).

The tradition-based *Colgate* doctrine explains the permissive approach followed by US antitrust law: according to the categorical imperative (*quasi* fundamental freedom) embedded in this doctrine, a trader is completely free to select his trading partners, and this natural right implies the right of the trader to announce his expectations towards the dealers (e.g. maintenance of resale prices) and to terminate business relations with the ones who fail to live up to these expectations. The *Colgate* defence is applicable even where all dealers comply.

EU competition law contains two theories of tacit agreement: 'continuous business relationship' and 'tacit acquiescence (assent)'.

For a while even genuine unilateral producer declarations could become part of the parties' vertical relationship and come within the purview of Article 101, provided that they occurred in the context of an ongoing business relationship. Nevertheless, in *Volkswagen*, the ECJ overruled this approach and held that the 'continuous business relationship' theory works only if the framework distribution agreement virtually contains an authorization for the producer to shape the parties' business relationship unilaterally; or to put it simply: to instruct the dealers. Though no express authorization is required, visionary authorization does not suffice. The 'continuous business relationship' theory is unknown for US antitrust law. Nevertheless, it is submitted that such an approach would be in accord with

US law only if the producer had clear and unambiguous authorization, resembling a contractual incorporation theory.

The second theory of EU competition law, i.e. 'tacit acquiescence (assent)', has its counterpart in US antitrust. Nevertheless, in the latter the scope of tacit acquiescence is rather limited. In EU law, the theory of tacit acquiescence has not been worked out because the 'continuous business relationship' theory made it unnecessary for the Commission to examine the actual conduct of the dealers; indeed, cases interpreting this theory are quite rare. While it is certain that silence infers no consent, it is questionable whether actual distributor compliance attached to the producer's call reveals an agreement according to Article 101. The ECJ's *Volkswagen* judgment suggests an affirmative answer.

On the other hand, in US antitrust, the actual compliance of the dealers does not turn a unilateral declaration into a tacit agreement. According to the *Colgate* doctrine, a producer is free to announce in advance the behaviour it expects from the dealers and to terminate those who are not complying. The fact that almost all dealers act in conformity with the producer's contemplated strategy does not prove the existence of an agreement. The Supreme Court went even further in *Monsanto* where its hostility towards the *per se* illegality of RPF heavily influenced the way the concept of agreement was shaped. It construed the term 'resale price fixing agreement' as narrow as possible: it held that only agreements relating specifically to a particular resale price or price levels are covered by the *per se* category of RPF; on the other hand, an agreement between a producer and a dealer on the basis of which the former terminates a price-cutter ('agreement to terminate') does not amount to resale price fixing.

The most obvious drawback of the American approach, before *Leegin* utterly abolished RPF's *per se* illegality, was that it was more favourable for producers with market power since these were the ones who were capable of coercing compliance through the threat of refusing to supply. Producers with minor bargaining power simply could not exploit the chances provided by *Colgate*. Nonetheless, economics suggests that vertical intra-brand restraints raise competitive perils only when the producer has market power. Now, granting more give to producers with some market power seems to be perverse.

Furthermore, before *Leegin* eliminated RPF's *per se* condemnation, the *Colgate* doctrine, underpinned by *Monsanto*, induced producers to engage in a very costly strategy in order to maintain prices. Producers were not deprived of the power to maintain resale prices but they were deprived of the cheapest means of maintaining prices (legally enforceable contracts).

On the other hand, the problem with EU competition law seems to be that it does not interdict attempts to coerce but it condemns successfully implemented coercion: a producer may urge its dealers not to discount or not to sell outside the contract territory but such an act is illegal if it is effective and the call is complied with.

The starting point of the question should be the competition law maxim that market operators, in principle, should determine their market behaviour independently. The distributor is certainly not acting independently if it behaves in a way envisaged by the producer simply because it is afraid of the consequences of non-compliance. It is submitted that if the producer calls the distributors to act in a certain way, including both public announcement and direct communication, and distributors do act in this way because of the call, the existence of an agreement cannot be denied since the parties do not act independently. Accordingly, the only way to escape competition law condemnation is to prove that the distributor would have acted in the incriminated manner anyway. In this regard the self-interests of the distributors should have a central role.

It is submitted that in EU competition law the concept of agreement should embrace all situations where independence of action is missing. Accordingly, the application of the 'tacit acquiescence' theory presupposes an 'announcement/call plus actual compliance' situation. The 'continuous business relationship' theory has already been rephrased by the ECJ so as to cover only situations where the producer is virtually authorized to amend or supplement the business relationship between the parties. Nevertheless, in the absence of such a mandate, the Commission or the plaintiff is required to prove actual compliance. Finally, it is submitted that, contrary to *Monsanto*, all debate about and hostility towards RPF's *per se* condemnation should be channelled into the analysis of the substance of the rule on restrictive agreements and should leave the concept of agreement intact.

The substance and architecture of the rule on restrictive agreements

Both US antitrust and EU competition law distinguish between agreements of automatic condemnation (*per se* illegal agreements in the US; agreements anti-competitive by object or hardcore agreements in the EU) and arrangements subjected to effects-analysis (rule of reason agreements in the US; agreements anti-competitive by effect in the EU).

The concept of agreements interdicted without an effects-analysis is based on two principles: 'automatic condemnation' rule, i.e. the agreement is afforded only a formal examination the purpose of which is to ascertain whether it can be brought under one of the pre-determined categories of *per se* illegality; and 'no defence' rule, i.e. the defendant has no chance to submit justifications: once the agreement comes under one of the pre-determined categories its anti-competitiveness is conclusively presumed.

The above firm propositions are supplemented with qualifications in both systems. In US antitrust law the concept of 'quick look' introduced a narrow corridor from *per se* agreements to the rule of reason: in some cases the court can give a limited chance to the defendant to name its justifications and if these are facially plausible, the court will go on with a full-blown rule of reason, where, nevertheless, the anti-competitive impact of the agreement is presumed. The Supreme Court was not clear about the purview of 'quick look'; however, it seems that this concept applies to professional services and markets that inevitably require some horizontal cooperation. Likewise, in EU competition law, even agreements anti-competitive by object might benefit from an individual exemption under Article 101(3); theoretically, automatic condemnation is restricted to Article 101(1). Nevertheless, it is submitted that it is normally not realistic for anti-competitive by object agreements to attach hopes to Article 101(3).

Per se categories in US antitrust law are inflexible compared to the concept of object type agreements in EU competition law. It is submitted that this inflexibility was probably the main reason that hastened the introduction of the 'quick look'. In *U.S. v Socony-Vacuum Oil Co*, the Supreme Court held that all arrangements tampering with price structures amount to *per se* illegal price-fixing. In *Broadcast Music, Inc. v Columbia Broadcasting System, Inc.*, the Supreme Court encountered an arrangement that did tamper with prices but was apparently not naked. 'Quick look' was introduced to save such agreements from the rigidity of *per se* rules.

In the scholarship the view emerged that there is a fundamental difference between anti-competitive object and *per se* illegality: the individual exemption of Article 101(3) is, theoretically, available to all agreements and no categories of agreements are excluded outright from the chance to meet the requirements of Article 101(3), contrary to US antitrust law, where the prohibition of *per se* agreements is watertight. It is submitted that this position is falsified, first, by the Supreme Court's introduction of 'quick look' and, second, by the fact that Article 101(3), in practice, is not a realistic but rather a theoretical perspective for agreements anti-competitive by object.

Agreements not warranting automatic condemnation deserve a full market analysis on both sides of the Atlantic (rule of reason analysis in the US; agreements anti-competitive by effect in the EU). At the end of the day the two regimes enable the examination of the same issues: the analysis of effect type agreements under Article 101(1) and 101(3) embraces all the aspects that are covered by the rule of reason, and *vice versa*. Nevertheless, the architecture of the analysis and the allocation of the burden of proof are not the same in the two systems.

The analysis under Article 101 is bifurcated: Article 101(1) centres around competition in the sense of rivalry, while Article 101(3) centres around efficiency.

In the first layer of the analysis the burden of proof is on the competition authority (in administrative procedures), including the Commission, or the plaintiff (in private actions). The question under Article 101(1) is whether the agreement has anti-competitive effects. It is submitted that in this regard competition means rivalry. It is also submitted that the 'market context' approach and the concept of 'comparison', i.e. comparing the competitive situation with and without the agreement, entail that the arrangement's net effect on competition (rivalry) is to be ascertained; competition-neutral and competition-enhancing agreements are not caught by Article 101(1).

In the second layer of the analysis the burden of proof shifts to the defendant. Here, the question is not whether the agreement interferes with the competitive process; this must have been already established under Article 101(1) if the case has reached Article 101(3). Instead, the question is whether the agreement increases efficiency and whether these efficiency benefits outweigh the harm caused by restricting competition; in other words, the relevant question is whether the ultimate effect on consumer welfare is positive or negative.

In US antitrust law, the statutory language of Section 1 of the Sherman Act suggests a monistic analysis. Nevertheless, the judicial practice developed a structured examination. Here, the analysis has the following layers: first, the plaintiff has to present a *prima facie* case, i.e. it has to prove anti-competitive impact or, as a surrogate, market power; if the plaintiff is successful, the burden of proof shifts to the defendant to present justifications, which may relate both to competition (rivalry) and efficiency. If the defendant meets the burden of proof, the court exercises a balancing; the perception is that in case of substantiated justifications courts tend to decide for the defendant.

It is to be stressed that under Article 101(3) undertakings bear a very heavy burden, as compared to the burden of the defendant in US antitrust law after the plaintiff's having showed a *prima facie* case. Contrary to US antitrust law, where perception suggests that in case of substantiated justifications it is decided for the defendant, in Europe undertakings are advised to act very carefully if their agreement is under the necessity to be examined under Article 101(3).

Legal certainty, predictability and judicial convenience all justify that there should be agreements that are condemned automatically, without the need to accomplish a costly market analysis and without considering the justifications proffered. The concept of 'quick look' and the notion that even object type agreements can meet the conditions of Article 101(3) are applicable only in highly exceptional cases and, thus, do not endanger the brightness of these rules.

Since both US antitrust and EU competition law cover the same issues when analysing the competitive repercussions of an arrangement and ask basically the same question, i.e. whether consumer welfare is enhanced or decreased at the end of the day, the real question of evaluation is how these tests are structured. In this regard EU competition law's method, if properly construed, could be preferable, as it allocates the burden of proof in accordance with the probable effects. Since common sense suggests that consumer welfare is maximized if there is rivalry, it is assumed that agreements setting back rivalry are illegal, while rivalry-neutral and rivalry-enhancing ones are lawful. On the other hand, though it is normally not the case, cooperation sometimes may have a beneficial impact on consumer welfare: accordingly, EU competition law provides for the analysis of this issue as well, nevertheless, as experience shows that cooperation is the exception and not the rule from the point of view of welfare maximization, in this regard the burden shifts to the defendant. All in all, this construction minimizes the risks of false positives and false negatives[1] as far as possible: on this level of regulation this is the maximum that could be done.

1 A false negative is when it is incorrectly concluded that the agreement does not violate competition law, i.e. an anti-competitive or inefficient practice is granted leave (under-enforcement); a false positive is when it is incorrectly concluded that the agreement violates competition law (over-enforcement), i.e. a pro-competitive or efficient practice is interdicted.

Nonetheless, the merits of the European system are called into question, because the above structure of analysis is not applied consistently: not all justifications relating to rivalry are considered under Article 101(1), and they are occasionally exiled into Article 101(3).

The economics of vertical intra-brand restraints

Economics suggest that vertical intra-brand restraints have a significant potential of enhancing consumer welfare, albeit they may also raise competition concerns. It seems to be settled that they may certainly have advantages and drawbacks; nevertheless, it depends on the circumstances which effects prevail.

Territorial protection presents a clear scenario of tackling the problem of free-riding, and the vast majority of the economic literature shares the common ground that such arrangements have very strong pro-competitive effects.

The treatment of RPF is more controversial in the scholarship. Nevertheless, the opinion that RPF merits a full-blown effects-analysis, though a closer one than in case of territorial protection, seems to be prevalent. Essentially, the controversy does not relate to whether but to how RPF arrangements should be analysed. Both horizontal and vertical perils are put on RPF; nevertheless, both empirical and theoretical evidence shows that horizontal projections, i.e. producer cartel and dealer cartel, do not raise substantial risks. RPF normally raises no horizontal concerns; although a cartel may use RPF as a tool, in such cases the source of the problem is horizontal and not vertical in nature. Accordingly, the analysis of the vertical projections should have priority.

The treatment of RPF

There is a fundamental divergence between US antitrust and EU competition law, both in law and in fact, concerning the treatment of the fixing of concrete and minimum resale prices, while the approaches of the two regimes regarding maximum resale price fixing and recommended resale prices roughly coincide.

Maximum and recommended resale prices are examined under the rule of reason in US antitrust law, while in EU competition law they are considered as lawful if neither the supplier's, nor the buyer's market share exceeds 30 per cent and even above this threshold they can be condemned only if they have anti-competitive effects.[2]

In EU competition law, RPF is treated as anti-competitive by object under Article 101(1) and it is highly unlikely that is could benefit from an individual exemption under Article 101(3); the chances of RPF surviving under Article 101(3) are theoretically always, although practically almost never, realistic.

2 Articles 3 and 4(a) of the BER.

In US antitrust law, the *per se* illegality of RPF was abolished in *Leegin* (2007). Nevertheless, it is to be emphasized that most parts of the *per se* illegal treatment were removed already in *Monsanto* (1984), where the Supreme Court restricted the application of *per se* illegality to agreements that relate positively to the resale price, i.e. prior announcements to terminate in case of discounting, communication between the producer and non-discounting dealers and agreements to terminate the price-cutter were not covered by *per se* illegality. Accordingly, the virtual divergence between US antitrust and EU competition law, in this regard, started 23 years before *Leegin*.

Recent developments and the European reaction to *Leegin* suggest that a change in the policy on RPF is emerging in EU competition law. There is, nevertheless, a danger that the enthusiasm for and the issues of RPF will be forced into Article 101(3)'s bed of Procrustes, which is, nevertheless, not the proper field for examining them. The 2010 *Guidelines on Vertical Restraints* foreshadow this approach and seem to turn this danger into a reality: they expressly encourage undertakings to test RPF agreements under Article 101(3) and declare that the exemption of such arrangements is a highly exceptional but not an always unrealistic perspective. As noted above, Article 101(3) focuses, or rather should focus, on questions of (productive) efficiency, while the vast majority of economic justifications for RPF assert that it increases rivalry, i.e. the intensity of competition. A very strong argument for RPF is that if implemented by a small supplier and it is not widespread in the industry (no cumulative effects), it is simply not capable of being harmful; an argument that does not fit in Article 101(3); on the other hand, this argument suggests that instead the *Notice on Agreements of Minor Importance* should be amended so as to cover agreements containing RPF if market share is low.

It is submitted that after *Leegin* the two regimes, even if taking into account the above perspectives, are not in line with each other, because the defendant has a much stronger position under the rule of reason in US antitrust law than an undertaking that is under the necessity of leaning on the broken reed of Article 101(3). First, under the rule of reason the plaintiff, before the defendant ought to say anything, has to show a *prima facie* case, i.e. it has to prove that the RPF arrangement had an anti-competitive impact or the supplier has market power; on the other hand, RPF is anti-competitive by object under Article 101(1) and its mischief is conclusively presumed. Second, the position of the defendant is also stronger under the rule of reason when presenting justifications. Perception suggests that US courts appreciate substantiated defendant justifications, while Article 101(3) places a heavier burden of proof on undertakings; and indeed, there has been no formal Commission decision or EU court judgment that would have exempted an RPF agreement.

The treatment of territorial exclusivity

Territorial exclusivity is subject to effects-analysis in both US antitrust and EU competition law, with the exception of the special treatment of absolute territorial protection in Europe. It is a sign of convergence that in EU competition law relative territorial protection is block exempted below 30 per cent market share, while in the US the plaintiff normally tries to present a *prima facie* case by proving market power as a surrogate of anti-competitive impact, which is usually not present below 30 per cent market share. Nevertheless, the distinction between absolute and relative territorial protection (active and passive sales) is unknown in the judicial practice of the Supreme Court: the Court refused to attach any significance to this distinction and absolute territorial protection and areas of primary responsibility have been treated alike.

While subjecting territorial exclusivity to effects-analysis is in accord with sound economic theory and a very welcome approach, the treatment of absolute territorial protection in Europe warrants fierce criticism. Namely, relative territorial exclusivity often fails to afford sufficient protection against free-riding; the success of relative territorial protection depends on the ratio between search costs and the price of the merchandise. If search costs are relatively small – either because their absolute value is small, or because the merchandise is very valuable – the ban on active sales has a modest capability for tackling free-riding. Furthermore, while this European specialty is a missing brick in the wall of territorial protection that in some markets can make the whole building crumble, the arguments that are raised for its defence are rather dubious. First, the argument that European citizens have the natural right to purchase goods and services in the common market wherever they want could be valid only on the retail level and only regarding final consumers; on the other hand, territorial exclusivity is normally, though certainly not always, imposed in wholesale markets. Second, it is questionable whether the purpose of market integration is really served by the outright ban on absolute territorial protection, as territorial exclusivity is the most popular means of penetrating new markets. Accordingly, the foregoing rule may even hinder market integration.[3] Third, the purpose of market integration seems to be to abolish artificial hurdles to intra-Union trade; vertical territorial protection is not an artificial hurdle, it is a private measure based on sound and efficient market considerations. Fourth, the outright prohibition of absolute territorial exclusivity may be especially harmful for poor Member States: as the profit-maximizing price is lower in poor countries, if parallel trade cannot be restricted, producers may find it reasonable not to supply cheap markets or to set a much higher price for them than the price charged if re-exportation was limited.

---

3 *Cf.* Sandra Marco Colino, Vertical agreements and competition law: a comparative study of the EU and US regimes 69-70 (2010). (Contending that if the purpose of market integration 'is prioritised even before the protection of competition *strictu sensu*, the results can be detrimental to the single market'.)

The synergies between the conclusions of the book: *quo vadis* EU competition law?

The construction of Article 101, as applied in practice, is inconsistent. Article 101(1) centres around the competitive process (rivalry), while Article 101(3) centres around efficiency. Unfortunately, in practice these two focuses are not clearly distinguished and the analysis under the bifurcated Article 101 is often blurred.

The current treatment of vertical intra-brand restraints in EU competition law is not in accord with sound economics; economic theory suggests that such restraints may have both pro- and anti-competitive effects, while EU competition law treats RPF and absolute territorial protection as restraints that are always or almost always harmful.

There is an emerging criticism against the *de facto* outright prohibition of RPF and absolute territorial protection in the EU, which was reinforced by the *Leegin* judgment. Nevertheless, the rising substantive analysis of vertical intra-brand restraints in EU competition law seems to be misplaced; there is a danger that all analysis related to RPF and absolute territorial protection will be done under Article 101(3). While the advantages of vertical intra-brand restraints normally relate to the enhancement of the competitive process, Article 101(3) centres around (productive) efficiency. Furthermore, the most compelling argument for RPF and absolute territorial protection is that if the producer has low market share and the practice is not widespread, the vertical intra-brand restraint is simply not capable of having any anti-competitive impact; this argument certainly fits the *de minimis* concept of Article 101(1) but has no place under Article 101(3).

Bibliography

Books and periodical materials

Deirdre Ahern, Case Comment, *Hemat v The Medical Council: the Wouters Legacy revisited*, 28 European Competition Law Review 366 (2007)

Femi Alese, *Unmasking the Masquerade of Vertical Price Fixing*, 28(9) European Competition Law Review 514 (2007)

Philip Andrews, *Self-regulation by professions – the approach under E.U. and U.S. competition rules*, 23(6) European Competition Law Review 281 (2002

PHILLIP AREEDA, ANTITRUST LAW (1986)

Phillip Areeda, *A Second Century of the Rule of Reason*, 59 Antitrust Law Journal 143 (1990)

Phillip Areeda, *The Rule of Reason – A Catechism on Competition*, 55 Antitrust Law Journal 571 (1986)

Jean-Yves Art and Dirk van Liedekerke, *Developments in EC Competition Law in 1994 – an Overview*, 32(4) Common Market Law Review 921 (1995)

Thomas C. Arthur, *A Workable Rule of Reason: a Less Ambitious Antitrust Role for the Federal Courts*, 68 Antitrust Law Journal 337 (2000)

Thomas C. Arthur, *Farewell to the Sea of Doubt: Jettisoning the Constitutional Sherman Act*, 74 California Law Review 263 (1986)

Thomas C. Arthur, *Workable Antitrust Law: the Statutory Approach to Antitrust*, 62 Tulane Law Review 1163 (1988)

Tyler A. Baker, *The Leegin Case: Some Personal Observations About How It Began and Where It Will Take Us Next*, 9 Sedona Conference Journal 125 (2008)

Brenda B. Balzon, *Leegin Creative Leather Products, Inc. v. PSKS, Inc. 127 U.S. 2705* (2007), 12 Intellectual Property Law Bulletin 95 (2007)

Matthew Bennett and A. Jorge Padilla, *Article 81 EC Revisited: Deciphering European Commission Antitrust Goals and Rules*, *in* COMPETITION POLICY IN THE EU (Xavier Vives ed., 2009)

Donald L. Beschle, *What, Never? Well, Hardly Ever: Strict Antitrust Scrutiny as an Alternative to Per Se Antitrust Illegality*, 38 Hastings Law Journal 471 (1987)

Oliver Black, *Per Se Rules and Rules of Reason: What Are They?*, 18(3) European Competition Law Review 145 (1997)

ROBERT H. BORK, THE ANTITRUST PARADOX (1978)

Ward Bowman, *The Prerequisites and Effects of Resale Price Maintenance*, 22 University of Chicago Law Review 825 (1955)

Morten Broberg and Peter Stig Jakobsen, *The concept of agreement in Article 81 E.C.: on the manufacturers' right to prevent parallel trade within the European Community*, 23(3) European Competition Law Review 127 (2002)
Christopher Brown, *Note, Bayer v Commission: the ECJ agrees*, 25(7) European Competition Law Review 386 (2005)
Mary Claire Butt, *Not a Surprise, Per Se: the Advent of the Rule of Reason for Vertical, Minimum Resale Price Maintenance Agreements in Leegin Creative Leather Products, Inc. v. PSKS, Inc.*, 61 Arkansas Law Review 531 (2008)
David A. Butz and Andrew N. Kleit, *Are Vertical Restraints Pro- or Anticompetitive? Lessons from Interstate Circuit*, 44 Journal of Law and Economics 131 (2001)
Stephen Calkins, *California Dental Association: Not a Quick Look but not the Full Monty*, 67 Antitrust Law Journal 495 (2000)
Terry Calvani, *Some Thoughts on the Application of the Rule of Reason and the Per Se Rule*, SH064 ALI-ABA 27 (2003)
D. W. Carlton and J. M. Perloff, Modern Industrial Organization (2000)
Jason A. Casey, *The Rule of Reason After Leegin: Reconsidering the USE of Economic Analysis in the Antitrust Arena*, 42 Suffolk University Law Review 919 (2009)
Edward D. Cavanagh, *Vertical Price Restraints After Leegin*, 21 Loyola Consumer Law Review 1 (2008)
David A. Clanton, *The FTC and the Professions*, 52 Antitrust Law Journal 209 (1983)
Bruce Clark, *Leegin Creative Leather Products, Inc. v. PSKS, Inc. 127 S. Ct. 2705 (2007)*, 34 Ohio Northern University Law Review 657 (2008)
Crystal J. Clark, *Leegin Creative Leather Products, Inc. v. PSKS, Inc.: Loosening the Belt on Price Fixing*, 59 Mercer Law Review 767 (2008)
R. H. Coase, *The Nature of the Firm*, 4 Economica 386 (1937)
William E. Cohen, *Per Se Illegality and Truncated Rule of Reason: the Search for a Foreshortened Antitrust Analysis* (1997) (available at http://www.ftc.gov/opp/jointvent/persepap.shtm)
Sandra Marco Colino, Vertical agreements and competition law: a comparative study of the EU and US regimes (2010)
William S. Comanor, *Vertical Price-Fixing, Vertical Market Restrictions, and the New Antitrust Policy*, 98 Harvard Law Review 983 (1985)
William S. Comanor and John B. Kirkwood, *Resale Price Maintenance and Antitrust Policy*, 3(3) Contemporary Policy Issues 9 (1985)
Eric D. Daniels, *Did the Supreme Court Fumble?: the Supreme Court's Failure to Endorse a Market Power Threshold to the Application of the Rule of Reason for Cases under Section 1 of the Sherman Act in NCAA v. Board or Regent*, 27 Boston College Law Review 579 (1986)
Elspeth Deards, *Case Comment, Closed shop versus one stop shop: the battle goes on*, 27 European Law Review 618 (2002)

Raymond Deneckere, Howard P. Marvel and James Peck, *Demand Uncertainty, Inventories, and Resale Price Maintenance*, 87 American Economic Review 619 (1997)

Michael L. Denger and Joshua Lipton, *The Rule of Reason and 'Leegin Policies': the Supreme Court's Guidance*, 22 Antitrust Fall 45 (2007)

Daniel Denman, *Case Comment, European Court of Justice: anticompetitive agreements – professional rules – Netherlands Bar*, 23 European Competition Law Review N73 (2002)

Alan Devlin, *On the Ramifications of Leegin Creative Leather Products, Inc. v. PSKS, Inc.: Are Tie-Ins Next?*, 56 Cleveland State Law Review 387 (2008)

F. Enrique Gonzalez Diaz, *The Notion of Ancillary Restraints under EC Competition Law*, 19 Fordham International Law Journal 951 (1996)

Ashley Doty, *Leegin v. PSKS: New Standard, New Challenges*, 23 Berkeley Technology Law Journal 655 (2008)

Richard A. Duncan and Alison K. Guernsey, *Waiting for the Other Shoe to Drop: Will State Courts Follow Leegin?*, 27 Franchise Law Journal 173 (2008)

Frank H. Easterbrook, *The Limits of Antitrust*, 63 Texas Law Review 1 (1984)

Frank H. Easterbrook, *Workable Antitrust Policy*, 84 Michigan Law Review 1696 (1986)

Claus-Dieter Ehlermann, *The Contribution of EC Competition Policy to the Single Market*, 29 Common Market Law Review 257 (1992)

Claus Dieter Ehlermann, *The Modernization of EC Antitrust Policy: a Legal and Cultural Revolution*, 37 Common Market Law Review 537 (2000)

Peter M. Ellis, *Leegin Creative Leather Products v. PSKS and Vertical Restraints*, 34 North Carolina Journal of International Law and Commercial Regulation 569 (2009)

David A. Ettinger and Gerard Mantese, *The Rule of Reason*, 64 Michigan Bar Journal 36 (1985)

European Commission, *Communication from the Commission on the application of the Community competition rules to vertical restraints. Follow-up to the Green Paper on Vertical Restraints.* COM (98) 544 final, 30 September, 1998. OJ [1998] C 365/3

European Commission, *Green Paper on Vertical Restraints in EC Competition Policy.* COM (96) 721 final. 22 January 1997

European Commission, *White Paper on Modernisation of the Rules Implementing Article 85 and 86 of the EC Treaty. Commission Programme 99/027. COM (99) 101 final.* OJ [1999] C 132/1

Erich M. Fabricius, *The Death of Discount Online Retailing? Resale Price Maintenance After Leegin v. PSKS*, 9 North Carolina Journal of Law and Technology 87 (2007)

Mario Filipponi, Luc Peeperkorn and Donncadh Woods, *Chapter 9: Vertical Agreements*, *in* THE EC LAW OF COMPETITION (Jonathan Faull and Ali Nikpay ed., 2007)

Ian Forrester and Christopher Norall, *The Laicization of Community Law: Self-help and the Rule of Reason: How Competition Law is and could be Applied*, 21 Common Market Law Review 11 (1984)

Eleanor M. Fox and Lawrence A. Sullivan, *Antitrust-Retrospective and Prospective: Where are We Coming from? Where are We Going?*, 62 New York University Law Review 936 (1987)

FTC and DOJ, *Guidelines for Collaborations Among Competitors*, April 2000

Baden Fuller, *Economic Issues Relating to Property Rights in Trade Marks, Important Bans, Differential Pricing, Restrictions on Resale and Repackaging*, 6 European Law Review 162 (1981)

Richard J. Gilbert and Paul Klemperer, *An Equilibrium Theory of Rationing*, 31(1) Rand Journal of Economics 1 (2000)

Jennifer E. Gladieux, *Towards a Single Standard for Antitrust: the Federal Trade Commission's Evolving Rule of Reason*, 5 George Mason Law Review 471 (1997)

Roger J. Goebel, *Metro II's Confirmation of the Selective Distribution Rules: Is This the End of the Road?*, 24 Common Market Law Review 605 (1987)

J. R. Gould and L. E. Preston, *Resale Price Maintenance and Resale Outlets*, 32 Economica 302 (1965)

JOANNA GOYDER, EU DISTRIBUTION LAW (4th ed., 2005)

Mark Griffiths, *A Glorification of De Minimis – The Regulation on Vertical Agreements*, 21(5) European Competition Law Review 241 (2000)

Warren Grimes, *Spiff, Polish, and Consumer Demand Quality: Vertical Price Restraints Revisited*, 80 California Law Review 815 (1992)

Warren S. Grimes, *The Path Forward After Leegin: Seeking Consensus Reform of the Antitrust Law of Vertical Restraints*, 75 Antitrust Law Journal 467 (2008)

Luc Gyselen, *Vertical Restraints in the Distribution Process: Strength and Weakness of the Free Rider Rationale under EEC Competition Law*, 21 Common Market Law Review 647 (1984)

Barry E. Hawk, *System Failure: Vertical Restraints and EC Competition Law*, 32 Common Market Law Review 973 (1995)

THOMAS HAYS, PARALLEL IMPORTATION UNDER EUROPEAN UNION LAW (2003)

DORIS HILDEBRAND, THE ROLE OF ECONOMIC ANALYSIS IN THE EC COMPETITION RULES (1998)

Jonathan Hillel, *Legal Turbulence After Leegin: New Possibilities for Patent Licensing at Research Institutions*, 7 Northwestern Journal of Technology and Intellectual Property 84 (2008)

Donald L. Holley, *EEC Competition Practice; a Thirty-Year Retrospective*, 16 Fordham International Law Journal 342 (1992)

Herbert Hovenkamp, *Distributive Justice and the Antitrust Laws*, 51 George Washington Law Review 1 (1982)

HERBERT HOVENKAMP, FEDERAL ANTITRUST POLICY. THE LAW OF COMPETITION AND ITS PRACTICE (1999)

Robert L. Hubbard, *Protecting Consumers Post-Leegin*, 22 Antitrust 41 (2007)

Pauline M. Ippolito, *Resale Price Maintenance: Empirical Evidence from Litigation*, 34 Journal of Law and Economics 263 (1991)

Ryan T. Jardine, *Economic Law – Vertical Minimum Pricing in Leegin – Adrift with the Rule of Reason; Sinking with Stare Decisis, Leegin Creative Leather Prod., Inc. v. PSKS, Inc.*, 127 S. CT. 2705 (2007), 8 Wyoming Law Review 683 (2008)

René Joliet, The Rule of Reason in Antitrust Law; American, German and Common Market Laws in Comparative Perspective (1967)

Alison Jones, *Resale Price Maintenance: a Debate about Competition Policy in Europe*, 5(2) European Competition Journal 479 (2009)

Joseph Kattan, *The Role of Efficiency Considerations in the Federal Trade Commission's Antitrust Analysis*, 64 Antitrust Law Journal 613 (1996)

Christopher S. Kelly, *Leegin Creative Leather Products, Inc. v. PSKS, Inc.: the Final Blow to The Use of Per Se Rules in Judging Vertical Restraints – Why the Court Got It Wrong*, 28 Northern Illinois University Law Review 593 (2008)

Leon J. de Keyser, *Territorial Restrictions and Export Prohibitions under the United States and the Common Market Antitrust Laws*, 2 Common Market Law Review 271 (1965)

James A. Keyte, *What It Is and How It Is Being Applied: the 'Quick Look' Rule of Reason*, 11-SUM Antitrust 21 (1997)

Benjamin Klein and Kevin M. Murphy, *Vertical Restraints as Contract Enforcement Mechanisms*, 31 Journal of Law and Economics 265 (1988)

Andrew N. Kleit, *Efficiencies without Economists: the Early Years of Resale Price Maintenance*, 59 Southern Economic Journal, 597 (1993)

Mart Kneepkens, *Resale Price Maintenance: Economics Call for a More Balanced Approach*, 28(12) European Competition Law Review 656 (2007)

Michael Komenda, *The Course Correction a Century in the Making: Leegin Creative Leather Products, Inc. v. PSKS, Inc.*, 31 Harvard Journal of Law and Public Policy 855 (2008)

Valentine Korah, Intellectual Property Rights and the EC Competition Rules (2006)

Valentine Korah, *Draft Block Exemption for Technology Transfer*, 25(5) European Competition Law Review 247 (2004)

Valentine Korah, *EEC Competition Policy – Legal Form or Economic Efficiency*, 39 Current Legal Problems 85 (1986)

Valentine Korah, *Goodbye, Red Label; Condemnation of Dual Pricing by Distillers*, 3 European Law Review 62 (1978)

Valentine Korah, *Rule of reason: apparent inconsistency in the case law under Article 81*, 1 Competition Law Insight 24 (2002)

Valentine Korah, *The Rise and Fall of Provisional Validity: The Need for a Rule of Reason in EEC Antitrust*, 3 Northwestern Journal of International Law and Business 320 (1981)

Valentine Korah and Denis O'Sullivan, Distribution Agreements under the EC Competition Rules (2002)

John E. Kwoka, *The Federal Trade Commission and the Professions: a Quarter Century of Accomplishment and Some New Challenges*, 72 Antitrust Law Journal 997 (2005)

Marina Lao, *Comment, The Rule of Reason and Horizontal Restraints Involving Professionals*, 68 Antitrust Law Journal 499 (2000)

Maija Laurila, *The De Minimis Doctrine in EEC Competition Law: Agreements of Minor Importance*, 14(3) European Competition Law Review 97 (1993)

Thomas B. Leary, *Should Leegin Finally Bury Old Man Miles?*, 21 Antitrust Spring 66 (2007)

Erick S. Lee, *Price Fix Away? Does the Supreme Court's Decision in Leegin Creative Leather Products Strengthen the Ability of Businesses to Engage in Vertical Price Restraints with Impunity?*, 8 University of Pittsburgh Journal of Technology Law and Policy 6 (2008)

Ioannis Lianos, *Collusion in Vertical Relations under Article 81 EC*, 45 Common Market Law Review 1027 (2008)

Wesley J. Liebeler, *Intrabrand 'Cartels' under GTE Sylvania*, 30 University of California at Los Angeles Law Review 1 (1982)

Robert C. Lind and Paul Muysert, *The European Commission's Draft Technology Transfer Block Exemption Regulation and Guidelines: a Significant Departure from Accepted Competition Policy Principles*, 25(4) European Competition Law Review 181 (2004)

Michael A. Lindsay, *Resale Price Maintenance and the World After Leegin*, 22 Antitrust 32 (2007)

Michael J. Lockerby, *Franchising After Leegin: a License to Fix Prices?*, 27 Franchise Law Journal 112 (2007)

Scott Looper, *Reading Roberts: a Critical Framework for Analyzing the Supreme Court's Decision in Leegin Creative Leather Products, Inc. v. PSKS, Inc.*, 46 Houston Law Review 177 (2009)

Edith Loozen, *Professional ethics and restraints of competition*, 31(1) European Law Review 28 (2006)

Pietro Manzini, *The European Rule of Reason – Crossing the Sea of Doubt*, 23 European Competition Law Review 392 (2002)

Aaron O. Martin, *The American Consumer Is Not Well: Where Is Dr. Miles?*, 47 Washburn Law Journal 581 (2008)

Howard P. Marvel, *The Resale Price Maintenance Controversy: Beyond the Conventional Wisdom,* 63 Antitrust Law Journal 59 (1994)

Howard P. Marvel and Stephen McCafferty, *Resale Price Maintenance and Quality Certification*, 15(3) Rand Journal of Economics 346 (1984)

Emmanuel P. Mastromanolis, *Insights from U.S. Antitrust Law on Exclusive and Restricted Territorial Distribution: The Creation of a New Legal Standard for European Union Competition Law,* 15 University of Pennsylvania Journal of International Business Law 559 (1994).

Lance McMillian, *The Proper Role of Courts: the Mistakes of the Supreme Court in Leegin*, 2008 Wisconsin Law Review 405 (2008)

Alan J. Meese, *Farewell to the Quick Look: Redefining the Scope and Content of the Rule of Reason*, 68 Antitrust Law Journal 461 (2000)

Alan J. Meese, *Price Theory, Competition and the Rule of Reason*, 2003 University of Illinois Law Review 77 (2003)

ERNST-JOACHIM MESTMÄCKER AND HEIKE SCHWEITZER, EUROPÄISCHES WETTBEWERBSRECHT (2004)

Giorgio Monti, *Article 81 EC and Public Policy*, 39 Common Market Law Review 1057 (2002)

Timothy J. Muris, *The New Rule of Reason*, 57 Antitrust Law Journal 859 (1989)

CSONGOR ISTVÁN NAGY, KARTELLJOGI KÉZIKÖNYV (2008)

Csongor István Nagy, *Refusal to Deal and the Doctrine of Essential Facilities in US and EC competition law: a Comparative Perspective and a Proposal for a Workable Analytical Framework*, 32(5) European Law Review 664 (2007)

Phedon Nicolaides, *The Balancing Myth: The Economics of Article 81(1) and (3)*, 32(2) Legal Issues of Economic Integration 123 (2005)

Ali Nikpay, Jonathan Faull and Lars Kjølbye: *Article 81*, *in* THE EC LAW OF COMPETITION (Jonathan Faull and Ali Nikpay ed., 2007)

Daniel B. Nixa, *Internet Retailers and Intertype Competition: How the Supreme Court's Incomplete Analysis in Leegin v. PSKS Leaves Lower Courts Improperly Equipped to Consider Modern Resale Price Maintenance Agreements*, 11 Vanderbilt Journal of Entertainment and Technology Law Winter 461 (2009)

Okeoghene Odudu, *Interpreting Article 81(1): Demonstrating Restrictive Effect*, 26(3) European Law Review 261 (2001)

Okeoghene Odudu, *Interpreting Article 81(1): Object as Subjective Intention*, 26(1) European Law Review 60 (2001)

OKEOGHENE ODUDU, THE BOUNDARIES OF EC COMPETITION LAW (2006)

Julie M. Olszewski, *Overruling a Nearly Century-Old Precedent: Why Leegin Got It Right*, 94 Iowa Law Review 375 (2008)

Stanley I. Ornstein, *Resale Price Maintenance and Cartels*, 30 Antitrust Bulletin 401 (1985)

H. J. OSTLUND AND C. R. VICKLAND, FAIR TRADE AND THE RETAIL DRUG STORE (1940)

THOMAS OVERSTREET, RESALE PRICE MAINTENANCE: ECONOMIC THEORIES AND EMPIRICAL EVIDENCE (Bureau of Econ., Fed. Trade Comm'n 1983)

Mark R. Patterson, *The Market Power Requirement in Antitrust Rule of Reason Cases: a Rhetorical History*, 37 San Diego Law Review 1 (2000)

Luc Peeperkorn, *E.C. Vertical Restraints Guidelines: Effects Based or Per Se Policy? – a Reply*, 23(1) European Competition Law Review 38 (2002)

Luc Peeperkorn, *Resale Price Maintenance and Its Alleged Efficiencies*, 4(1) European Competition Journal 201 (2008)

Luc Peeperkorn, *Revision of the 1997 Notice on Agreements of Minor Importance (de minimis Notice)*, 2001(2) Competition Policy Newsletter 4 (2001)

Jan Peeters, *The Rule of Reason Revisited: Prohibition on Restraints of Competition in the Sherman Act and in the EEC Treaty*, 37 American Journal of Comparative Law 521 (1989)

Rudolph J. R. Peritz, Competition Policy in America 1888-1992 (1996)
Randal C. Picker, *Twombly, Leegin, and the Reshaping of Antitrust*, 2007 Supreme Court Review 161 (2007)
Thomas A. Piraino, *Reconciling the Harvard and Chicago Schools: A New Antitrust Approach for the 21st Century*, 82 Indiana Law Journal 345 (2007)
Thomas A. Piraino, *Reconciling the Per Se and Rule of Reason Approached to Antitrust Analysis*, 64 Southern California Law Review 685 (1991)
Richard A. Posner, Antitrust Law. An economic perspective (1976)
Richard A. Posner, *Vertical Restraints and Antitrust Policy*, 72 University of Chicago Law Review 229 (2005)
Patrick Rey and Jean Tirole, *The Logic of Vertical Restraints*, 76 American Economic Review 921 (1986)
Derek Ridyard and Simon Bishop, *E.C. Vertical Restraints Guidelines: Effects Based or Per Se Policy*, 23(1) European Competition Law Review 35 (2002)
Lennart Ritter and W. David Braun, European Competition Law: a Practitioner's Guide (3d ed., 2005)
Beverley Robertson, *What is a Restriction of Competition? The Implications of the CFI's Judgment in O2 Germany and the Rule of Reason*, 28(4) European Competition Law Review 252 (2007)
Vivien Rose and Peter Roth, *Article 81(1), in* Bellamy and Child's European Community Law of Competition (Peter Roth and Vivien Rose ed., 2008)
Stephen F. Ross, Principles of Antitrust Law (1993)
Alexander Schaub, *Continued focus on reform: recent developments in EC competition policy, in* 2001 Annual proceedings of the Fordham Corporate Law Institute 44 (Hawk ed., 2002)
Mark Clifford Schechter, *The Rule of Reason in European Competition Law*, 1982(2) Legal Issues in European Integration 1 (1982)
Frederic M. Scherer and David Ross, Industrial Market Structure and Economic Performance (3d ed. 1990)
Frederic M. Scherer, *The Economics of Vertical Restraints*, 52 Antitrust Law Journal 687 (1983)
Jakob Schröter, Kommentar zum Europäischen Wettbewerbsrecht (2003)
Greg Shaffer, *Rendering Alternative Offerings Less Profitable with Resale Price Maintenance*, 3(4) Journal of Economics and Management Strategy 639 (1995)
Kassie Smith, *Vertical Agreements Affecting Distribution or Supply, in* Bellamy and Child's European Community Law of Competition (Peter Roth and Vivien Rose ed., 2008)
A. Michael Spence, *Monopoly, quality, and regulation*, 6 Bell Journal of Economics 417 (1975)
J. J. Spengler, *Vertical Integration and Antitrust Policy*, 58 Journal of Political Economy 347 (1950)
Kenneth G. Starling, *Antitrust Defenses in Physician Peer Review Cases*, 63 Antitrust Law Journal 399 (1995)

Ernst Steindorff, *Article 85 and the Rule of Reason*, 21 Common Market Law Review 639 (1984)

Robert L. Steiner, *Sylvania Economics – a Critique*, 60 Antitrust Law Journal 41 (1991)

Romano Subiotto and Filippo Amato, *The Reform of the European Competition Policy Concerning Vertical Restraints*, 69 Antitrust Law Journal 147 (2001)

LAWRENCE A. SULLIVAN AND WARREN S. GRIMES, THE LAW OF ANTITRUST: AN INTEGRATED HANDBOOK (2000)

Erika Szyszczak, *Competition and sport*, 32(1) European Law Review 95 (2007)

Jessica L. Taralson, *What Would Sherman Do? Overturning the Per Se Illegality of Minimum Vertical Price Restraints Under the Sherman Act in Leegin Creative Leather Products, Inc. v. PSKS, Inc. Was Not As Reasonable As It Seemed*, 31 Hamline Law Review 549 (2008)

Paul M. Taylor, *The Vertical Agreements Regulation*, 3 The Cambridge Yearbook of European Legal Studies 525 (2000)

Lester G. Telser, *Why Should Manufacturers Want Fair Trade?*, 3 Journal of Law and Economics 86 (1960)

Christopher Thomas, *Article 81(3)*, *in* BELLAMY AND CHILD'S EUROPEAN COMMUNITY LAW OF COMPETITION (Peter Roth and Vivien Rose ed., 2008)

Ivo Van Bael, *Heretical Reflections on the Basic Dogma of EEC Antitrust: Single Market Integration*, 10(1) Revue Suisse du Droit International de la Concurrence 39 (1980)

ROGER J. VAN DEN BERG AND PETER D. CAMESASCA, EUROPEAN COMPETITION LAW AND ECONOMICS (2001)

Stefaan Van den Bogaert and An Vermeersch, *Sport and the EC Treaty: a tale of uneasy bedfellows*, 31(6) European Law Review 821 (2006)

Frederik Van Doorn, *Resale Price Maintenance in EC Competition Law: The Need for a Standardised Approach* (November 6, 2009) (available at SSRN: http://ssrn.com/abstract=1501070)

James S. Venit, *Brave New World: the Modernization and Decentralization of Enforcement under Articles 81 and 82 of the EC Treaty*, 40 Common Market Law Review 545 (2003)

James S. Venit, *Pronuptia: Ancillary Restraints or Unholy Alliances?*, 11 European Law Review 213 (1986)

Vincent Verouden, *Vertical Agreements and Article 81(1) EC: the Evolving Role of the Economic Analysis*, 71 Antitrust Law Journal 525 (2003)

Louis Vogel, *EU Competition Law Applicable to Distribution Agreements: Review of 2010 and Outlook for 2011*, 2(3) Journal of European Competition Law and Practice 245 (2011)

Rein Wesseling, *The Commission White Paper on Modernisation of E.C. Antitrust Law: Unspoken Consequences and Incomplete Treatment of Alternative Options*, 20(8) European Competition Law Review 420 (1999)

RICHARD WHISH, COMPETITION LAW (2008)

Richard Whish, *Regulation 2790/99: the Commission's 'New Style' Block Exemption for Vertical Agreements*, 37 Common Market Law Review 887 (2000)
Richard Whish and Brenda Sufrin, *Article 85 and the Rule of Reason*, 7 Yearbook of European Law 1 (1987)
Urs Wickihalder, *The distinction between an 'agreement' within the meaning of Article 81(1) of the EC Treaty and unilateral conduct*, 2 European Competition Journal 87 (2006)
Frank Wijckmans and Filip Tuytschaever, *Active Sales Restrictions Revisited*, 25(2) European Competition Law Review 107 (2004)
FRANK WIJCKMANS, FILIP TUYTSCHAEVER AND ALAIN VANDERELST, VERTICAL AGREEMENTS IN EC COMPETITION LAW (2006)
Oliver E. Williamson, *Economies as an Antitrust Defense Revisited*, 125 University of Pennsylvania Law Review 699 (1977)
OLIVER E. WILLIAMSON, MARKETS AND HIERARCHIES: ANALYSIS AND ANTITRUST IMPLICATIONS (1975)
Geert Wils, *'Rule of Reason': Une Regle Raisonnable en Droit Communautaire?*, 26 Cahiers de Droit Européen 19 (1990)
BASIL S. YAMEY, THE ECONOMICS OF RESALE PRICE MAINTENANCE (1954)

Commission decisions

73/322/EEC *Deutsche Philips GmbH* OJ [1973] L 293/40
76/172/EEC *Bayer/Gist-Brocades* OJ [1976] L 30/13
77/66/EEC *GERO-fabriek* OJ [1977] L 16/8
80/1333/EEC *Hennessy-Henkell* OJ [1980] L 383/11
85/617/EEC *Sperry New Holland* OJ [1985] L 376/21
86/506/EEC *Peugeot* OJ [1986] L295/19
86/507/EEC *Irish Banks' Standing Committee* OJ [1986] L 295/28
87/406/EEC *Tipp-Ex* OJ [1987] L 222/1
87/409/EEC *Sandoz* [1987] OJ L 222/28
91/128/EEC *Sippa* OJ [1991] L 60/19
92/426/EEC *Viho/Parker Pen* OJ [1992] L 233/27
93/46/EEC *Ford Agricultural* OJ [1993] L 20/1
93/174/EEC *Tariff structures in the combined transport of goods* OJ [1993] L 73/38
93/554/EEC *Zera/Montedison, Hinkens/Stähler* OJ [1993] L 272/28
94/29/EC *Grundig's EC distribution system* OJ [1994] L 20/15
94/987/EC *Tretorn and others* OJ [1994] L 378/45
95/477/EC *BASF Lacke+Farben AG, and Accinauto SA* OJ [1995] L 272/16
96/478/EC *ADALAT* [1996] OJ L 201/1
Organon, XXVth Report on Competition Policy 1995 37-38 (1996)
97/123/EC *Novalliance/Systemform* OJ [1997] L 47/11

97/780/EC *Unisource* OJ [1997] L 318/1
97/781/EC *Uniworld* OJ [1997] L 318/24
1999/6/EC *Sicasov* OJ [1999] L 4/27
1999/230/EC *Whitbread* OJ [1999] L 88/26
1999/267/EC *EPI code of conduct* OJ [1999] L 106/14
1999/473/EC *Bass* OJ [1999] L 186/1
1999/474/EC *Scottish and Newcastle* OJ [1999] L 186/28
1999/573/EC *Cégétel + 4* OJ [1999] L 218/14
Newspaper distribution contracts in Belgium – AMP Cases IV/C-2/31.609 and 37.306, XXIXth Report on Competition Policy 1999 161 (2000)
2001/135/EC *Nathan-Bricolux* OJ [2001] L 54/1
2001/146/EC *Opel* OJ [2001] L 59/1
2001/478/EC *UEFA's broadcasting regulations* OJ [2001] L 171/12
2001/696/EC *Identrus 511* OJ [2001] L 249/12
2001/711/EC *Volkswagen* OJ [2001] L 262/14
Case COMP/29.373 *Visa International* OJ [2001] L 293/24
IV/36.957/F3 *Glaxo Wellcome*, IV/36.997/F3 *Aseprofar and Fedifar*, IV/37.121/F3 *Spain Pharma*, IV/37.138/F3 BAI, IV/37.380/F3 *EAEPC* OJ [2001] L 302/1
2002/190/EC *JCB* OJ [2002] L 69/1
2002/758/EC *Mercedes-Benz* OJ [2002] L 257/1
2002/914/EC *Visa International – Multilateral Interchange Fee* OJ [2002] L 318/17
2003/675/EC *PO Video Games, PO Nintendo Distribution and Omega – Nintendo* OJ [2003] L 255/33
Case COMP/37.975 *PO/Yamaha* Commission decision of 16.07.2003 (unpublished but available at http://ec.europa.eu/competition/antitrust/cases/decisions/37975/en.pdf)
2004/841/EC *Société Air France/Alitalia Linee Aeree Italiane SpA* OJ [2004] L 362/17
Case COMP/B-1/38348 *Repsol CPP SA* OJ [2004] C 258/03
Case COMP/34.579 – *MasterCard*, COMP/36.518 – *EuroCommerce*, COMP/38.580 – *Commercial Cards* (unpublished but available at http://ec.europa.eu/competition/antitrust/cases/dec_docs/34579/34579_1889_2.pdf

GC and ECJ judgments

Joined Cases 56/64 and 58/64 *Consten and Grundig v Commission* [1964] ECR 299
Case 56/65 *Société Technique Minière (L.T.M.) v Maschinenbau Ulm GmbH (M.B.U.)* [1966] ECR 235
Case 5/69 *Franz Völk v S.P.R.L. Ets J. Vervaecke* [1969] ECR 295
Case 1/71 *Société anonyme Cadillon v Firma Höss, Maschinenbau KG* [1971] ECR 351

Case 26/76 *Metro SB-Großmärkte GmbH and Co. KG v Commission* ECR [1977] 1875
Case 19/77 *Miller International Schallplatten GmbH v Commission* [1978] ECR 131
Case 28/77 *Tepea BV v Commission* [1978] ECR 1391
Joined Cases 32/78, 36/78 to 82/78 *BMW Belgium SA and others v Commission* [1979] ECR 2435
Case 258/78 *L.C. Nungesser KG and Kurt Eisele v Commission* [1982] ECR 2015
Case 31/80 *NV L'Oréal and SA L'Oréal v PVBA 'De Nieuwe AMCK'* [1980] ECR 3775
Joined Cases 100 to 103/80 *SA Musique Diffusion française and others v Commission* [1983] ECR 1825
Case 262/81 *Coditel SA, Compagnie générale pour la diffusion de la télévision, and others v Ciné-Vog Films SA and others* [1982] ECR 3381
Case 86/82 *Hasselblad (GB) Limited v Commission* [1984] ECR 883
Case 107/82 *Allgemeine Elektrizitäts-Gesellschaft AEG-Telefunken AG v Commission* [1983] ECR 3151
Case 35/83 *BAT Cigaretten-Fabriken GmbH v Commission* [1985] ECR 363
Case 243/83 *SA Binon and Cie v SA Agence et messageries de la pressem* [1985] ECR 2015
Joined Cases 25/84 and 26/84 *Ford-Werke AG and Ford of Europe Inc. v Commission* [1985] ECR 2725
Case 42/84 *Remia BV and others v Commission* [1985] ECR 2545
Case 161/84 *Pronuptia de Paris GmbH v Pronuptia de Paris Irmgard Schillgallis* [1986] ECR 353
Case 27/87 *SPRL Louis Erauw-Jacquery v La Hesbignonne SC* [1988] ECR 1919
Case C-277/87 *Sandoz Prodotti Farmaceutici v Commission* [1990] ECR I-45
Case T-14/89 *Montedipe SpA v Commission* [1992] ECR II-1155
Case T-148/89 *Tréfilunion SA v Commission* [1995] ECR II-1063
Case C-234/89 *Stergios Delimitis v Henninger Bräu AG* [1991] ECR I-935
Case T-29/92 *Vereniging van Samenwerkende Prijsregelende Organisaties in de Bouwnijverheid and others v Commission* [1995] ECR II-00289
Case T-43/92 *Dunlop Slazenger International Ltd v Commission* [1994] ECR II-441
Case T-66/92 *Herlitz AG v Commission* [1994] ECR II-531
Case T-77/92 *Parker Pen Ltd v Commission* [1994] ECR II-549
Case C-49/92 *Commission v Anic Partecipazioni SpA* [1999] ECR I-4125
Case C-199/92 *Hüls AG v Commission* [1999] ECR I-4287
Case C-235/92 *Montecatini SpA v Commission* [1999] ECR I-4539
Case T-17/93 *Matra Hachette SA v Commission* [1994] ECR II-595
Case C-399/93 *H. G. Oude Luttikhuis and others v Verenigde Coöperatieve Melkindustrie Coberco BA* [1995] ECR I-4515
Joined Cases T-374/94, T-375/94, T-384/94 and T-388/94 *European Night Services Ltd (ENS) et altera v Commission* [1998] ECR II-3141

Case C-219/95 *P Ferriere Nord v Commission* [1997] ECR I-4411
Case T-41/96 *Bayer AG v Commission* [2000] ECR II-3383
Case C-306/96 *Javico International and Javico AG v Yves Saint Laurent Parfums SA (YSLP)* [1998] ECR I-1983
Case T-62/98 *Volkswagen v Commission* [2000] ECR II-2707
Case T-65/98 *Van den Bergh Foods Ltd v Commission* [2003] ECR II-4653
Joined Cases C-180/98 to C-184/98 *Pavel Pavlov and Others v Stichting Pensioenfonds Medische Specialisten* [2000] ECR I-06451
Case T-112/99 *Métropole téhlévision (M6), Suez-Lyonnaise des eaux, France Télécom and Télévision française 1 SA (TF1) v Commission* [2001] ECR II-2459
Case C-309/99 *J. C. J. Wouters, J. W. Savelbergh and Price Waterhouse Belastingadviseurs BV v Algemene Raad van de Nederlandse Orde van Advocaten, intervener: Raad van de Balies van de Europese Gemeenschap* [2002] ECR I-1577
Case T-368/00 *General Motors Nederland BV and Opel Nederland BV v Commission* [2003] ECR II-4491
Case C-338/00 *Volkswagen AG v Commission* [2003] ECR I-9189
Case T-67/01 *JCB Service v Commission* [2004] ECR II-49
Case T-168/01 *GlaxoSmithKline Services Unlimited v Commission* [2006] ECR II-02969
Case T-208/01 *Volkswagen v Commission* [2003] ECR II-5141
Joined Cases C-2/01 and C-3/01 *Bundesverband der Arzneimittel-Importeure eV and Commission v Bayer AG* [2004] ECR I-23
Case T-328/03 *O2 (Germany) GmbH and Co. OHG v Commission* [2006] ECR II-1231
Case C-551/03 *General Motors BV, formerly General Motors Nederland BV and Opel Nederland BV v Commission* [2006] ECR I-03173
Case C-519/04 *David Meca-Medina and Igor Majcen v Commission* [2006] ECR I-6991
Joined Cases C-468/06 to C-478/06 *Sot. Lélos kai Sia EE and Others v GlaxoSmithKline AEVE Farmakeftikon Proionton, formerly Glaxowellcome AEVE* [2008] ECR I-07139
Case C-209/07 *Competition Authority v Beef Industry Development Society Ltd and Barry Brothers (Carrigmore) Meats Ltd* [2008] ECR I-08637

US judgments

Albrecht v Herald Co., 390 U.S. 145 (1968)
American Ad Management, Inc., v GTE Corp., 92 F.3d 781 (1996)
American Medical Association, 455 U.S. 676 (1982)
Arizona v Maricopa County Medical Soc., 457 U.S. 332 (1982)
Black Gold, Ltd. v Rockwool Industries, Inc., 729 F.2d 676 (1984)

Board of Trade of City of Chicago v U.S., 246 U.S. 231 (1918)
Broadcast Music, Inc. v Columbia Broadcasting System, Inc., 441 U.S. 1 (1979)
Business Electronics Corp. v Sharp Electronics Corp., 485 U.S. 717 (1988)
California Dental Association v FTC, 526 U.S. 756 (1999)
Chicago Professional Sports Ltd. Partnership v National Basketball, 95 F.3d 593 (1996)
Continental T. V., Inc. v GTE Sylvania Inc., 433 U.S. 36 (1977)
Dart Drug Corp. v Parke, Davis and Co., 221 F.Supp. 948 (1963), aff'd 344 F.2d 173 (1965)
Dictograph Prods., Inc. v FTC, 217 F.2d 821 (1954)
Dr. Miles Medical Co. v John D. Park & Sons Co., 220 U.S. 373 (1911)
Fashion Originators' Guild of America v FTC, 312 U.S. 457 (1941)
Frey and Son v Cudahy Packing Co., 256 U.S. 208, 41 S.Ct. 451 (1921)
FTC v Beech-Nut Packing Co., 257 U.S. 441 (1922)
FTC v Brown Shoe Co., 384 U.S. 316 (1966)
FTC v Indiana Federation of Dentists, 476 U.S. 447 (1986)
Girardi v Gates Rubber Co. Sales Division, Inc., 325 F.2d 196 (1963)
In re California Dental Association, 121 F.T.C. 190 (1996)
International Salt Co. v U.S., 332 U.S. 392 (1947)
Jack Walters and Sons Corp. v Morton Bldg., Inc., 737 F.2d 698 (1984)
Kiefer-Stewart Co. v Joseph Seagram and Sons, Inc., 340 U.S. 211 (1951)
Klein v American Luggage Works, Inc., 323 F.2d 787 (1963)
Klor's, Inc. v Broadway-Hale Stores, Inc., 359 U.S. 207 (1959)
Leegin Creative Leather Products, Inc. v PSKS, Inc., 127 S.Ct. 2705 (2007)
Matter of Massachusetts Board of Registration in Optometry, 110 F.T.C. 549 (1988)
Monsanto Co. v Spray-Rite Service Corp., 465 U.S. 752 (1984)
National Bancard Corporation (NaBANCO) v VISA U.S.A., Inc., 596 F.Supp. 1231 (1984).
National Collegiate Athletic Ass'n v. Board of Regents of University of Oklahoma, 468 U.S. 85 (1984)
National Soc. of Professional Engineers v U. S., 435 U.S. 679 (1978)
Northern Pac. Ry. Co. v U.S., 356 U.S. 1 (1958)
Northwest Wholesale Stationers, Inc. v Pacific Stationery and Printing Co., 472 U.S. 284 (1985)
Parke, Davis and Co. v Health Cross Stores, Inc., 364 F.2d 214 (1966)
Pink Supply Corp. v Hiebert, Inc., 612 F.Supp. 1334 (1985)
Russell Stover Candies, Inc. v FTC, 718 F.2d 256 (1983)
Schwegman Bros. v Calvert Distillers Corp., 341 U.S. 384 (1951)
Simpson v Union Oil Co., 377 U.S. 13 (1964)
Standard Oil Co. of New Jersey v U.S., 221 U.S. 1 (1911)
Standard Oil of Cal. v U.S., 337 U.S. 293 (1949)
State Oil Co. v Khan, 118 S.Ct. 275 (1997)

Theatre Enterprises, Inc. v Paramount Film Distributing Corp., 346 U.S. 537 (1954)
Times-Picayune Pub. Co. v U.S., 345 U.S. 594 (1953)
U.S. v A. Schrader's Son, 252 U.S. 85, 40 S.Ct. 251 (1920)
U.S. v Addyston Pipe and Steel Co., 175 U.S. 211 (1899)
U.S. v Addyston Pipe and Steel Co., 85 F. 271 (1898)
U.S. v Arnold Schwinn Co., 388 U.S. 365, 382 (1967)
U.S. v Bausch and Lomb Optical Co., 321 U.S. 707 (1944)
U.S. v Brown University in Providence in State of R.I., 5 F.3d 658 (1993)
U.S. v Colgate and Co., 250 U.S. 300 (1919)
U.S. v Joint-Traffic Ass'n, 171 U.S. 505 (1898)
U.S. v National Lead Co., 63 F.Supp. 513 (1945)
U.S. v Parke, Davis and Co., 362 U.S. 29 (1960)
U.S. v Realty Multi-List, Inc., 629 F.2d 1351 (1980)
U.S. v Richfield Oil Corp., 99 F. Supp. 280 (1951)
U.S. v Socony-Vacuum Oil Co., 310 U.S. 150 (1940)
U.S. v Topco Associates, Inc., 405 U.S. 596 (1972)
U.S. v Trans-Missouri Freight Ass'n, 166 U.S. 290 (1897)
U.S. v Trenton Potteries Co., 273 U.S. 392 (1927)
White and White, Inc. v American Hosp. Supply Corp., 723 F.2d 495 (1983)
White Motor Co. v United States, 372 U.S. 253 (1963)
World of Sleep, Inc. v La-Z-Boy Chair Co., 756 F.2d 1467 (1985)
Yentsch v Texaco, Inc., 630 F.2d 46 (1980)

Index

www.ingramcontent.com/pod-product-compliance
Ingram Content Group UK Ltd.
Pitfield, Milton Keynes, MK11 3LW, UK
UKHW011005180926
475701UK00004B/566
* 9 7 8 0 3 6 7 6 0 1 8 1 2 *